The Dimensions of Job

The Dimensions of Job

A Study and Selected Readings

PRESENTED BY
Nahum N. Glatzer

SCHOCKEN BOOKS · NEW YORK

Manufactured in the United States of America

To the Memory of

T. HERZL ROME

1914–1965

Artist, Publisher, Friend

"I read this book as it were with my heart. . . .
You surely have read Job? Read him, read him
over and over again. . . . because everything about
him is so human."

KIERKEGAARD

"Job, you have cried through all vigils
but one day the constellation of your blood
shall make all rising suns blanch."

NELLY SACHS

Contents

INTRODUCTION: A STUDY OF JOB   1

I   The Book Itself / II   Job and His God / III   The
Issue of Interpretation / IV   The Folk Tale Tradition
/ V   The Classical Judaic Interpretation / VI   The
Christian Interpretation / VII   Modern Interpretations

SELECTED MODERN READINGS OF JOB

PREFACE

Much praise has been lavished upon the biblical book of Job. The profundity of its substance, the beauty of its form, the grandeur of its hero have found expression in a profusion of utterances. Francis Bacon thought the book "will be found pregnant and swelling with natural philosophy." Thomas Carlyle called it "one of the grandest things ever written with . . . pen. A noble book, all men's book!" Of the book's imagery he wrote: "Sublime sorrow, sublime reconciliation; oldest choral melody as of the heart of mankind; so soft, and great . . . There is nothing written, I think, in the Bible or out of it, of equal literary merit."

Daniel Webster described Job as "the most wonderful poem of any age and language." Tennyson considered it to be "the greatest poem of ancient and modern times." James Anthony Froude, author of a Job essay included in his *Short Studies on Great Subjects,* predicted that "one day [Job] will be seen towering up alone, far above all the poetry of the world." And Thomas Wolfe felt: "The most tragic, sublime and beautiful expression of loneliness which I have ever read is the Book of Job" ("The Anatomy of Loneliness"). The book's influence extends to the great works of world literature, to Dante's *Divine Comedy,* John Donne's sermons, Milton's *Paradise Regained* and *Samson Agonistes,* Klopstock's *Messias,* Goethe's *Faust.*

The purpose of this volume is not the pursuit of this line of praise, but to attempt a survey of how the book of Job was read and understood through the ages and, through pertinent examples, to observe how it is being read and interpreted in modern times. The latter aspect is presented in the main body of the volume. The introduction, after rendering a brief account of the book and discussing some of its central issues, addresses itself to the various dimensions of Joban interpretation. The short prefaces to the chapters in the body of the volume give the basic information on the authors and their work. The titles of the selections are the authors', whenever available; when not available they were chosen from the context. Omissions are marked by three dots in brackets. Spelling and transliteration of names and terms have been unified, except when the character of a selection suggested the retention of the original style. Biblical quotations appear in the form used by the various authors. In the introductory study I have used the translation of the Jewish Publication Society, unless the context required a different version. Chapter and verse in parentheses refer, naturally, to the book of Job. Details on the origin of each selection are listed under "Sources and Acknowledgments," where permissions to use copyrighted material are recorded.

The enterprise grew out of a number of college courses, lectures, and seminars on the book of Job and on writings on Job. The students' response and the insights gained in the process of teaching and discussions with students of various backgrounds and professional aims suggested that such a presentation may be of use to others who wish to approach this biblical work in the context of the history of ideas.

A note of sincere gratitude for personal, editorial, and technical assistance, respectively, is due to my daughter Judith Wechsler, to Professor Oscar Shaftel, Miss Hanna Gunther, Miss Sonia Volochova, and Miss Beverly Colman.

NAHUM N. GLATZER

Brandeis University
June 1968

Introduction: A Study of Job

I The Book Itself

For over two thousand years people have been attracted by the biblical book of Job and its hero. His fall from a state of happiness to utmost misery and degradation, the "behind-the-scene" manipulations of Satan, the hero's debates with his traditionalist, self-righteous comforters, the outbursts of indignation over the evils in the world, the occasional glimpses of hope, the appearance of God in all His mystery and majesty, the final reconciliation of the sufferer with God, world, and man—these images have agitated, provoked, and vexed the reader. He could not but identify with Job. Job is man.

The author of this book is unknown; that he was a Hebrew, writing in the language of his people, is generally (but not unanimously) accepted. The hero of the book was long believed to have been a real person and the book to be a poetic record of his experiences. Together with Noah and Daniel, a Job is mentioned by Ezekiel (14:14) as one of the righteous men of the past. But as early as the third century a talmudic master stated that "Job never was and never existed, but is only a parable."[1] Like the identity of the author, so too is the time of the composition unknown; half a millennium (from the fifth to the first pre-Christian centuries) is allowed as the probable range of its origin. Considering the efforts, from ancient times to this day, to re-form, recast, reconstruct the work in various media, it is, in a sense, timeless.

Let us, however briefly, recall the structure of the book, not as it developed and grew, but as it appeared to many generations of readers and as it lies before us.

1

The book opens with a prologue, a prose folk tale of a prosperous, pious man who through all adversity remains loyal to his God. "The Lord gave, the Lord has taken away, blessed be the name of the Lord." The cause of his adversity is a wager—unknown to Job—between Satan, the Accuser, and God that, once deprived of his possessions, his children, and, finally, of his physical well-being, Job would forsake his faith. His wife counsels him to "curse God and die," but Job rejects the "foolish" thought and patiently, humbly, accepts evil "at the hand of God," as he has previously accepted good. Three friends—Eliphaz, Bildad, and Zophar—come from afar to comfort the stricken hero (1:1–2:10).

Against this background, the substance of the book (3:1–42:6), written in poetic form, presents a different Job: not a submissive, saintly sufferer, but a rebel against the injustice rampant in the affairs of the world, against the reign of evil, against a creator who refuses to answer the creature's outraged address to Him.

The poetic part starts with a lament: Job curses the day of his birth and longs for a way out of the terrors of life (chapter 3). Then follows a series of three cycles of dialogue between the friends and Job. The friends—no comforters they!—proclaim the God of biblical tradition who exercises providence, rewards the just, and punishes the wicked; Job's sorry fate is an indication of his own (or his children's) guilt. Each friend in turn affirms the conventional doctrine of divine justice and of just, if at times delayed, retribution, and exhorts Job to make his peace with this God. Job answers each of the friend's affirmations, accusations, and pious advice; he protests his integrity, cries out against the disorder evident in a world that seems to have been handed over into the hands of the wicked. Job is a rebel, with a difference. He is ready to face the One against whose government, or rather non-government, he rises; he asks for the seemingly impossible: to be heard and to be spoken to. Yet, as it stands, "As God liveth, who hath taken away my right . . . I will not put away my integrity from me" (chapters 4–27).

Chapter 28 is a poem on wisdom, unassigned to any one of the participants; it declares that "wisdom" is divine, beyond the reach of man, unless it be by "the fear of the Lord" and ethical behavior. The three chapters that follow (29–31) are Joban soliloquies: the hero recalls his former happy state and honorable position in society

(29), contrasts this with his present "days of affliction" (30), and concludes with an "oath of clearance," affirming once more his integrity and ending his plea with, "Here is my signature, let the Almighty answer me!" (31).

Now a fourth friend enters the debate, young Elihu. In four verbose speeches (chapters 32–37) he refutes the notion that suffering is necessarily the consequence of wrongdoing and rejects Job's rebellious assertion of God's injustice. By inflicting suffering, he maintains, God chastens man; He speaks to man in dreams, in nightly visions, to warn him against pride; erring man may hope for an intercessor to vouch for him and to evoke divine grace; yet God's actions, executed in "terrible majesty," are beyond human understanding.

In a dramatic turn of events, "the Lord answered Job out of the whirlwind." In two speeches (38:1–40:2 and 40:6–41:26) He reveals to Job the marvelous order of the universe, while bypassing Job's quest for an explanation of his predicament. It's all there: the earth, the sea, light and darkness, the deep, snow and hail, wind and rain, and "the ordinances of the heavens"; the lion and the raven, goats and hinds, the wild ass and the wild ox, the ostrich, the war horse, the hawk and the vulture; the hippopotamus (*behemoth*), who is just "the beginning of the ways of God," and the crocodile (*leviathan*)—"will he make a covenant with you?" The inference follows logically: "Whatsoever is under the whole heaven is mine."

Job's rebellion subsides. After the first of the speeches he concedes, "I am of small account; what shall I answer Thee? I lay my hand upon my mouth" (40:3 ff.). And after the second speech he fully acknowledges that he has uttered that which he knew not, that previously he had heard of Him "by the hearing of the ear, but now mine eye seeth Thee" (42:1–6).

The book then, in an epilogue, resumes the thread of the prose folk tale of the pious Job. The hero prays for his friends; his former fortunes are restored (42:7–17).

Modern biblical scholarship has been questioning the authenticity of certain parts of the book. The third cycle of the dialogue (chapters 22–27) is incomplete and out of order; the poem on wisdom (28) appears to have been originally an independent creation; some scholars consider the Elihu speeches (chapters 32–

37) a later interpolation, and the Lord's speeches (chapters 38–41)
—at least the second of the two, or at the very least the description
of some of the animals—a secondary composition. Yet, urgent as
these issues are to the biblical critic, the "nonprofessional" reader
beholds a remarkable dramatic unity and a superb structure—the
work of the final editor of the book. Throughout the ages the reader
has viewed the book as *one* composition.

II Job and His God

The book of Job can be read on a variety of levels. Job, the
sufferer "without cause," the man whose steadfastness is being
tested, man confronting indifference and evil in the world, the
pawn between God and Satan, the lonely challenger of divine
justice and providence, man undergoing an Odyssey of faith, or
personifying the mystery of suffering, or conversely, personifying
the futility of asking ultimate questions, man the target of God's
unlimited power, or man in poignant struggle with his God—these
are some of the motifs that, singly or in various combinations, occur
in writings on Job.

The author placed the drama of Job in the "Land of Uz" (probably Edom), outside the realm of Israel. The personal names,
except one, Elihu, are non-Hebraic. The name of the God of Israel,
YHVH, recedes in the poetic parts of the book in favor of designations
of godhood in general—El, Elohim, Eloah, Shaddai. The author did
not refer to Judaic laws of conduct but to what he considered a
universal moral code. By such devices he intended to indicate the
universal character of the issues of suffering, evil, man confronting
God and world. Transcending the natural ethnic and cultural
boundaries, yet remaining within the sphere of monotheism, he
conceived his hero as representing man, man suffering, everywhere,
just as the author of the creation story in Genesis established Adam,
not as a Judaic Adam, but as what the name indicates, a creature
made out of "dust of the ground" *(adamah).*

The radical nature of Job's protest cannot be overemphasized;

the occasional rays of hope should not be overestimated. "The terrors of God do set themselves in array" against Job (6:4); God has set a watch over him and scared him with dreams (7:12, 14); He is the cause of destruction of both the innocent and the wicked (9:22, 24); He oppresses and despises His creatures, and shines "upon the counsel of the wicked" (10:3). Even the righteous cannot "lift up [his] head" (10:15); He controls "the deceived and the deceiver" (12:16). He hides His face and holds Job for His enemy; He puts the sufferer's feet in the stocks and watches his paths, so that he "wastes away like a rotten thing" (13:24, 27 f.); He destroys the hope of man (14:19). In His wrath He has torn Job, hated him, gnashing at him with His teeth; He has cast him into the hands of the wicked and broken him asunder; He runs upon him like a warrior (16:9, 11, 12). Job cries "violence," but "there is no justice"; in His wrath He counted Job "as one of His adversaries" (19:7, 11). He has alienated Job from his kinsfolk, friends, and servants (19:13 ff.); His presence spells terror and dread (23:15). God has "turned to be cruel" to him and hates him "with His mighty hand" (30:21). From God comes destruction, and because of His majesty Job can do nothing (31:23).

God's existence is unquestionable, as is the fact that He created this world and fashioned man. But now divine existence and creation have ceased to imply concern and benevolence. Order and justice are no longer in evidence. To the contrary, God has turned to being a wrathful attacker of humanity, as represented by Job. The notion of punishment for wrongdoing (adduced by the friends as an "explanation" of Job's fate) is here utterly inadequate. For here is a hostile deity and man is its antagonist. Job wishes to face his enemy, to reason with him, to speak and to receive an answer. But there is no breakthrough to this estranged God. All Job can do is to affirm his integrity, express his cruel experience, and cry out for the seemingly impossible: "Here is my signature, let the Almighty answer me" (31:35).

What is the cause of God's anger and open hostility on the one side, and Job's rebellious defiance on the other? Hopefully, we may find the clue to the understanding of this issue, which underlies the Job drama, by examining the key words employed by the author in presenting the argument between Job, the friends, and God.

The key words are knowledge, wisdom, and understanding, and their verbal forms. Job says what he says because he "knows." "I know that it is so" (9:2), "I know that this is with Thee" (10:13). "Who knoweth not such things as these?" (12:3), and "What ye know, do I know also" (13:2). He is sure in his stand: "I know that I shall be justified" (13:18). He wishes his friends "to know" that God has wronged him (19:6); as for himself, "I know that my vindicator liveth" (19:25). He is charged with the notion that God does not know (22:13), but Job affirms that "He knoweth the way I take" (23:10), yet prevents those "that know Him from seeing His days" (24:1). If Job would but reach His presence, he "would know the words which He would answer" him (23:5). He is certain that he has knowledge, and it is on this basis that he utters his invective and makes his rebellious pleas.

The friends maintain the position that Job does not "know," in fact, that "we . . . know nothing" (8:9). Zophar argues that "deep things" and a "purpose of the Almighty" leave man impotent to "do" or to "know"; it is God who "knows" (11:7, 8, 10). Eliphaz terms Job's a "windy knowledge" (15:2), and Bildad points to Job as one "that knoweth not God" (18:21). Elihu especially hears Job speaking "without knowledge" (34:35), multiplying words "without knowledge" (35:16). Disobedient men, he declares, "shall die without knowledge" (36:12), whereas God is great "beyond our knowledge" (36:26). He asks Job to behold the works of God "who is perfect in knowledge" (37:16), whereas man does not "know" the facts of nature (37:15). He adds sarcastically: "Let us know what we shall say unto Him" (37:19). Thus repudiating Job's, and man's, ability to know, Elihu concludes his speeches on the note that God rejects the "wise of heart" (37:24).

The chapter on wisdom (28) gives credit to man's accomplishments in the material world, but as for "wisdom," man "knoweth not the price thereof" (28:13); only God "knoweth the place thereof" (28:23). Wisdom (knowledge) remains with God; it is not communicated to man. Man's wisdom is but "the fear of the Lord . . . and to depart from evil" (28:28), traits that characterized Job's life in the happy days (1:1) before the controversy began, before he rebelled against the injustice in the world, in reliance on his own possession of "knowledge"—and encountered as his antagonist Him "who is perfect in knowledge" (37:16).

The key word "knowledge" runs throughout the answer from the whirlwind. These speeches that review the grandeur and multi-fariousness of the created world take the form of questions addressed to Job, challenging his power to know and to act. The key word appears in the introductory question: "Who is this that darkeneth counsel by words without knowledge?" (38:2). Job is asked about the earth's foundation, if indeed he has "understanding," if he "knows" (38:4 f.). Does he "know" about "the recesses of the deep"? (38:16). Light and darkness—"thou knowest it, for thou wast then born" (38:21). And: "Knowest thou the ordinances of the heavens?" (38:33). Turning from inanimate nature to the animal kingdom, the voice asks: "Knowest thou the time when the wild goats . . . bring forth? . . . Doth the hawk soar by thy wisdom?" (39:1, 26). Man, whose knowledge is thus disputed, is therefore impotent to act, to take part in the maintenance of creation: "Hast thou commanded the morning . . . ?" (38:12). "Canst thou number the months that they [the hinds] fulfill?" (39:2).

Throughout the dialogue Job speaks of a hostile God who has withdrawn from the world and become estranged from man. All this he asserts because he "knows." The voice from the whirlwind makes him aware of the root of the tension: Job's affirmation of his own knowledge is an affront to the true possessor of knowledge: God. In claiming knowledge, Job has overstepped the boundary between God and man and provoked the wrath of divinity. He thinks he has acquired knowledge, but this faculty makes him conscious only of death and the ills and suffering, his own and mankind's, and exposes him to the revenge for his *hubris*.

Now that the voice has subsided, Job realizes how infinitely small a part he is of the vast universe and the limits of his knowledge (and his action) in the view of Him who knows (and acts). "I know that Thou canst do everything" (42:2). He had "without knowledge" attempted to obscure the purpose of God (42:3) and "uttered that . . . which [he] knew not" (42:4). Now he can only pray that he be granted knowledge: "I will ask Thee and do Thou make me know" (42:4).

Job's question concerning the moral order is not referred to in the divine answer. Instead, the answer concerns itself with the basis of man's intellectual existence: the fact of his knowledge (man is the only being to whom the creator can address Himself) and the painful limitation of this knowledge. Now a sense of hostility no longer prevails; man has attained comprehension of the human condition. Rebellious response is replaced by calm, wise, even resigned, acceptance. The sense of distance remains; it is even accentuated. The only experience that can bridge the distance is man's reconstructed knowledge. God remains distant, but it is direct communication from God that has conveyed this fact to man. Man's (reconstructed) knowledge is both: awareness of his limitation *and* of his capacity to live with this limitation in the context of the universe. No longer does he need to pin his hope on a vindicator to take up his cause (19:25); his own eye has seen Him (42:5).

The moral issue is, by implication, left to man to deal with. Justice and loving concern in the affairs of man and the world have not been restored, but Job's wish for instruction and understanding (6:24) has been fulfilled.

I have alluded to the motif of God's wrath over Job's (i.e., man's) appropriation of knowledge that rightfully belongs to Him. This calls to mind the story in Genesis 3, where Adam (and Eve) are tempted to eat from the Tree of Knowledge and bear the consequences of this step—suffering, expulsion—that make them truly human. It therefore seems probable that the author of Job had this ancient legend in mind when writing his work and expected the reader to view the Job drama against the background of Genesis 3. A number of more or less subtle allusions and parallels are possibly not coincidental, but may point to the intended relationship between the two biblical stories about man. Eve's prompting of Adam to act counter to the divine order is paralleled by the suggestion of Job's wife that he "blaspheme God and die" (2:9). The serpent in the Genesis story reappears as Satan in the book of Job. Adam's fate, caused by his appropriation of knowledge, corresponds to Job's agony, which in the dialogue portion of the book is related to the hero's assertion of the possession of knowledge; in both cases there is an interrelationship between the loss of innocence, knowledge, and estrangement from God. Adam (and Eve) are informed of God's wrath; Job experiences this wrath bodily throughout the poem. "I had heard of Thee by the hearing of the ear" (42:5) is a possible reference to "I heard Thy voice" in the Adam story. Adam "hides" before God, so as not to be seen and not to have to see. This state is overcome in Job's triumphant assertion: "But now mine eye seeth Thee" (42:5). "Where wast thou?" (38:4) at the beginning of the Lord's speeches echo His question to Adam: "Where art thou?" (Gen. 3:9). The review of the created world thundered at Job = man, who is excluded from the picture, corresponds to Adam's exclusion from the paradisiac world, originally created for his sake. "Unto dust shalt thou return" (Gen. 3:19) is paralleled by Job's reference to "dust and ashes" in his final confession (42:6).

In the internal history of biblical Israel, Adam, man, expelled from Paradise and from the presence of God, is progressively recalled into that presence: in Noah, in Abraham, in Moses. Forbidden, death-causing knowledge is re-formed into one that is freely given and life-sustaining. Later, in Christian thought, the curse of Adam is lifted by the experience of the cross. The author of Job stands outside the biblical tradition and its theory of man. His Job is Adam after the expulsion. He is presented as an upright, God-fearing heathen. He has remained "Adam"—up to the point when a divine communication makes him recognize his place in a wider, extrahuman, universe.

Neither the motif of knowledge in the book of Job nor (to a lesser degree) the parallel Adam-Job escaped the attention of medieval commentators of various religious traditions.[2] Moses Maimonides goes so far as to use the concept of knowledge as the key to the interpretation of the book.

The first fruits of Adam's "knowledge" were toil and trouble, "thorns and thistles," and awareness of his mortality. "Dust thou art, and unto dust shalt thou return" (Gen. 3:19). Access to the Tree of Life was barred forever. Life meant progression toward death.

Death as an inescapable reality appears as a primary motif in Job's speeches addressed to his friends. It is second only to the references to knowledge. I know; I shall die. Job dreads death; but under the conditions of pain and agony he views death as relief.

Death not only terminates life; it penetrates life; it destroys life in the very process of living. And since it is God—Job's enemy—who causes the inescapable end, Job anticipates death in an attitude of self-pity, mixed with bitter impatience and longing.

"Why died I not from the womb, why did I not perish at birth?" (3:11). "Wherefore is light given to him . . . who longs for death, but it cometh not?" (3:20 f.). "While Thine eyes are upon me, I am gone" (7:8). "My soul chooseth strangling and death rather than these my bones" (7:15). "Now I shall lie down in the dust; and Thou wilt seek me, but I shall not be" (7:21). "Wilt Thou bring me into dust again?" (10:9). "I should have been carried from the womb to the grave" (10:19). "Let me alone . . . before I go whence I shall not return" (10:20 f.). "Man . . . is of few days and full of trouble . . . his days are determined" (14:1–5). "Man dieth, and lieth low, yea, man perisheth and where is he?" (14:10). "If a man die, may he live again?" (14:14). "The years that are few are coming on, and I shall go the way whence I shall not return" (16:22). "The grave is ready for me" (17:1). "My days are past, my purposes are broken off" (17:11). The man at ease and the man with bitter soul "lie down alike in the dust, and the worm covereth them" (21:26). Referring to himself, Job affirms: "He hath cast me into the mire, and I am become like dust and ashes" (30:19). And, finally, "I know that Thou wilt bring me to death" (30:23).

It has been pointed out that Near Eastern mythological motifs and epics of the dying god and of the Ugaritic Môt, ruler of the Canaanite nether world, influenced the imagery and the vocabulary of the author of Job.[3] The parallels between the two bodies of writings are indeed conclusive. But if the assumption of a relationship between Job and the Adam story is correct, the death passages in Job should be read also with reference to the death sentence imposed upon Adam. However, as the turning point in the Job drama is reached and his claim to knowledge undergoes its catharsis, so, too, does the dread of death disappear. The calm that pervades his admission, "I know that Thou canst do everything" and "do Thou make me know" (42:2, 4), is evident in his last words in the book, "I am dust and ashes" (42:6). With his new knowledge, Job is reconciled to his mortality. Death is not removed, but it is no longer an issue. Job does not become immortal, he does not return to the Garden of innocence, but—and this is the meaning of the epilogue—he can taste the sweetness of life, undisturbed by the prospect of its end. Life, no longer focused on itself, becomes acceptable, even worthwhile. Family and friends come and "eat bread with him in his house" and bring gifts of money and rings of gold (42:11); he enjoys possession of cattle; he has again sons and daughters, women of beauty, and he lives to see the fourth generation of children, so that when death does come, it finds him "old and full of days" (42:17). Thus the epilogue, though of a different origin from the poem itself, came to serve the purpose of the poem's author: it complements the hero's reform and restoration that commenced with the concluding portion of the poetic part. The drama of Job's reconciliation is complete.

III The Issue of Interpretation

In reviewing the major trends in the entire range of literature on the book of Job, one cannot fail to notice that, with some notable exceptions, Jewish interpreters in the premodern period Judaized Job and Christian expositors Christianized him. Both sides, again with exceptions, avoided a direct confrontation with the text of the book, in order not to be exposed (or not to expose the pious reader) to the bluntness of the hero's speeches and the shattering self-revelation of God in His answer to Job. The heritage of faith and the belief in a benevolent, providential deity were too strong to admit a position so greatly at variance with the accepted basic religious attitudes. The book's frame, the folk tale, offered an escape clause. By concentrating on the story of the patient, *saintly* Job, the reader could absorb the shock of the drama of the impatient, *rebellious* hero; he could "interpret" the latter in the light of the former.

Whatever difficulties the text still presented in this process of adaptation could be taken care of, reduced, or eliminated by skillful exegesis. Thus, the interpretations of Job in the premodern period advance our understanding of the book very little; instead, they add to our appreciation of the periods, the writers, and their concerns. And, by indirection, we are placed in the position of viewing with admiration or with pity, of condemning or laughing at the ingenuity displayed by the commentators in bypassing the stubborn soil of the book and in fashioning its hero in their own image, or in the image of their respective traditions.

In the early modern period the established religions lost their all-embracing grip on the interpreter; man became increasingly ready to explore an ancient text on its literary merits, and the techniques of literary analysis improved and gained refinement. Obviously, a book like Job benefited from this general liberalization of the mind.

Yet it is curious to observe that even in the modern period and in some contemporary writing the interpreter's intellectual preoccupation still tends to determine his reading of the book and causes an adaptation of Job to his own thinking or needs. The rationalist, the idealist, the psychologist, the existentialist—each is tempted to appropriate the book of Job as documentation of his own interest. With notable exceptions, the book's challenge is, at best, only partially admitted. A partial acceptance, however, is not enough in the case of this radically unorthodox work.

Still, compared with the periods of theological certainty and conformity to tradition, the modern era has evoked a sensitive understanding of the book. More and more contemporary students ask the simple question: What does the book really say? They are prepared to approach the text with a naked eye.

In the sections that follow I shall examine, however briefly, the major trends prevalent in the treatment of Job. First, by surveying the folk tale tradition (IV); second, by citing examples of the classical Judaic and authoritative Christian inquiries into Job (V and VI); third, by recording some of both early and more recent modern writings, selections from which could not be included in the body of the volume, mainly for reasons of space (VII).

IV   The Folk Tale Tradition

The folk tale of Job has a history of its own. Its hero caught the imagination of Jews, Christians, and Moslems. It was elaborated on and expanded, to form independent literary creations. Its image of Job often infiltrated the interpretation of the main part of the book and displaced its hero or modified his rebellious character. Its scenario was adapted by a succession of dramatists, up to Goethe ("Prologue in Heaven" in *Faust*) and Archibald MacLeish (*J. B.*). Its figure of Satan (which in the book disappears with chapter 2) fascinated theologians and homilists, and, in the modern period, poets, painters, and psychologists. In the context of this volume I cannot do more than point to the early developments of this tradition, starting with the so-called *Testament of Job*.

The *Testament of Job* is an anonymous, apocryphal work that reinterprets the story of Job in the form of parting words addressed by the hero to the ten children born to him after his restoration to his former estate. The Hebrew original, composed probably in the last pre-Christian century, is lost. Two Greek versions based on the Hebrew were discovered in the nineteenth century.[4]

In this *Testament*, Job, or Jobab, a king in the land of Ausitis (Uz), dares to destroy a popular idol, built in the image of Satan, though he knows that the latter will exact revenge for the deed. Job says: "I shall from love of God endure until death all that will come upon me, and I shall not shrink back." Satan obtains from God the power to persecute Job. He destroys Job's possessions, his children, his health. The hero endures for seven years, sitting on a dunghill. His wife, her heart greatly troubled by the Seducer, loses her faith in God and tries to persuade her husband to "speak some word against God and die." Convinced finally of Job's firmness, Satan admits defeat and yields to him. At this time four kings come to visit the sufferer. They lament their friend's sorry fate, whereas Job remains steadfast: "Kings perish and rulers vanish, and their glory and pride is as the shadow in a looking glass, but my kingdom lasts forever, and its glory and beauty are in the chariot of my Father.'" He proclaims his "hope in the living God," and answers the friends' doubts by stating: "Who understands the depths of the Lord and of His wisdom to be able to accuse God of injustice?" He refuses to accept the help of the friends' physicians: "My cure and my restoration cometh from God, the Maker of physicians." The friends consider Job's faith to be mere boastfulness and overbearing pride, and Elihu, "imbued with the spirit of Satan," speaks hard words to him. Finally, God appears in a storm and in clouds, pardons three kings but accuses Elihu of "loving the beauty of the serpent." Job is restored to his former glory and resumes his benefactions to the needy. When his end approaches, God kisses him, takes his soul, and soars upward. "It is written that he will rise up with those whom the Lord will reawaken. To our Lord be glory. Amen."

Job's last admonition to his children is: "Do not forsake the

Lord. Be charitable toward the poor; do not disregard the feeble. Take not unto yourselves wives from strangers."

In this work Job represents the eternal Kingdom of God against the mighty but perishable realm of the Evil One. The sad state of this world is unable to disturb the communion between God and man.

The tradition presenting Job as a man of perfect, unquestioning faith appears also in an Addendum to the midrashic work *Abot de-Rabbi Nathan,* compiled sometime between the seventh and the ninth centuries. This Addendum, found in a manuscript in the Vatican Library,[5] tells of a Job who throughout his troubles "acknowledged and praised the Lord for all His attributes" until "all the world believed that there was none like him in all the land." Satan, who has not succeeded in destroying Job's trust in God, is finally condemned and cast down from heaven. Job's trial lasts one full year—symbolic of a perfect unit of time—after which he is returned to his former estate.

The early Christian church maintained the ideal of the saintly Job. The Apostle James, first bishop of Jerusalem, addresses his faithful, "You have heard of the patience of Job and you have seen the end of the Lord, that the Lord is merciful and compassionate."[6] "The First Epistle of Clement to the Corinthians," written about A.D. 100, refers to Job as the "righteous and blameless, true worshipper of God," in the company of Abraham and Moses, Elijah and Elisha, Ezekiel and the other prophets, who were "heralding the coming of Christ" and whose piety and humility is to be imitated by the faithful.[7]

The Syriac version of the "Apocalypsis Pauli"[8] (end of the fourth century) has Satan threaten Job daily, saying, "Curse thy God and die!" The Evil One prompts Job's sons to make their father "blaspheme against the living God." But Job "does not cease from blessing His name . . . for what is the affliction of this world, compared with the promises of God, which He prepared for His called, and for those who delight in His love?"

The "Apostolic Constitutions" (*Constitutiones Apostolorum,* Syria, *ca.* A.D. 380) contains a "Form of Prayer for the Ordination of a Bishop." Job is listed among the priests "fore-ordained from the beginning for the government of Thy people." He is preceded by "Abel, Seth, Enos, Enoch, Noah, and Melchisedec," and followed by "Abraham and the rest of the patriarchs."[9]

Bishop Theodore of Mopsuestia (died 428), disciple of Diodorus of Tarsus and the most influential teacher of the theological school of Antioch (he repudiated the doctrine of Original Sin), mentions an "outstanding and much esteemed story of the saintly Job, retold orally by everybody in a similar form, not only among Israelite people but also by others.[10] He accepted this popular story of Job as the true account, dismissing the biblical book of Job as a mere literary product written by a man anxious to parade his learning and to gain repute. The speeches attributed to Job by the biblical author Bishop Theodore thought unbefitting a man "who mastered his life with great wisdom and virtue and piety."

The Islamic sources and later traditions extol Job as the pious and righteous servant of Allah. He was the recipient of revelation, as were Abraham, Ishmael and Isaac and Jacob, Jesus and Jonah, Aaron, David and Solomon (Qur'ān 4:161). His righteousness was recompensed, as was that of Abraham, Joseph, Moses and Aaron, David and Solomon (6:84). When he cried to his Lord ("Thou art the most merciful of those who show mercy"), the burden of his woe was lightened (21:83 f.). 'Verily, We found him patient! How excellent a servant! Verily he was one who turned to Us" (38:44).

The Qur'ān commentary by al-Bayḍāwī (thirteenth century) stresses Job's patience. Those who serve Allah "should be patient like he was patient, then they would be rewarded as he was rewarded" (comment on 21:83 f.). Indeed, Job was patient "in what befell him in himself, and in his people, and in his wealth. And his complaint to God concerning Satan was not a falling short in patience, for it, like longing for health and seeking healing, is not called impatience; and, besides, he said that out of fear lest Satan should tempt him and his people in the Faith." Job was one "who brought his burden to God" (comment on 38:44).[11]

The Islamic version of the folk tale of Job appears in various formulations; all of them present Job as a saint.

As in the biblical tale, the Islamic version, in one of its formulations,[12] credits Satan, Iblīs, with the instigation of Job's troubles; Satan was given permission to test the hero's faith. Another reason for Iblīs' action is mentioned in the course of the tale: The Evil One was angered by the lack of veneration accorded to him by Job and his wife, Raḥma. This motif is reminiscent of the reason for Satan's work given in the *Testament of Job* and, as we shall note later, in the *Zohar*.

Rahma's character differs from both the character of Job's wife in the biblical story and that of the wife in the *Testament of Job*. Iblīs tries to win her to his side, but Job prevents her from taking this fateful step. His own faith is strong and unshakable. Calmly he accepts the news of his children's death: "My children were but a loan from the almighty God." Iblīs finds Job in a mosque, praying: "Behold, the misfortune that Thou hast brought upon me only served to increase my gratitude and my patience." His examples are the prophets and messengers of God. He bids his wife to proclaim: "There is no strength nor power except in God." Neighbors lament Job's sad condition, but he replies, "I am the servant of my Master and His messenger; I satisfy my hunger by calling upon His name, and my thirst by praising Him." His stench becomes unbearable, and people no longer allow Rahma to enter their homes in search of food. Iblīs appears in the guise of a physician; Job rejects the cure that would have involved a departure from the religious law. (The physician motif parallels the reference to the friends' physicians in the *Testament of Job*.)

After a period of suffering that—corresponding to the years of Job's happiness—lasts eighty years, God reveals Himself, announcing Job's deliverance. To restore his health and his appearance, he is given pure water from a spring to drink, a quince from Paradise—half of which he offers to Rahma—to eat, and is clothed in garments from Paradise. And God revives his children.[13]

At the base of these traditions of Job as saint—in Judaism, Christianity, and Islam—lies the simple biblical tale that, in the book of Job, was to serve as a mere prologue to the drama. It was fascination with the figure of the submissive, trusting, pious sufferer that lent an independent existence to this single aspect of the biblical Job. It helped to create a profusion of literary images that can be traced through many centuries of the book's interpretation.

V The Classical Judaic Interpretation

For the classical Judaic tradition we must first turn to the talmudic-midrashic literature, which forms the basis of the majority of later writings in that tradition, and then follow with an analysis of the Job image as delineated in the Bible commentary of Solomon ben Isaac ("Rashi") and in the work of one of the exegetes whose interpretation stems from Rashi's. Medieval philosophical thought on the subject is represented by Moses Maimonides, and the mystical view by the *Zohar* ("Book of Splendor").

The talmudic-midrashic literature (primarily of the first centuries) treats Job as the most pious Gentile that ever lived,[14] one of the seven prophets who prophesied to the nations of the world.[15] According to this conception he was a grandson of Jacob's brother Esau; after his trial he married Dinah, Jacob's daughter, who became his second wife. Some exegetes considered Job to have been a Jew. Still others believed that Job never existed: "the purpose of the story was to serve as an example."[16] Certain sages thought that Job was one of four men who came to know God through their own thinking, the others being Abraham, King Hezekiah, and the future Messiah.[17] In this conception he sought to free the world from divine judgment by pointing to the all-powerful divinity; his friends rebutted his argument by reference to the Torah, which allows man to counter evil with good.[18]

For a better understanding of Job's piety, the talmudic masters compared him to Abraham. Some thought that he served God only "from fear" (see Job 1:1), whereas Abraham was a lover of God; others concluded that in both Abraham and Job "fear" and "love" were interrelated; still others believed that Job's deeds were motivated by pure love.[19] Satan's actions were conceived as stemming from a sacred intent; he thought that God, in favoring Job, had forgotten the love of Abraham. When Satan heard this interpretation, he came and kissed the interpreter's feet.[20]

Nevertheless, under the impact of his tribulations, Job became a rebel. As such he spoke "as if there were an equality with heaven on the part of man." He, the servant, dared "to argue against his master." He accused God of confusing *Iyov* [Job] with *Oyev* [enemy] and thus multiplying his wounds "without cause" (Job 9:17). In his answer "out of the whirlwind," God proffered examples of His paternal providence, evinced in nature; how, then, could he mistake Job for another?[21] God rebuked him for his lack of patience when suffering was inflicted upon him: Adam, whose sentence was death, did not murmur; Abraham, who was told his seed would be slaves in Egypt, did not murmur; Moses was prevented from entering the promised land, yet he too did not murmur; neither did Aaron when his two sons died.[22] On the other hand, some sages excused Job's outbursts, since "man is not held responsible for things done under duress."[23] However, had he stood firm during the great trial, his name would have been included in prayer, and men would have called upon the "God of Job" as they now call upon the "God of Abraham, Isaac, and Jacob."[24] The day of Job's accusation was the New Year's Day, when God judges the good and the evil deeds of man.[25] The atmosphere of stern divine justice prevailed "as long as Job stood against his friends and his friends against him." The turning point came "after they made peace with each other and Job prayed for his friends." Then God returned to him, as it is said: "And the Lord changed the fortune of Job, when he prayed for his friends" (42:10).[26]

In sum, the talmudic-midrashic tradition avoided reference to the extremes of Job's rebellion against evil and injustice and their Author; glossed over the motifs of Job's isolation, despair, and alienation; maintained a state of communion between the actors of the drama; and presented God as more concerned for the weal of Job, and Satan as more "human," than the two are portrayed in the book of Job. The book taught Yohanan of Tiberias, the great third-century talmudist, that "the end of man is death and the end of cattle is slaughter—all are doomed to die." But "blessed is he who has grown in the Torah . . . and who is giving pleasure to his Maker: he goes through life with a good name and with a good name departs from this world."[27]

The medieval Jewish Bible commentator who expounded the book of Job was faced with the task of reconciling the story of the pious Job presented in the prose section and the epilogue of the book with the rebellious Job of the body of the text. The text made it impossible to ignore the hero's outbursts, but exegetical skill helped to reduce the measure of his impetuousness and hostility. In addition, the talmudic and midrashic heritage, which presented Job in a rather positive light, largely determined the stand of the medieval Jewish interpreter. Thus Job was viewed as a saintly person, a man, however, whose piety was not perfect, requiring correction.

This view is best typified by Solomon ben Isaac ("Rashi," 1040–

1105), the classical commentator of the Hebrew Bible and the Babylonian Talmud. On the text "I would not believe that He would hearken unto my voice" (9:16), Rashi commented: "because of my fear of Him, and how could I not fear Him." To the verse "Though I be righteous, mine own mouth shall condemn me" (9:20), he added, "fear [of Him] would silence my voice." On the verse "Though He slay me" (13:15), he noted, "I shall not separate myself from Him and shall always trust in Him; therefore, there is no rebellion and transgression in my words." On the verse that follows and states that Job's only salvation shall be that no hypocrite shall come before Him, Rashi commented: "As I am wholly with Him, so is He salvation to me."

By such exegesis, Job's protest was turned into affirmation of faith. But the text itself spoke too clearly to be muted. Job did say, after all, that God "destroyeth the innocent and the wicked" (9:22) and asked Him not to frighten him by His terror (13:21). Such utterances were admitted to be signs of weakness and imperfection. This state required correction rather than an overall reprimand, which is the substance of chapters 38 to 41. The correction was achieved by Elihu's pointing to man's insignificance in the cosmos (Rashi's comment on 33:12) and God's pointing to Abraham, whose faith, in contrast to Job's, was perfect because unquestioning (comment on 38:2).

Similarly, the northern French Bible exegete Joseph Kara (eleventh–twelfth centuries) presents Job as an example of imperfect piety.[28] Job, a generally good man, is overwhelmed by the "evil urge" and knows himself to be guilty before God (comments on 12:4, 7:20, and 9:20). He trusts in God, but is astounded that God, who knows him, should have had to put him on trial (comment on 13:15). Yet, in all his agony, he does not abandon faith that God will be his salvation (comment on 13:16). Elihu praises both God's independence from the world and His compassionate concern for man. He advises doubting Job that his suffering was inflicted upon him to save his soul from darkness. "He reproves you because He loves you" (comment on 33:24). God confirms Elihu's advice: "I am full of compassion for the beasts and animals . . . and I feed them, and all the more for man created in my image and likeness" (comment on 28:26 f.). No more was needed to dispel the shadows from the suffering hero's soul, to make him understand God's ways, and to restore the perfection of his faith.

Like Rashi's, Kara's reading of Job does not call for an inquiry into the problem of evil; in their view Job never doubted God's providence, he was only confused concerning its evidence in the world.

The interpretation of Job given by Samuel ben Nissim Masnut of Aleppo (twelfth–thirteenth centuries) is contingent on Rashi's. His *Maayan Gannim,* a midrashic exposition of Job,[29] attributes Job's angry invectives to events of the past, to Pharaoh, or to Sodom and Gomorrah. Thus, except for such historical events, the world is seen as harmoniously conducted, and it is Job himself who voices humble recognition of divine goodness: "I do not rely on my prayer and on myself, because I am not worthy that He answer me and hearken unto my voice" (comment on 9:16). "I cannot justify myself so as to accuse Him, because He is high above all glory and praise" (comment on 9:22). What upset Job's thinking was the seeming undeservedness of his suffering. But God, in His speeches, "made him realize that he had no knowledge and that he was unable to understand His ways" (comment on 38:1). Through this address Job attained "true understanding," and his piety, previously inhibited and weakened, now became strong and complete (comments on 42:2, 6).

These and other (but not all) medieval Hebrew commentators desired to preserve the traditional image of the pious Job. The evidence of the text compelled them to confirm the element of doubt and error—but not the rebellion—in Job's mind. It cannot be said that the attempt to reconcile the two tendencies in Job was successfully executed. A certain amount of artificiality and inconsistency is quite evident. Nor did commentaries of this type have any reason for delving into the intent of the book: Job's grappling with the problem of evil and the drama of his transformation.

Moses Maimonides (1135–1204), author of the most significant work in the field of Jewish religious philosophy, *The Guide of the Perplexed,*[30] analyzed the book of Job in chapters 22 and 23 of the third book of his work. He firmly believed that he had "explained the story of Job up to its ultimate end and conclusion"; one of his insights Maimonides, the rationalist and Aristotelian, attributed to "something similar to prophetic revelation."

He noted that the biblical text ascribed to Job uprightness and moral virtues—but not knowledge (1:1). Job's belief in the existent disorder and in the meaninglessness of his sufferings stemmed from his lack of knowledge. Satan—and here Maimonides refers to a talmudic tradition[31]—is identical with the "evil inclination" that is inherent in man from his birth onward, long before the "good inclination" enters his life, "when his intellect is perfected." Thus Job's erroneous beliefs, instigated by Satan (the evil inclination), were an earmark of that period in his life when discernment and knowledge were not yet in operation. Knowing God only from tradition and lacking independent understanding and, in addition, plagued by his affliction, Job conceived of God as "contemptuous of the human species; He has abandoned it . . . laughs at the calamity of the innocent and allows the wicked to prosper." However, once Job's intellect had developed and "he knew God with a certain knowledge, he admitted that true happiness, which is the knowledge of the deity, is granted to all who know Him and that a human being cannot be troubled by any or all of the misfortunes in question." This knowledge, and not "the things thought to be happiness, such as health, wealth, and children, [is] the ultimate goal."

Elihu, "among the friends the most perfect in knowledge," rejects their opinions on providence as "senile drivel" and introduces the notion of an angel who intercedes for afflicted man until "he is raised from his fall" and restored. To Maimonides, this is the principal objective of Elihu's speeches—an emphasis that is by no means obvious to the text's ordinary reader. The philosopher probably considered such an interceding angel the counterpart of Satan: a helper of man standing against the adversary of man and man's evil inclination. The transformation of Job, the man without knowledge, to the intellectually mature Job ready for the knowledge of God is symbolized by the replacement of the angel of error by an angel of correction and intercession: "the good inclination." Thus transformed, Job receives what Maimonides terms "the prophetic revelation" of the Lord's speeches. They communicate to Job the radical difference between divine creation and human production, between God's rule, providence, and purpose, and the things men rule over, provide for, and purpose. True wisdom, true knowledge, is attained only when man has freed himself from the "error that His knowledge is like our knowledge or that His purpose is like our purpose." With such knowledge of

man's position in the universe, "every misfortune will be borne
lightly by him." Such humble recognition will silence man's doubts
concerning "whether He does or does not know and whether He
exercises providence," and will, on the contrary, "add to His love."
Many medieval Hebrew interpreters of Job have attempted to read
an affirmation of providence into the text of the Lord's speeches,
thus providing questing Job with an answer to his problem. Not
so Maimonides. In sensitive attention to the text's meaning, he
removed the issue of providence from the area of human concern.
In this reorientation of human thought, Maimonides perceived the
potential basis for what Job, "who feared the Lord," was lacking
before his conversion: the love of God.

Medieval Jewish mystical thought is best represented by the
Zohar ("Book of Splendor"), composed in Spain toward the end
of the thirteenth century by Moses de Leon.[32] Written in Aramaic,
the *Zohar* imitated the form of the midrashic works of the early
Christian centuries. For three centuries after 1500, the *Zohar* "came
to fulfill [in Judaism] the great historical task of a sacred text
supplementing the Bible and Talmud on a new level of religious
consciousness" (G. G. Scholem). The Zoharic writings offer a
number of observations on Job; in several instances they show
kinship to the talmudic-midrashic thinking on the theme, retaining
at the same time their profound, fanciful, and daring originality.

The *Zohar* presents Job as a scapegoat for Israel. On New
Year's Day (which is taken to be the scene of chapter 1 of Job),
God sits in judgment on the world and, with special exaction, on
Israel. In the time of Job the world was balanced exactly between
the good and the wicked, and its fate depended on but a single
person's turning the scale in either direction. Satan, the Accuser,
eager to denounce the world, was therefore impelled to concentrate
all his attention upon one man, and this happened to be Job.
Through God's testing of this man, the power of the Evil One was
to be weakened and Israel enabled to obtain forgiveness. Job was
singled out because he "was known to be apart from his people";
his separation from the community made him a target "in the upper
realm." But, "though he did sin in his mind and later also in his
speech," he did "not go so far as to attach himself to the 'other
[the Satanic] side,'" as Satan had predicted. Therefore, after the

trials that lasted twelve months, "the Lord blessed the latter end of Job" (42:12).³³

In another interpretation, Job is seen as a member of the heathen branch of Abraham's family and an adviser to Pharaoh in his scheme to enslave Israel. Once, when Satan arraigned Abraham for having substituted an animal sacrifice for the offering of Isaac, a deed whose iniquity fell upon the whole seed of Abraham, Job was given to the Evil One as a scapegoat; he deserved to be judged according to the plot he devised for Israel in Egypt: his possessions were taken away, his body was afflicted, but his life was spared.³⁴

Comparing Job with Abraham, the *Zohar* finds that the latter was tempted by *God* to sacrifice his only begotten son, whereas "Job gave nothing to him." "Indeed, he was not bidden to do anything of the kind, as God knew that he would not be equal to the trial"; he was merely delivered to the Accuser to test his faith.³⁵

In still another reflection, the *Zohar* makes Job the symbol of the man who failed to be "cognizant of both good and evil." Cognizance of evil is demonstrated by allowing a portion of one's sacrifice to go to Satan, "the other side." Job permitted his offerings to ascend entirely to heaven and gave no portion to the "other side." Had he given Satan his due, the latter would not have been able to prevail against him. The "unholy side" would have separated itself from the holy, and the holy side would have risen undisturbed to the highest spheres. "As Job kept evil separate from good and failed to fuse them, he was judged accordingly: first he experienced good, then what was evil, then again good. For man should be cognizant of both good and evil, and turn evil itself into good. This is a deep tenet of faith."³⁶

In a note on Elihu—like Job, a descendent of Abraham, and also of the prophet Ezekiel—the *Zohar* discusses divine justice and mercy and the meaning of the suffering of a righteous man.³⁷ Such suffering is declared to stem "from the love which God bears for him; He crushes his body in order to give more power to his soul, so that He may draw him nearer in love."³⁸

The Zoharic observations—only loosely related to each other—deal primarily with the Job of the folk tale, rather than with the hero of the dialogue. Most of the Zoharic texts view Job in the context of the reality of evil, as represented by Satan; they attempt to probe into the deeper reasons for Job's fate and to detect his place in the cosmic drama of the fall and redemption.

In introducing a sequence of reflections on Job, the author of the *Zohar* has Rabbi Judah declare: "And in all this the ways of the Holy One are hidden, and it is beyond me to follow them, for these are the statutes of the Holy One, which men must not examine too closely, save those who walk in the ways of wisdom and are in truth worthy to penetrate into the veiled paths of the Torah, and to comprehend the hidden truths contained therein."[39]

Despite the common core of traditions, the postbiblical Jewish interpreters enjoyed a measure of freedom in approaching the subject of Job. Yet rarely did they allow themselves to look at the book itself and to explore its original meaning. The personality and intellectual circumstances of the exegete, modified by the heritage of his faith, determined his position in commenting on Job.

VI   The Christian Interpretation

It can be maintained that, generally speaking, Christianity was in a more advantageous position than Judaism in approaching the book of Job. It saw in Job a type, symbol, prefiguration of Jesus and could concentrate on and elaborate this understanding of the book. Judaism, on the other hand, had no corresponding single focus of interpretation. This made for a greater variety of outlook and greater freedom of exposition, but militated against a singleness of purpose such as is evident in the Christian reading of Job.

In presenting samples of Christian interpretation, I have chosen John Chrysostom and Jerome as representative of the last period of the ancient Greco-Roman, and the incipient Christian, civilization; Gregory the Great as the author of a major exposition of Job; Luther and Calvin as leaders of the Protestant Reformation.

John Chrysostom of Antioch and Constantinople (second half of the fourth century) is considered to be the greatest preacher of the Eastern Church. Author of a great number of homilies, mainly on New Testament texts, he opposed the philosophical tendency and allegorizing method of Origen of Alexandria (died 254) and strove for a literal interpretation of the Scriptures.

Chrysostom's monastic and ascetic drive shines through his presentation of Job as "a wrestler of self denial."[40] He practiced "freedom from all despondency"; despising wealth, he was "not confounded at its being taken away, since he desired it not when present." He strove for continence, loved his wife, "not however immoderately," and was ready for "bodily mutilation and indignity"; thus "nothing of what happened confounded him."[41] His life "displayed an endurance firmer than any adamant."[42]

In the "Homily on the Power of Man to Resist the Devil,"[43] Chrysostom compares Adam, Eve, and the Serpent with Job, his wife, and the devil, and finds Job's trial to have been far more grievous than Adam's, Job's temptation by his wife far more persuasive than Adam's by his, and Satan more powerful than the Serpent. Yet Adam was defeated and Job emerged a conqueror. The lesson: "This man will give us greater zeal, so that we may raise our hands against the devil." Let us, therefore, "avoid the imitation of Adam ... and imitate the piety of Job."[44] In temptation and in moments of weakness, "remember that body and that saintly flesh, for it was saintly and pure even when it had so many wounds." In sorrow "have recourse to this just man," in calamity "consider this saint." Living "before the day of grace and of the law ... when the grace of the Spirit was not so great and death prevailed," Job "exhausted the misfortunes of the universe" and bore its travails. "So let us always flee to this book."

Most famous among Chrysostom's sermons are the "Homilies on the Statues," delivered in Antioch in 387 or 388, after the people of the city rioted against the imposition of heavy taxes and demolished the statues of the Emperor Theodosius and his wife. In these twenty-one homilies, he exhorts the people to bear with fortitude and patience the impending wrath of the Emperor. Throughout his exhortations he refers repeatedly to the example of Job, who withstood his trials. His is the Job of the folk tale; certain passages from the dialogue are adduced only in support of the folk tale's hero.[45]

In his happy days, says Chrysostom, Job "was not visible to the many what a man he was. But when, like a wrestler, that strips off his garment, he threw it aside, and came naked to the conflicts of piety, thus unclothed, he astonished all who saw him." To the devil, God said: "I am sure of this wrestler; therefore I do not forbid thee to impose on him whatever struggles thou desirest." He was not as illustrious when he opened his house to the poor and clad the naked with the fleece of his flock as when misfortunes befell him. "Before, he was a lover of man; now he was a lover of wisdom. Before, he had compassion on the poor; but now he gave thanks to the Lord." He knew "that God was dispensing all things to the good." His happy state had aroused the devil's suspicion; his endurance in suffering "dealt the devil a heavy blow . . . and his shameless mouth was stopped." "Before, there was much benignity to his fellow servants; now, there was exceeding love shown toward the Lord."[46] "When he lost all . . . he bore away an illustrious victory from the devil."[47]

Comparing Job to Adam, Chrysostom expounds that Paradise was of no profit to Adam when he provoked God, whereas pious Job sitting naked on his dunghill prevailed.[48] That dunghill is "more to be venerated than any kingly throne." A royal throne affords "only a temporary pleasure . . . but from the sight of Job's dunghill one may derive . . . much divine wisdom and consolation." It is "a golden statue set with gems." Job's wounds "struck the devil with utter blindness. . . . He fled, defeated." Thus "poverty is much better . . . than riches, and infirmity and sickness than health, and trial than tranquillity." Job's body "became more venerable when pierced . . . by these wounds." "After the royal throne comes death; but after that dunghill, the kingdom of heaven."[49] Chrysostom exhorted the faithful to imitate the example of Job. When soldiers encircle the city and are about to plunder its wealth, "flee to thy Lord" and repeat the expression of Job's resignation: "The Lord gave," etc.[50]

The rebel of the dialogue, the perceptive listener to the Lord's majestic speeches, was of no use to the fiery preacher. Moreover, being ignorant of Hebrew, he had to rely on translations in which Job's heroic stand is toned down considerably. The saintly, submissive Job of the folk tale, on the other hand, appealed to him and to his flock. The homilies succeeded in pacifying the city; the Emperor sent his gracious pardon.

Jerome (died 420), head of a monastery in Bethlehem and author of the Vulgate translation of the Bible into Latin, was, like other Fathers of the period, involved in the controversy over the doctrines of Origen of Alexandria. Origen's *Peri archon* (On First Principles) was interpreted as denying the divinity of Jesus and the resurrection of the body. In an acrimonious letter against John of Jerusalem,[51] a monk who was a follower of Origen, Jerome (in his early years himself an admirer of Origen) adduced Joban texts to prove "the hope and reality of resurrection." Citing Job 19:23 ff. ("I know that my Redeemer liveth," etc.), Jerome exclaims: "No one since the days of Christ speaks so openly concerning the resurrection as he did before Christ. . . . He knew and saw that Christ, his Redeemer, was alive, and at the last day would rise again from the earth. The Lord had not yet died, and the athlete of the Church saw his Redeemer rising from the grave." The verse "Then in my flesh[52] shall I see God" (19:26) is interpreted: "When all flesh shall see the salvation of God, and Jesus as God, then I, also, shall see the Redeemer and Savior, and my God. But I shall see him in that flesh which now tortures me. . . . In my flesh shall I behold God, because of His own resurrection He has healed all my infirmities." Jerome felt that he had given final and convincing evidence for bodily resurrection, for he adds: "Does it not seem to you that Job was then writing against Origen, and was holding a controversy similar to ours against the heretics, for the reality of flesh?" If this view is not accepted, Jerome continues, the statement that "Job will rise again" is but a "hollow phrase."[53]

It is curious to note that Job, who, in the book, opposed his friends and a hostile deity, became, in Jerome's polemic, an opponent of the third-century Alexandrian. And of all "solutions" of the Job problem resurrection is the least feasible. Had the author of Job shared the later Jewish (and Christian) belief in resurrection in a redeemed world, he could not have written the book. But in the context of ancient and medieval scriptural interpretation this is beside the point.

Gregory I, the Great (*ca.* 540–604), prefect of Rome, later monk, Abbot of St. Andrew's Monastery, and finally Pope (590–604), is the author of *Magna Moralia,* or "Exposition of the Book of Job." The work originated in lectures, delivered in Constantinople, in which Gregory "desired to lay open the deep mysteries it [the book of Job] contains, so far as the Truth should inspire me with the power of doing so." Edited later in Rome, the work comprised thirty-five "books"; the English version consists of four volumes.[54]

Gregory's exposition of Job has a threefold purpose: to offer, first, and least important, a literal (historical), second, an allegorical (mystical), and third, a moral interpretation, the latter addressed to the Church or to the individual Christian. It is the allegorical mode that matters most to the author. Since Scripture "holds out in promise the Redeemer of the world in all its statements" (VI, 1), the book of Job, too, is but a record of the Christian message, and its hero a prefiguration of Jesus. "The blessed Job, who uttered those high mysteries of His Incarnation," was by his life "a sign of Him, whom by voice he proclaimed" (Preface, 14). Job's seven sons refer, symbolically, to the twelve Apostles ($7 = 3 + 4$; $3 \times 4 = 12$); his three daughters typify the "three orders of the faithful." The 7,000 sheep refer to the Jews who have been led "from the pastures of the Law to the perfect estate of grace," and so on (I, 21). "Let it look for light, but have none" (3:9, in Job's curse of the day of his birth) refers to "the mischievous effects of [Judaea's] blindness . . . at the coming of the Redeemer" (IV, 20). This allegorical exposition is followed by a moral mode, in which such a verse as "Let that day be darkness" (3:4) teaches the faithful "to what end of ruin sin is hurrying us" (IV, 26).

Job's outcry against his God, "For the arrows of the Almighty are within me" (6:4), is addressed to the sinful Christian "at the same time pierced by the stroke of divine correction, and . . . which we apprehend of the terribleness of the Judge to come, and of His everlasting visitation" (VII, 13). Similarly, Job's accusation, "For He shall break me with a tempest" (9:17), speaks not of the innocent sufferer's fate, but of "that sinner, who seemed to be established in tranquillity . . . whom the long-suffering Above bears for long but the last strict Judgment destroys" (IX, 31). In the case of such verses, Gregory's literal and his moral interpretation merge into one. The two meanings supplement each other also when Job's protest against God as one who "destroyeth the innocent and the wicked" (9:22) is taken to mean: "The perfect man is destroyed by the creator, in that whatever his pureness may have been, it is swallowed up by the pureness of the divine immensity.

. . . The wicked likewise is destroyed by the creator, in that . . . his wickedness is caught in the noose of his own artifices" (IX, 40). Job's ultimate indictment of the world's management, "The earth is given into the hand of the wicked" (9:24), is viewed as an allegorical reference to the Crucifixion: "The hands of this wicked one [i.e., the devil] were they who were the aggressors in the death of our Redeemer. . . . His flesh [earth = flesh] he [Satan], being permitted, did by means of his ministers deprive of life for three days" (IX, 44). Job's plea to be relieved of divine terror ("Let Him take away His rod from me, and let not His terror make me afraid," [9:34]) is read as an allegorical allusion to the law (= the rod), which was removed by the Incarnation. "For He had no mind to be feared as God, but . . . loved as a Father" (IX, 62).

Job, pointing to the unconscious immortality of inanimate nature versus mortal man, says that "there is hope of a tree, if it be cut down, that it will sprout again. . . . But man dieth . . . where is he?" (14:7–10). In Gregory's exposition, "tree" is a symbol of the Cross, a just man, or of Wisdom of God Incarnate. Thus, there is indeed hope for a just man in his suffering, for "in the greenness of everlasting life he is recovered again. But the sinner [= man] "dies in guilt . . . and [is] consumed in punishment. . . . Where then is he, who is not in His love, where only it is truly to be?" (XII, 5–9).

The problem of evil is a main concern in the book of Job; it is of no concern in Gregory's commentary. For "sin," here identified with evil, "has no foundation; it has no subsistence in its own proper nature. For evil has no substance. But that [of evil] which anyhow exists, unites with the nature of good" (XXVI, 68, interpreting Job 36:16). Only "in proportion as the mind neglects to take account of the good that comes after, does it feel the ills of the present life" (X, 32, commenting on Job 11:16). In denying reality to evil, Gregory follows the teachings of Augustine (which he accepts also in other points of theology). "The Lord is the Author of nature, not of sin" (= evil); "He engendered therefore, by naturally creating, those whom He suffered . . . to remain in sin." As an example of this relationship of good and evil, nature and sin, Gregory offers "the hearts of the Jews, which before were tender, and easily penetrated by faith, [but] afterwards hardened in the obstinacy of unbelief" (XXIX, 55, commenting on Job 38:29).

Since, therefore, the Joban speeches raised no questions, the speeches of the Lord will bring no reply, even though the expositor seems to have sensed the major motif in chapter 38. He comments on 38:3: "I rouse thee by my words to consider sublime truths, and whilst thou perceivest that thou knowest not these things that are above thee, I make thee better known to thyself. For then thou answerest me truly, if thou understandest what things thou knowest not" (XXVIII, 13). But, rather than pursuing the implications of the motif of knowledge in the chapters on creation, Gregory resumes the application of the allegoric method to the text. Thus, "the foundations of the earth" (38:4) becomes the creation of the Church (XXVIII, 14); "the measures" of the earth (38:5) refers to Jesus, who "marked out the boundaries of the Church with the subtlety of His secret judgment" (XXVIII, 15). "The foundations" (38:6) are "the teachers of Holy Church" (XXVIII, 17), "the corner-stone" (38:6) is "He who taking into Himself from one side the Jewish, and from the other the Gentile people, unites, as it were, two walls in the one fabric of the Church" (XXVIII, 19). The "raven" (38:41) designates "the Gentile world blackened with sin," or "the people of the Jews, black with the demerit of unbelief"; the "young raven" *(ibid.)* symbolizes "the sons of the Gentiles, when their longing is refreshed by our conversion" (XXX, 28, 32). The "rhinoceros" (or wild ox [39:9]), to Gregory, signifies the Jewish people, who "with foolish pride confided in the works of the law, in opposition to the preaching of the truth" (XXXI, 29). The "ostrich" (39:13) refers to the synagogue, her "eggs" (39:14) to the Apostles "born of the flesh of the synagogue" (XXXI, 37). "She [the ostrich] raiseth her wings" (39:18) alludes mystically to the rise of the Antichrist, who "despises not only the Manhood of the Lord, but also His very Godhead" (XXXI, 42). *Behemoth* (40:15) is none else than Satan, the ancient enemy (XXXII, 16), whose habits Gregory discusses in great detail. But in the end, he declares, Jesus took Satan as it were "with a snare" (Job 40:24): "Our Lord, when coming for the redemption of mankind, made, as it were, a kind of hook of Himself for the death of the devil; for He assumed a body, in order that this *behemoth* might seek therein the death of the flesh, as if it were his bait. . . . He was quite ignorant that our Redeemer was piercing him by His own death" (XXXIII, 14). *Leviathan* (Job 40:25) is but another symbol for Satan (XXXIII, 17); the text "the hope of him is in vain" (41:1), which speaks of man's hope to catch the crocodile, is interpreted as the "cruel and mighty monster [that] is brought captive into the midst, and with his own body, that is, with all reprobates, consigned to the eternal fires of hell" (XXXIII, 37). The commentator adds: "O what a spectacle will that be!"

Now, since the Lord's speeches, in Gregory's reading, contained nothing to affect Job's thought, his final admission that he had uttered that which he understood not (42:3) does not refer to his, Job's, dramatic experience, but to man in general: "All human wisdom, however powerful in acuteness, is foolishness, when compared with divine wisdom" (XXXV, 3).

In Job's restoration, Gregory sees an allegorical meaning: The seven bullocks offered by the friends (42:8) refer to the Apostles, "who were to be filled with the Spirit of sevenfold grace . . . ; they were sent in the four quarters of the world to make known the Trinity, which is God" (XXXV, 15). In the end, "the Lord blessed the latter end of Job more than his beginning" (42:12), which is a mystical allusion to the final "admission of the people of Israel [into the Church], when . . . the Lord consoles the pain of Holy Church by a manifold ingathering of souls" (XXXV, 35).

To sum it up, the chief purpose of the book of Job, as Gregory views it, is, like that of all of Scripture, the teaching of the doctrines of the Church: Trinity, Incarnation, Death and Resurrection, Grace, the function of the Church, the merit of suffering, the victory over the demons and the devil, the fate—promise and predicament—of Israel, sin and punishment, hell and Redemption. A literal, "historical" meaning of the book of Job admittedly existed, but, to Gregory, such meaning was irrelevant. The author of Job, he postulated, had elevated his work above national, ethnic, and cultic peculiarities and had raised a purely human issue; thus Gregory read the text as being either a testimony of salvation to be consummated or a warning to the sinner. He made it the spokesman of his own religious aim, which to him, however, signified the divine purpose. The book's "man" became divided into man the saint and man the sinner, Christian and Jew.

The success of the commentary was phenomenal. The work is not as profound as Augustine's, nor as structured as that of Thomas Aquinas. Its author was neither scholar, nor theologian, nor original thinker, but, basically, a preacher. However, he brought to fruition

the work that was initiated by the Latin doctors who preceded him—
Ambrose, Augustine, and Jerome: the establishment of the spiritual
power of the Church. In the centuries following its publication, the
Magna Moralia was many times translated from the Latin and
epitomized, and read as a textbook and compendium of Christian
dogma and thought. The book of Job as such proffered no message
beyond the one that Gregory's commentary saw documented in it.

In his Preface to the translation of the book into German,[55]
dated 1524, Martin Luther stated that his rendition used "language
that is clear and that everybody can understand, giving the genuine
sense and meaning." For if it were literally translated "as the Jews
and foolish translators would have it done," no one would understand
it. As Luther sees it, the theme of the book is "whether misfortune
can come to the righteous from God." Job holds that God does
indeed chastise even the good "without reason, to His praise." To
be sure, being in danger of death, Job "talks in his human weakness
too much against God, and thus sins amid his sufferings." Though
Job was right in asserting his innocence when he replied to his
friends, he had, in God's judgment, "spoken wrongly by speaking
against Him." For Luther, the chief point of the text is the fact
that "God alone is righteous, and yet one man is more righteous
than another, even before God." The book was written "for our
comfort, in order that we may know that God allows even His
saints to stumble." In adversity, even a holy man may get the
notion "that God is not God, but only a judge and wrathful tyrant,
who applies force and cares nothing about the good life." The text
is best understood by those "who experience and feel what it is to
suffer the wrath and judgment of God, and to have His grace
hidden from view."

Luther, who read the Psalter as "a clear promise of Christ's
death and resurrection" and as typifying "His kingdom and the
condition and nature of all Christendom,"[56] omitted the chris-
tological motif in his Preface to Job. In view of the fact that
many Christian interpreters before and after Luther introduced
this motif, it is noteworthy that he did not. His Job is a man
tempted by God, and the book tells the story of the hero's stand.
The element of skepticism and rebellion is reduced in scope, and
the speeches of the Lord are not adduced as the answer to Job.

John Calvin (1509–64) wanted to be known more as a preacher than as a theologian; he considered his sermons to be more important than his famous *Institutes of the Christian Religion.* Indeed, both his personality and his thinking express themselves most fully in his sermons.[57] In contradistinction to the Jesus-centered Luther, Calvin was God-centered. He emphasized God's incomprehensible majesty, His providence and sovereign grace, the doctrine of election and of man's nothingness. Seven hundred of his originally French sermons became known in English, first published in 1553. Foremost among his sermons are the 159 based on the book of Job —one of the few major biblical books on which he wrote no commentary. Owing to the spread of Calvinism in England, the sermons on Job, in their English translation, enjoyed great popularity up to the beginning of the seventeenth century.[58]

A fair example is Sermon 147, on the Lord's answer to Job from a whirlwind.[59] It is because of our rebellion, says Calvin, that God must show Himself in terror. When He perceives our hardness of heart, He must cast us down at the beginning. (Just as, when He gave His law on Sinai, "He moved the thunderbolts . . . in order to bring down the haughtiness of the people.") And if a saint like Job, who humbled himself under His majesty, needed to be checked, what about us? Man, full of pride and rebellion against God, must be beaten down into rightful obedience. God speaks to us out of a whirlwind because we did not hear Him when He spoke to us graciously, and in a humane and fatherly manner. For a time He lets us run like escaped horses, yet in the end we shall experience His terrible majesty to be frightened by it.

Turning to the phrase "Who is this that darkeneth counsel" (38:2), Calvin has God mock Job—and all men—with the question: "And who are you, man?" We ourselves may imagine that we have dignity, power, and wisdom, but God knows that in us reside only odor and stink; the wisdom of man is only foolishness and vanity, he is only a vessel full of filth and villainy. It is God's intent to lead us to a correct knowledge of our poverty, so that we may be void of all pride and presumption, and learn to be ashamed of ourselves, in the realization that it is up to Him to call one man to salvation and reject another. The condemnation of man in the Scriptures is not aimed simply at the vulgar and the contemptible; it encompasses the greatest, those who supposedly touch the clouds.

We must be completely emptied, God must void us, that He may not leave a single drop of virtue in us. What we do receive from Him proceeds from His pure goodness.

Job (= man) speaks "without knowledge" (38:2). We should come to God's Word with fear and solicitude rather than coughing up what comes to us in fancy. As an example of folly Calvin cites the Papists, who turn upside down, falsify, deprave, and corrupt all the Holy Scriptures and mock God. Others too wish to be theologians but are in fact stupid and wholly brutish; wine rules them like pigs, and they chat and babble what seems good to them.

So, Calvin concludes, let us learn to keep our mouths shut rather than open them to vomit up what is unknown to us; let us learn not to presume to answer our God, and correct this arrogance that is in us. Filled with His glory, we may glorify ourselves, not in us, but in Him alone.

A fiery, vigorous sermon indeed. The tension between the majesty of God and the low state of man's knowledge is most forcefully presented. But in crudely identifying Job with "us," or, rather, "us" with Job, Calvin missed both the sincerity of Job's quest for justice and God's intent in displaying the miraculous universe before him. However, as is the case with other interpreters, Calvin's scheme was not to analyze the book but to use it as a foil for his own views. In this he succeeded magnificently.

To sum up: The Christian interpreter reads Job as an allegory, as a text that calls for symbolic analysis. For him, the book of Job is but a testimony to the central event in Christianity and, later, to some of the theological and moral teachings of the Church. Though greater "use" was made of Job in Christian than in Jewish thought, the Christian contribution to the understanding of the issues of the book itself is even less evident than in the Jewish counterpart.

VII Modern Interpretations

In approaching the early modern and more recent interpretations of Job, the reader will note the strong shift from testimonies and adaptations rooted in tradition and doctrine to freer expressions of attitudes (even when they are based on the writer's intellectual stance rather than the evidence of the text), a greater variety of insights, a profounder appreciation of the human and literary aspects of the book.

Thomas Hobbes (1588–1679), the first "modern" political philosopher, considered (as is well known) hereditary monarchy to be the only legitimate and the most workable form of government. While in his earlier writings he proposed a monarchy that makes concessions to, and use of, both democracy and aristocracy, in his *Leviathan* (1651) he demanded the exercise of absolute power by the sovereign. The Christian, he postulated, is duty bound to render unconditional obedience to the secular ruler; religion must serve the state. The Kingdom of God, both in Judaism and in Christianity, is a kingdom on earth.

Hobbes made use of biblical arguments, or, better, his own interpretation of certain scriptural passages, to support and lend authority to his political theory. This tendency decreased in the progression of his writings but is still evident in *Leviathan*.[60] In the chapter "Of the Kingdom of God by Nature,"[61] he argues that "The Right of Nature, whereby God reigneth over man, and punisheth those that break his Lawes, is to be derived not from his Creating them . . . but from his Irresistible Power." He refers to Job:

> And *Job*, how earnestly does he expostulate with God, for the many Afflictions he suffered, notwithstanding his Righteousness? This question in the case of Job, is decided by God Himselfe, not by arguments derived from Job's Sinne, but His own Power. For whereas the friends of Job drew their arguments from his Affliction to his Sinne, and he defended himselfe by the conscience of his Innocence, God Himselfe taketh up the matter, and having justified the Affliction by arguments drawn from His Power, such as this, *Where wast thou when I layd the foundations of the earth* [38:4], and the like, both approved Job's Innocence, and reproved the Erroneous doctrine of his friends. Conformable to this doctrine is the sentence of our Saviour, concerning the man that was born Blind, in these words, *Neither hath this man sinned, nor his fathers: but that the works of God might be made manifest in him* [John 9:3].[62]

It would not have served Hobbes's interest to inquire into the source of this power. The element of seemingly arbitrary might in the Lord's speeches suited his purposes; he did not need to go any further.

Spinoza (1632–77) had no immediate interest in the Bible, and his philosophy required no recourse to Scripture. Yet he examined the biblical writings, both as an antidote to the intolerance of the age and in order to secure for the believer the freedom to engage in philosophy. He attempted to distinguish clearly between the objective content of a given book and the interpreters' subjective beliefs.[63] Speaking of the book of Job in his *Theologico-political Treatise,* Spinoza twice quotes the opinion of the medieval Hebrew Bible exegete Abraham ibn Ezra, that the book is a translation into Hebrew (rather than an original Hebrew work)[64] and twice that Job (or the author of the book) was a heathen,[65] which suggests that pagans, too, were in possession of sacred books. The fate of Job (fortune, tragedy, restored fortune) and the strength of his character caused people to reflect upon divine providence and moved the author to compose the dialogue. Viewing the argument of the book and its style, Spinoza was prompted to assert that the writer could not have been the sufferer himself, sitting on his dunghill, but must have been a man given to quiet reflection in his study.[66] In the firm belief that the Bible is a human book and a work of imagination, the philosopher could have been expected to do more for Job, this most human and most imaginative of biblical writings.

Voltaire (1694–1778) has a satirical article on Job in his *Dictionnaire Philosophique,* published in 1764.[67] He was intrigued by Job's possessions, referred to in the first verses of the book, and figured out their value: Seven thousand sheep "at three livres ten sous apiece" make 22,500 livres; three thousand camels "at fifty crowns apiece" make 450,000 livres, and so on, until he arrived at a total of 562,500 livres, "without reckoning thy furniture, rings and jewels." Yet he, Voltaire, though having been much richer than Job, had not murmured against God when he lost a great part of his property. Satan was mistaken in his scheme against Job. In the state of poverty and illness, "men always have recourse to divinity; they are prosperous people who forget God." At the time "Satan

knew not enough of the world," but "he has improved himself
since." The good friends offered advice, but none lent him a crown.
"I would not have treated thee thus." In the end, God "condemned
them to a fine of seven bullocks and seven rams, for having talked
nonsense."

As to the authorship of the book, "it is evident," says Voltaire,
"that it is the work of an Arab" before the time of Moses, since it
mentions "Arcturus, Orion, and the Pleiades" and the Hebrews
"never had the least knowledge of astronomy," whereas the Arabs,
"living in tents, were continually led to observe the stars." And
monotheism? "It is an absurd error to imagine that the Jews were
the only people who recognized a sole God; it was the doctrine of
almost all the East, and the Jews were only plagiarists in that as
in everything else." But regardless of such puny details of history,
the historian Voltaire continues, "there is not at present any little
physical treatise that would not be more useful than all the books
of antiquity."

In 1791 Immanuel Kant (1724–1804) published his essay "On
the Failure of All Philosophical Essays in the Theodicy," which he
defined as a defense of the supreme wisdom of the world's creator
against the accusation raised by human reason aware of the in-
expediency in the world. Following a keen analysis of the rational
and moral implications of this employment of reason, the philosopher
reaches the conclusion that thus far no theodicy has succeeded in
harmonizing the concept of moral wisdom in the rule of the world
and man's worldly experience with the end of justifying the former.
Our reason, says Kant, gives us no insight whatsoever into the relationship between the world of our experience and the supreme
wisdom (of God). The world may be considered as the proclama-
tion of the intentions of the divine will; as such, it is all too often
a sealed book; it is always a sealed book if we try to read in it
the ultimate, moral intentions of the creator. Terming this approach
"doctrinal theodicy," Kant differentiates from it the approach he
calls "authentic theodicy," a theodicy rooted not in speculative
reason but in the authoritative divine dictum conceived by our
reason but preceding experience. In such theodicy, God, rather than
our reason, becomes the interpreter of His will as documented in
the created world.

In this discourse, Kant restated his critique of dogmatic metaphysics and of its belief that our reason is capable of an objective knowledge of God and world. Man's intellect is subjective, finite, and therefore unable to know the unconditional, the infinite, the perfect—God. God as a reality can be known to man only to the degree in which He reveals Himself. Man's knowledge is limited to the *idea* of God, the world, the soul. This type of knowledge, which is "practical" (rather than "speculative" or "scientific") and accessible to man as a subject that wills and acts, is the root of our moral existence, moral will, and moral faith.

In this essay on theodicy, Kant noted that he found the above theme allegorically presented and authentically interpreted in the "ancient, sacred book" of Job. Job's friends, according to Kant's conception, represent speculative reason; their reasoning explains evil in the world as punishment for sins, and by so doing asserts divine justice; they argue a priori that otherwise (i.e., without an assumption of Job's sin) divine justice could not be reconciled with man's misfortunes. Before a court of dogmatic theologians, a synod, a bench of the Inquisition, or a contemporary religious consistory, Job would indeed have suffered an evil fate. Job's point was that the divine decree is absolute. "He is at one with Himself . . . what He desireth, even that He doeth" (23:13), Kant quotes, implying that human reason cannot understand divine action. He further quotes 13:7–11, 16: "Will ye speak for God with unrighteousness. . . . Will ye show Him favor? Will ye contend for God? . . . He will surely reprove you, if ye do secretly show favor. . . . A hypocrite cannot come before Him."

In Kant's interpretation, Job's honesty and intellectual integrity (he cites 27:5 f.) earned him the answer out of the whirlwind. In this revelation God pointed to the inscrutableness of creation, which, from man's point of view, includes creatures of destruction and with no apparent purpose. The physical order of things is hidden from us; even more impenetrable is the connection of the physical with the moral order. In the face of this instruction, Job admitted to have spoken words without wisdom. His ethically honest admission of lack of knowledge and the limits of reason is the basis of Job's faith. Thus his faith was founded upon moral conduct, which makes it an authentic faith, and his attitude to God an authentic theodicy.

It is fascinating to observe how Kant made the book of Job fit his critical system and his neat distinction between metaphysical knowledge and moral will and faith, or, between morality based on faith and faith based on moral consciousness. However, his Job is a rather stationary figure; Job the rebel against universal disorder and injustice is reduced to a minimum, while his candor and integrity are projected as central characteristics. Be this as it may, the book of Job gave Kant the opportunity to separate what he termed doctrinal from authentic theodicy.

This essay was followed, two years later, by *Die Religion inner-halb der Grenzen der blossen Vernunft* (Religion Within the Bounds of Mere Reason). Fearing the opposition of the religious traditionalist, the king of Prussia requested Kant to refrain from further publications on the touchy subject. Kant, always a good citizen, complied.

The English poet and illustrator William Blake (1757–1827) personifies the unusual paradox of mythology and thought, apocalypse and humanism. A Christian, he denounced the Church and a supernatural God, but believed in a deity "who is the intellectual fountain of Humanity" and interpreted Christianity as the advocate of "the liberty both of body and mind to exercise the Divine Arts of Imagination." He rejected material, mechanical creation as the Fall of God, the dark power and originator of the Book of Law—and of evil. It is this god ("Urizen" in Blake's mythology) who allows Jesus to be crucified "on the Tree of Mystery." Yet (especially in Blake's earlier writings) Jesus, "divine humanity," represents revolt, dynamism, man's liberated energy; and Crucifixion implies that "Man is Love as God is Love." Both Jesus and the revolutions of the late eighteenth century aimed at one and the same thing: freedom. The ideal goal was the exuberant exercise of imagination, of poetic genius, the "Contraries" redeemed, and man's eyes opened "inwards into the Worlds of Thought, into Eternity."

Blake's thinking about God and deities refers not to an extra-human reality but to states of mind. "All deities reside in the human breast," he said, and "God only Acts and Is in existing beings or Men."

Such a process of internalization is also evident in Blake's *Illustrations of the Book of Job* (1820–25).[68] Here God, Satan, Job's wife, children, and friends are all symbols of what in reality takes place in the hero's soul. Satan is the Accuser within; the search for God, a search for Job's self.

In Blake's vision—there is no better term for designating his reading of the book—Job is an innocent, pious man, who, however, is bound by the letter of the law, the "book," a symbol contrasted by the spiritual "scroll." He prides himself on his ability to do his duty and to "fear" (not "love") God—who in Blake's strikingly beautiful illustrations has the facial characteristics of Job himself. His self-assurance gives rise to doubt, symbolized by Satan, the Accuser. His rigid adherence to the law causes his children's estrangement, symbolized by their violent death. The bereaved parents sit under heavy crosses, symbols of distorted faith. In a scene absent from the biblical text (Illustration V), Blake has Job sharing his bread with a beggar in a spirit of duty, not of love: the gift is given and received with the left hand, indicative of the negative aspect, not with the right hand, sign of the positive aspect. (The symbolism of right and left in Blake is Wicksteed's discovery.) Now Satan is free to act his part—until, through suffering, anguish, and indignation, Job is ready to re-examine his life, past and present. The friends—parts of Job's consciousness—remain in their former adherence to dogma; they crouch under the stone cross. The turning point comes to Job when he realizes (Illustration XI) that the God of Justice and Morality to whom he had appealed is none but the Accuser. It is Elihu, pointing to Job's pride, who prepares the hero for the vision of the true God "out of the whirlwind": Jesus, "the divine imagination," offering mercy and forgiveness, opening "Eternity in Time and Space" (Illustration XIII). The vision widens to embrace a perception of the universe—body, intellect, emotion, and imagination held together by the divine force (Illustration XIV). This vision, this perception, marks the end of Satan's rule; Job, freed from the shackles of self, and his wife (who throughout Blake's presentation remained the hero's loyal companion) ascend to the divine realm. He prays for his friends and receives gifts from them, offered in a spirit of love. His three daughters return, the sons are restored. Job, purified, lives a full life again. In the final illustration he plays the harp which, in Wicksteed's words, "stands upon the earth, but seems to soar to Heaven."

Blake created Job in his own image. Though biblical quotations appear on the margins of the illustrations, the ones most typical of the original Job—the utterances of protest and rebellion against the established tradition—eluded the mystic illustrator. The elusion is noteworthy, for in Job's protest Blake could have sensed an echo of his own protest against dogma and institutionalized Christianity. But he was determined to present Job as living in error, in the sin of pride, in clinging to the law and its Satanic God—until the true God appeared and Job himself became an expression of "Humanity Divine."

This concept of the deity, too, strongly deviated from the biblical text. For in the latter, the God who inflicts torment upon Job and He who answers him from the whirlwind are one and the same; the Lord's answer in chapters 38–41 explains His silence in the course of the dialogue. The entire composition of the book rests upon this identity. It is Job who undergoes a change, a radical transformation. And in no way is Job akin to, or a reflection of, this God. Antagonism separates him from God during the dialogue, and a sense of wonderment and distance prevails in the speeches from the whirlwind; but the creature, first ignored, then addressed, and the creator, the silent and the speaking one, never merge. Against this drama, Blake posits a duality within the realm of divinity: the divine justice on the one hand, and the divine imagination (Jesus), a better God, on the other. This dualism makes for a smoother, more plausible transition in the mind of Job, but it destroys the majestic turnabout, his "conversion," as posited in the biblical presentation.

In the biblical drama, what happens between Job and his God is a confrontation, or rather, a renewal of the confrontation the hero was ardently waiting for. In Blake's interpretation, "what is Above is Within"; what happens is an internal process: "in every bosom a Universe expands."

Further, like many Job readers, both predecessors and successors, Blake was deeply intrigued by Satan, the demonic faculty in man; his figure ranks prominently in the illustrations. He pointed to the paradoxical nature of the devil by saying of Milton that "in the Book of Job his Messiah is call'd Satan." Blake's was an internalized, spiritualized vision of the biblical world. "As to the natural sense, that Voltaire was commissioned by God to expose."

Alphonse de Lamartine (1790–1869), a religiously motivated poet within French romanticism, read the book of Job as a document of aged humanity, coming to us "from the depths of centuries."

In this epic poem of the soul, in this dream of man's thought, in this lyrical work of philosophy, in this elegiac, moaning lament, everything betokens the wisdom and melancholy of declining age. How many years, how many centuries had to pass for humanity to gather, delve into, and examine its innermost thoughts, in order to arrive finally at these metaphysical judgments on the miseries of man's destiny and the mysteries of divine providence!

What! can it be that from the very beginning, from the first wailing of his soul, man could have spoken both as man and as God? This first cry of the human heart, bursting with the fullness of anger and pain; this first roar of anguish that a cruel destiny brings forth from the tortured lion-sinew of the human soul, how can these have surpassed all that the most cultivated art of thought and style has produced even to the present day? Where then, indeed, could Job have found his knowledge of nature, his understanding of human things, his weariness with life, his despairing annihilation of self, if not in the wealth of our wretchedness and our tears,—a treasure stored up through long centuries, in the abyss of an age already grown old?

If there is any book which has portrayed the special poetry of old age—first its discouragement, bitterness, irony, reproach, complaint, impiety, silence, prostration, and then its resignation: that impotence which, of necessity, is transformed into virtue; and finally, the consolation which by divine reverence raises up the crestfallen spirit;—then that book is most certainly the book of Job, that dialogue with the self, with one's friends, with God.

Lamartine dismisses the traditional view that ascribed the book to Moses. This is, he says, not the book of a statesman, a historian, a legislator, but of a poet.

Job speaks in the tongue of the greatest poet who ever uttered human speech. His language is eloquence and poetry fused together all at once into all the cries of mankind. He narrates, discusses, listens, replies; he grows angry, challenges, apostrophizes, rants and scolds; he cries out, sings, weeps, jeers, implores; he reflects, he judges himself, he repents, he grows calm, he worships, and soars on the wings of his religious enthusiasm far above his own anguish; from the depths of his despair he justifies God against his own self; he says: "It is good!"

Comparison between Job and Prometheus came to the minds of many sensitive readers. So to Lamartine: "Job is the Prometheus of the word, raised to the heavens still shrieking, still bleeding, in the very claws of the vulture gnawing at his heart. He is the victim become judge, by the sublime impersonality of reason, celebrating his own torture and, like the Roman Brutus, casting up to heaven the drops of his blood, not as an insult, but as a libation to a just God!"

In conclusion: "Job is no longer man; he is humanity! A race which can feel, think, and speak in such a voice is truly worthy of a dialogue with the divine; it is worthy of conversing with its creator."[69]

"I have always studied the Bible, but as a poet, not as an exegete," said Paul Claudel (1868–1955), French diplomat and a poet of the symbolist school. Arthur Rimbaud and Stéphane Mallarmé, members of that school, influenced him greatly. As a man of deep Catholic faith (Christmas, 1886, in Notre Dame, he experienced a spiritual awakening), he believed that true art always gravitates toward the sacred, that the divine is involved in the life of man, and that man is at all times exposed to eternity. In the last two decades of his life, he turned away from writing plays and poetry and devoted himself almost completely to putting down his intuitions on biblical themes.

His *Le Livre de Job* (1946) begins by stating that, of all biblical books, Job "is the most sublime, the most poignant, the most daring, and, at the same time, the most enigmatic, disappointing and . . . the most offensive." What is offensive is the fact that Job's plea for the cause of man should take the form of blasphemy. However, to Claudel, this aspect of the book is only the surface of things. In truth, Job's outcry is but "the prefiguration of the supreme interjection on the cross: 'My God, my God, why hast Thou forsaken me?'" Thus, "the eruption of human complaint," in which Job is a symbol of Jesus, is not rooted in man's awareness of evil and injustice in the world. Evil is no problem; it has been answered by the incarnation.

In reviewing Job's desperate reproaches, Claudel omits or tones down much of what is outrageous and blasphemous, and gives the rest a meaning that suggests faith rather than rebellion. Job defends his integrity: "This also shall be my salvation, that a hypocrite cannot come before Him" (13:16). Of this verse Claudel cites only the first half, translating "He will be my Savior," and omits the second half. Job counterposes the hope of a tree that, cut down, will sprout anew, against the finality of man's death, and leads to the bold assertion, "Thou destroyest the hope of man" (14:7–19). Claudel cites only the first part of verse 7, "for there is hope of a tree," rendering it "the wood has hope," uttered "mysteriously" by Job; human hopelessness, as expressed by Job, is replaced by faith.

The expressions of Job's agony did not escape Claudel, but to him they are part of a larger whole. Job "both hopes and despairs . . . he blasphemes and he adores, he is a sinner and he is innocent." Ultimately, he knows that "his Redeemer liveth" and that he will rise again on the last day and see God with his own eyes. And Claudel asks: "Isn't it here a question of the cross and of the crown of thorns?" In his view, Job mysteriously divines his rôle as symbol and prefiguration.

He continues: The Lord's answer to Job is, on the surface, no relevant answer at all; it hardly differs from the arguments of the friends. Why, for instance, did Job have to be informed that *behemoth* "has the nerves of his testicles intertwined?" (40:17). But on a deeper level the speeches interpret to Job the cause of evil. The source of evil is none but the Evil One. Satan is that power in creation which refused to give free consent to God's reign upon it. The parade of animals in the Lord's speeches proffers "figures of the devil." Each of them personifies a Satanic trait espoused by man. The wild goat and the hind personify unreliable theorists; the wild ass, rebels, parasites, antisocial men; the rhinoceros, egotists, positivists, humanists, pagans, educators who corrupt youth, materialists; the ostrich, heretics; the vulture, *philosophes*, and so on. *Behemoth* and *leviathan* symbolize the two aspects of the devil: passive refusal and active rebellion. By devouring man, the image of God, Satan endlessly tries to absorb God Himself. In contrast to Satan stands God, who is order, form, providence, grace: the path to be followed by man.

The divine reply is only apparently addressed to Job, but Job knows that God is speaking to someone within him who is not he, and that if he does not understand, that mysterious "other" within him, the "L'Homme-Dieu" of the future, does.

Claudel, who said that he had for fifty years struggled with the meaning of God's answer to Job, presented his thesis with dramatic power. He read the book in the light of his faith; Job, symbol of man, became symbol of the God-Man; the transformation within man himself—the great teaching of the book—Claudel replaced by the transfiguration of man. True, it is a poet's reading, not an exegete's. But the non-exegete Claudel professes "profound respect for the written *verbe*," and calls "every word a re-calling of the command that created it." Such respect, if applied to Job, would, for one thing, have ruled out the reintroduction of the Satan whom the biblical author so radically dismissed with the end of chapter 2.

In his *Answer to Job*,[70] Swiss psychologist and psychiatrist Carl Gustav Jung (1875–1961), one of psychology's Big Three and father of "collective myths" and "archetypes," proposes to deal "with the way in which a modern man . . . comes to terms with the divine darkness which is unveiled in the book of Job." For, in his view, the God of Job, far from being a free Lord of creation, is a demiurge, amoral, inconsistent, touchy, suspicious, ruthless, brutal. This God envies man for what he, man, alone possesses: "a somewhat keener consciousness." This envy explains God's yielding to Satan, His "surprising readiness to listen to Satan's insinuations against His better judgment," since He knows that Job is a good man. Job's realization of "God's inner antinomy" produces in him "a divine numinosity." Moreover, Job is "the outward occasion for an inward process of dialectic in God." In confronting poor Job (in chapters 38–41), God, who had "let Himself be bamboozled by Satan," actually addressed Himself to a much more formidable opponent, Satan. Because of Satan's "close kinship" to God, the situation is so compromising that God must hide the Evil One from His own consciousness and, instead, set up Job as "the bugbear."

Obviously (to Jung) Job emerges as the victor in this contest with God. Man, "in spite of his impotence, is set up as a judge over God." Nothing can "rescue the monotheistic conception of God from disaster." He has failed to rebuke Satan and to protect Job. "The reason He doubts Job is that He projects His own unfaithfulness upon a scapegoat."

Whereas the biblical Job closes with the recognition by Job of his place in the universe and with his restoration, Jung's drama continues beyond this point. God's fateful encounter with Job aroused in Him the desire to become man (who proved to be morally superior). To this end, He regenerated Himself "in the mystery of heavenly nuptials" with Sophia, primordial Wisdom, mentioned in Job 28. The virgin Mary, the incarnation of Sophia, elevated to the status of a goddess, "is chosen as the pure vessel for the coming birth of God." In Jesus "Job and Yahweh were combined in a single personality. Yahweh's intention to become man . . . is fulfilled in Christ's life and suffering."

God, in Jung's analysis, failed in the act of creation and is suffering from guilt over this failure—a guilt that makes Him "subject to ritual killing," as Jung terms the crucifixion of Jesus. Satan has "close kinship" to God; indeed, God is partly Satan. The Christian concept of Trinity is expanded to a Quaternity in order to give the devil his rightful place within divinity.

This weird analysis, which seemingly defines the nature of the biblical God and of Christian redemption, refers, however, neither to historical events nor to religious situations—but to man's unconscious. For, to Jung, God is an "autonomous psychic content" and "a function of the unconscious," and religion "a living relation to physical events which . . . take place on the other side of consciousness, in the darkness of the physical hinterland." It is a mere projection, or reflection, of events in man's soul if a God is spoken of who is both good and evil, both construction and destruction, both Lord and Satan. Thus "divine darkness" is in reality human darkness, and the psychologist's interpretation of Job "a purely subjective reaction" (as stated in the Preface to the book) but in no way an "Answer to Job."

The English novelist D. H. Lawrence (1885–1930), in writing to a young author, takes him to task for having his hero commit suicide. Egotism, which is the theme of the young man's book, should, in Lawrence's opinion, lead not to the death of the sinner but to the death of egotism itself. "Russia, and Germany, and

Sweden, and Italy, have done nothing but glory in the suicide of the Egoist." Against this tendency Lawrence points to the book of Job as "the greatest book on the subject."

> Job was a great, splendid Egoist. But whereas Hardy and the moderns end with "Let the day perish" (3:3) or, more beautifully, "the waters wear the stones; thou washest away the things which grow out of the dust of the earth; thou destroyest the hope of man; thou prevailest for ever against him, and he passeth: thou changest his countenance, and sendest him away" (14:19 ff.)—the real book of Job ends, "Then Job answered the Lord and said: I know that thou canst do everything, and that no thought can be withholden from thee. . . . Therefore have I uttered that I understood not: things too wonderful for me, which I knew not. . . . I have heard of thee by the hearing of the ear; but now mine eye seeth thee. Wherefore I abhor myself, and repent in dust and ashes" (42:2–6). If you want a story of your own soul, it is perfectly done in the book of Job—much better than in [Dostoevsky's] *Letters from the Underworld*. But the modern today prefer to end insisting on the sad plight. It is characteristic of us that we have preserved, of a trilogy which was really Prometheus Unbound, only the Prometheus Bound and terribly suffering on the rock of his own egotism.

Thus Lawrence interprets Job as the man who conquered his concern with himself and his justification—his egotism—and rose to a perception of what is greater than he. Similarly, Lawrence thought that "Christianity should teach us now, that after our Crucifixion . . . we shall rise again . . . acknowledging the Father, and glorying in his power, like Job."[71]

"Here endeth chapter forty-three of Job." Thus Robert Frost (1874–1963) concluded his *A Masque of Reason* (1945), a serio-comic dramatic postscript to the forty-two deeply serious chapters of the biblical work. The humanist, "Old Testament Christian" Frost knew well that the confrontation between the rebellious, noncon-formist, heroic man and the God who wishes to be free "from moral bondage to the human race" is a perennial issue, and that the notion of reward and punishment stands in the way of freedom for both. At first, God had to adjust Himself to human understanding; in order not to risk loss of worship, He rewarded good and punished evil.

"You changed all that. You set me free to reign. You are the Emancipator of your God."

Finally, there is one great modern writer whose world bordered on Job's yet who failed to make any references to him: Franz Kafka (1883–1924). It was Martin Buber who considered Kafka's work to be the most important Job commentary in our generation—but a commentary that came to a sudden end at the point where God begins to speak. Kafka knew (Buber continues, alluding to the biblical Jacob story) that the place where "he stayed at night" was "awesome," though he had heard no voice, and the ladder he saw in his dream was broken and its top did not reach to heaven. Kafka was the strong-willed Jew who was not enticed by Marcion, although he sensed the terrible paradox of existence. The fact that the voice does not reach us and that instead we perceive demonic noises, Kafka attributed not to the hostile power of a demiurge but to a strange derangement in the process of communication caused by intermediary forces.[72] — How intriguing that Kafka himself was silent on the motif of Job.

While the samples of reflections on, and references to, Job summarized in this chapter follow a roughly chronological sequence, the selections from modern writings on Job to which we now turn in the body of this volume are arranged according to categories. Naturally, different groupings would have been possible. Basically, each author speaks his own mind and is in a measure independent of the others, although some similarities and some parallels do occur. Viewed as a whole, modern writings on Job testify to the book's appeal to the spirit, the imagination, and, above all, to a grappling with the issues raised by the book.

SELECTED MODERN READINGS

OF JOB

I

In the Judaic Tradition

LEO BAECK :
JOB AND KOHELET: BOOKS OF WISDOM

Leo Baeck (1873–1956), theologian, rabbi, writer, is the most representative figure of German Jewry before and during the Nazi period. His major work, *Das Wesen des Judentums* (*The Essence of Judaism*), 1905, was a critical response to Adolf von Harnack's *Das Wesen des Christentums* (*The Essence of Christianity*), 1900; in it he interpreted Judaism as a religion of the divine commandment, of moral decision, of both faith and action. In 1933, he became the official spokesman for German Jewry. Thrown into the concentration camp of Theresienstadt, he sketched out his second work, *Dieses Volk: Jüdische Existenz* (*This People: The Meaning of Jewish Existence*), published in 1955 and 1957. In this work he considers the book of Job together with Ecclesiastes (Kohelet) as documents of the biblical doctrine of wisdom. It is significant that, to him, it is not Job's rebellion nor the divine answer that constitutes the high point of the book; as he sees it, the book culminates in chapter 28, the hymn on wisdom, and in the commandment to fear the Lord and to depart from evil. It is in this chapter that he finds the true answer to Job—and to suffering man everywhere.

The men who arranged traditional writings in the canon of Holy Scriptures included two books between which a contrast extends almost to extremes. The whole breadth—one almost wants to say the infinity of the Bible—is manifested in the fact that these two have a place in it. [. . .] Mutually opposed, they stand together in the Holy Scriptures. Yet both are books of *hokhmah* [Wisdom].

One, the book of Job, is a volcanic book. Out of the depths the fiery glows, the lamentations, break forth with elemental force. The other, the book of Kohelet, Ecclesiastes, is a book of coolness.

It does not become excited. A playful muse spins, weaves, and unravels. Both are books of inquiry. But in the one the questions boil and burn, all the questions in which the torment of human need, inward and outward, seeks its way and outlet. The other one sorts and stacks questions, both those which the times in their changes bring near and those which the rise and descent of men or fate uncover. In one, a man struggles to the very last with God, and battles with the men who would be God's advocates, but who come to be the advocates of Satan the accuser. The words of his pain and his suffering urge and force themselves and rise before us. In the other, a man philosophizes about the world and God, dispassionately moving first to one, then to another curiosity existing on earth, ready to send them all away again, and he speaks no superfluous or insufficient word. One book forces its way down to the deepest human pain and agony and does not give way; it is a book of Either/Or. The other sets up mirrors and moves them here and there. It bids us examine—at times from this, at times from that angle—the concerns, the worries, which, after all, exist. It is a book of the "both this and that." In the one book Man speaks; in the other, a man speaks. Man speaks in the book of Job, and that is why many of the old teachers could say: "A man Job never existed, was never born; rather, Job is the representation of the human being."[1] In the book of Kohelet a man speaks, and therefore some of the old teachers could assume: "They thought him to be King Solomon, and he was one who traveled from place to place and did not show his actual features"[2]—a man.

In the book of Job, the old friends, his contemporaries, spoke to the man who had encountered all the suffering that a human being can. They thought to find shadows in his life, reasons for his affliction. They demanded of Job, who had been called "wholehearted and upright, and one that feared God, and shunned evil" (1:1), that he confess dark ways, that he accuse himself so that honor would go to God, who had punished him. He replies to them; before God, he engages these men for his justification, trying to illumine the path of his life. He is always ready to confess that God is God, and that man is man, but he will never deny the way of his life. Every hour will he humble himself before God, but he rejects casting himself to the ground before men and their reproaches. After he has spoken concerning himself, concerning that which his life needs and expresses, he then speaks of that which the world eternally needs, and which yet remains within God's mystery. And in all the mystery, in all the concealment which surrounds him in the world and which surrounds the world about him, he nevertheless hears an answer. It speaks of *hokhmah*. It is the answer that God gives the world and to the man who asks, which this people in all its suffering ultimately always knew.

With the fullness of poetry the answer which Job heard speaks:

> For there is a mine for silver,
> And a place for gold which they refine.
> Iron is taken out of the dust,
> And brass is molten out of the stone.
>
> He putteth forth his hand upon the flinty rock;
> He overturneth the mountains by the roots.
> He cutteth out channels among the rocks;
> And his eye seeth every precious thing.
> He bindeth the streams that they trickle not;
> And the thing that is hid bringeth he forth to light.
>
> But wisdom, where shall it be found?
> And where is the place of understanding?
> No mortal knoweth the pathway to it;
> Neither is it found in the land of the living.
> The deep saith: "It is not in me";
> And the sea saith: "It is not with me."
> It cannot be gotten for gold,
> Neither shall silver be weighed for the price thereof.
> The topaz of Ethiopia shall not equal it,
> Neither shall it be valued with pure gold.
>
> Whence then cometh wisdom?
> And where is the place of understanding?
> Seeing it is hid from the eyes of all living,
> And kept close from the fowls of the air.
> Destruction and Death say:
> "We have heard a rumour thereof with our ears."
> God understandeth the way thereof,
> And He knoweth the place thereof.
> For He looketh to the ends of the earth,
> And seeth under the whole heaven;
> When He maketh a weight for the wind,

And meteth out the waters by measure.
When He made a decree for the rain,
And a way for the storm of thunders;
Then did He see it, and declare it;
He established it, yea, and searched it out.

And unto man He said:
"Behold, the fear of the Lord, that is wisdom;
And to depart from evil is understanding." (28:1–28)

That is the answer which the mystery gives. It stands in the center of the book of Job. In it the life of Job finds its self-justification.

Kohelet, the "man of the assembly," heard the same answer. Kohelet always spoke only to men, unlike Job who speaks to God even when he addresses his word to men. Kohelet observes only what he is able to see. Everything is therefore in motion for him, in flux, rotating, coming and going. Only the world, this earthly foundation, abides, but nothing on it is certain. Standards are impossible. Nothing is affirmed, nowhere is there a straight way. "Who knows?" the universal question, is Kohelet's question. Only the hour counts, the giving and taking hour, the wondering hour— the hour rules. Everything therefore has its time. Basically, each hour is as every other hour. What is, was; what was, will be, "And there is nothing new under the sun" (Eccles. 1:9). Everything passes along, and everything returns. End and beginning, beginning and end find one another. The cycle completes itself to begin anew and come to the end again. Nothing endures and remains established. "Vanity of vanities, saith Kohelet; vanity of vanities, all is vanity" (1:2).

Yet for this man too one thing was certain: even he recognized the great "nevertheless," the other sphere out of which this people lives. First, he let the experiences speak, the days and the movements, the colors and the excitements, with all the variety of words which man can have for them. But then, in the end, he has the "And nonetheless" speak, the truth of this other, enduring domain. The experiences showed the many contrasts; they required the iridescent sentences. This truth has the one sentence. And so the author concludes, even through a final irony—mystery too has its irony, and the real irony lives by reason of the mystery—he concludes with the certainty that remains: "And furthermore, my son, be admonished: To make many books is not a goal, And much study is a weariness of the flesh. The conclusion, in which we will hear everything, is: fear God, and keep His commandments; for this is the whole man" (12:12–13).

That is his final word, the word of *hokhmah*. It is not just that this man philosophizes with his head and believes with his heart, a precursor of that romanticism which is derived from skepticism; for he remained, with all his rationality, one of this people, which is unable to understand itself or the world without the law of God, indeed, cannot live without it. This people can have its members who, like Job, militate against all that has been said because their fear of God is always firm, or, like Kohelet, can cast doubt on all else, because they never doubt the law of God.

Therefore the book of Kohelet found its place in the Book; the old teachers were able to say that in it too is "holy spirit."[3]

These two books are books of man. "And unto man He said" (Job 28:28), thus ends, in one of the books, the chapter concerning the search for wisdom, for the meaning of the world and life. And the phrase "this is the whole man" (Eccles. 12:13) is in the second book the final answer to all questioning about that which endures. Already the prophet had spoken: "It hath been told thee, O man, what is good" (Micah 6:8). All of these books of the revelation are the words of man, and therefore the words unto man.

What the word *hokhmah* means actually embraces what the contemplation of another people called humaneness, humanity. But the idea and the law of *hokhmah* contain more. They signify what man is, and what he should be out of the basic fabric of his humanness, which unites man with man, and signify also what unites man with the whole cosmos into which he has been placed. *Hokhmah* is that in which the revelation and therefore the creation prove true, that which speaks out of everything, out of the world and its laws, out of human life, and its laws too. It is that which testifies to the permanence of the creation, to the permanence of the revelation.

In *hokhmah*, as in very few other words, this people came to recognize itself. This was so true that at times even a meditative humor (which can be a form of self-understanding) could enter into this world. Because it succeeded in getting to know itself in

what this word meant, it consequently learned to understand nearby
peoples. This understanding, too, was at times imbued with that
humor behind which love may hide, behind which deep seriousness
may hide as well. Thus, Israel has an old expression of gratitude to
God, that "He has given unto mortal men of His *hokhmah*."[4] A
loving and serious knowledge of the universality of the revelation
also sounds in this untranslatable word. It is as untranslatable as
this people itself.

MARTIN BUBER :
A GOD WHO HIDES HIS FACE

Martin Buber (1878–1965), advocate of Jewish intellectual renaissance
in Europe, expounder of Hasidism, translator (with Franz Rosenzweig) of
the Hebrew Bible into German, propounder of the I-Thou relationship, the
dialogical communion and the way of response, was basically and ultimately
a religious humanist.

In his *Torat ha-Neviim* (*The Prophetic Faith*), 1942, he discusses the
book of Job, viewing it against the background of the prophecy of Ezekiel,
who was sent out as "watchman" and warner of *persons* (Ezek. 3:17–21) and
who proclaimed man's personal responsibility. Ezekiel, says Buber, spoke of a
God in whose justice it is possible to believe, a God whose recompense of the
individual is objectively comprehensible. Juxtaposed with this doctrine was
man's experience of injustice and evil.

In the actual reality of the catastrophe, "honest and wicked"
(Job 9:22) are destroyed together by God. In the outer reality,
the wicked who were left alive knew how to assert themselves
successfully in spite of all the difficulties: "they lived, became old,
and even thrived mightily" (21:7), whereas, for the pious, endowed
with weaker elbows and more sensitive hearts, their days were
"swifter than a weaver's shuttle, and were spent without hope"
(7:6). "The robbers' tents are peaceful, and they that anger God
have secure abodes" (12:6), whereas the upright is "become a
brother of jackals" (30:29). This is the experience out of which

the book of Job was born, a book opposed to the dogmatics of
Ezekiel, a book of the question which then was new and has persisted ever since.

I cannot ascribe this book—which clearly has only slowly grown
to its present form—in its basic kernel to a time later (or earlier)
than the beginning of the Exile. Its formulations of the question
bear the stamp of an intractable directness—the stamp of a first expression. The world in which they were spoken had certainly not
yet heard the answers of Psalm 73 or Deutero-Isaiah. The author
finds before him dogmas in process of formation, he clothes them
in grand language, and sets over against them the force of the
new question, the question brought into being out of *experience;*
in his time these growing dogmas had not yet found their decisive
opponents. The book, in spite of its thorough rhetoric—the product
of a long-drawn-out literary process—is one of the special events
in world literature, in which we witness the first clothing of a
human quest in form of speech.

It has rightly been said[1] that behind the treatment of Job's
fate in this discussion lie "very bitter experiences of a supra-
individual kind." When the sufferer complains, "He hath broken
me down on every side, and I am gone" (Job 19:10), this seems
no longer the complaint of a single person. When he cries, "God
delivereth me to the ungodly, and casteth me into the hands of the
wicked" (16:11), we think less of the sufferings of an individual
than of the exile of a people. It is true it is a personal fate that is
presented here, but the stimulus to speaking out, the incentive to
complaint and accusation, bursting the bands of the presentation,
are the fruit of suprapersonal sufferings. Job's question comes into
being as the question of a whole generation about the sense of its
historic fate. Behind this "I," made so personal here, there still
stands the "I" of Israel.

The question of the generation, "Why do we suffer what we
suffer?" had from the beginning a religious character; "why?"
here is not a philosophical interrogative asking after the nature
of things, but a religious concern with the acting of God. With
Job, however, it becomes still clearer; he does not ask, "Why does
God *permit* me to suffer these things?" but "Why does God *make*
me suffer these things?" That everything comes from God is

beyond doubt and question; the question is, How are these sufferings compatible with His godhead?

In order to grasp the great inner dialectic of the poem, we must
realize that here not two, but four answers stand over against each
other; in other words, we find here four views of God's relationship to man's sufferings.

The first view is that of the prologue to the book which, in the
form in which it has reached us, cannot have come from an ancient
popular book about Job, but bears the stamp of a poetic formation.
The popular view of God, however, stands here apparently unchanged.[2] It is a God allowing a creature, who wanders about
the earth and is subject to Him in some manner, the "Satan," that
is, the "Hinderer" or "Adversary," to "entice" Him (2:3)—the
verb is the same as is used in the story of David being enticed by
God or Satan to sin—to do all manner of evil to a God-fearing
man, one who is His "servant" (1:8; 2:3), of whose faithfulness
God boasts. This creature entices the deity to do all manner of
evil to this man, only in order to find out if he will break faith, as
Satan argues, or keep it according to God's word. The poet shows
us how he sees the matter, as he repeats in true biblical style the
phrase "gratuitously." In order to make clear whether Job serves
him "gratuitously" (1:9), that is to say, not for the sake of receiving a reward, God smites him and brings suffering upon him, as
He Himself confesses (2:3), "gratuitously," that is to say, without
sufficient cause. Here God's acts are questioned more critically
than in any of Job's accusations, because here we are informed of
the true motive, which is one not befitting deity. On the other
hand, man proves true as man. Again the point is driven home by
the frequent repetition of the verb *berekh,* which means both real
blessing and also blessing of dismissal, departure (1:5, 11; 2:5, 9)[3]:
Job's wife tells him, reality itself tells him to "bless" God, to dismiss Him, but he bows down to God and "blesses" Him, who has
allowed Himself to be enticed against him "gratuitously." This
is a peculiarly dramatic face-to-face meeting, this God and this
man. The dialogue poem that follows contradicts it totally: there
the man is another man, and God another God.

The second view of God is that of the friends. This is the dogmatic view of the cause and effect in the divine system of requital:
sufferings point to sin. God's punishment is manifest and clear to

all. The primitive conception of the zealous God is here robbed
of its meaning: it was YHVH, God of Israel, who was zealous
for the *covenant* with His *people*. Ezekiel had preserved the covenant faith, and only for the passage of time between covenant and
covenant did he announce the unconditional punishment for those
who refused to return in penitence; this has changed here, in an
atmosphere no longer basically historical,[4] into the view of the
friends, the assertion of an all-embracing empirical connection
between sin and punishment. In addition to this, for Ezekiel, it is
true, punishment followed unrepented sin, but it never occurred
to him to see in all men's sufferings the avenging hand of God;
and it is just this that the friends now proceed to do: Job's sufferings testify to his guilt. The inner infinity of the suffering soul
is here changed into a formula, and a wrong formula. The first
view was that of a small mythological idol, the second is that of
a great ideological idol. In the first the faithful sufferer was true
to an untrue God, who permitted His guiltless children to be slain;
whereas here man was not asked to be true to an incalculable
power, but to recognize and confess a calculation that his knowledge of reality contradicts. There man's faith was attacked by fate,
here by religion. The friends are silent seven days before the
sufferer, after which they expound to him the account book of sin
and punishment. Instead of his God, for whom he looks in vain—
his God, who had not only put sufferings upon him, but also had
"hedged him in" until "his way was hid" from his eyes (3:23)—
there now came and visited him on his ash heap *religion*, which
uses every art of speech to take away from him the God of his soul.
Instead of the "cruel" (30:21) and living God, to whom he clings,
religion offers him a reasonable and rational God, a deity whom
he, Job, does not perceive either in his own existence or in the
world, and who obviously is not to be found anywhere save only
in the very domain of religion. And his complaint becomes a protest against a God who withdraws Himself, and at the same time
against His false representation.

The third view of God is that of Job in his complaint and protest.
It is the view of a God who contradicts His revelation by "hiding
His face" (13:24). He is at one and the same time fearfully notice-
able and unperceivable (9:11), and this hiddenness is particularly
sensible in face of the excessive presence of the "friends," who are

ostensibly God's advocates. All their attempts to cement the rent
in Job's world show him that this is the rent in the heart of the
world. Clearly, the thought of both Job and the friends proceeds
from the question about justice. But, unlike his friends, Job knows
of justice only as a human activity, willed by God, but opposed
by His acts. The truth of being just and the reality caused by the
unjust acts of God are irreconcilable. Job cannot forego either
his own truth or God. God torments him "gratuitously" (9:17;
it is not without purpose that here the word recurs, which in the
prologue Satan uses and God repeats); He "deals crookedly" with
him (19:6). All man's supplications will avail nothing: "there is
no justice" (19:7). Job does not regard himself as free from sin
(7:20; 14:16 f.), in contradistinction to God's words about him in
the prologue (1:8; 2:3). But his sin and his sufferings are incommensurable. And the men, who call themselves his friends, suppose that on the basis of their dogma of requital they are able to
unmask his life and show it to be a lie. By allowing religion to
occupy the place of the living God, He strips off Job's honor (19:
9). Job had believed God to be just and man's duty to be to walk
in His ways. But it is no longer possible for one who has been
smitten with such sufferings to think God just. "It is all one—
therefore I say: He destroyeth the innocent and the wicked" (9:22).
And if it is so, it is not proper to walk in His ways. In spite of this,
Job's faith in justice is not broken down. But he is no longer able
to have a *single faith* in God and in justice. His faith in justice
is no longer covered by God's righteousness. He believes now in
justice in spite of believing in God, and he believes in God in spite
of believing in justice. But he cannot forego his claim that they
will again be united somewhere, sometime, although he has no
idea in his mind how this will be achieved. This is in fact meant
by his claim of his right, the claim of the solution.

This solution must come, for from the time when he knew God
Job *knows* that God is not a Satan grown into omnipotence. Now,
however, Job is handed over to the pretended justice, the "account
justice" of the friends, which affects not only his honor, but also his
faith in justice. For Job, justice is not a scheme of compensation. Its
content is simply this, that one must not cause suffering gratuitously. Job feels himself isolated by this feeling, far removed from
God and men. It is true, Job does not forget that God seeks just

such justice as this from man. But he cannot understand how God
Himself violates it, how He inspects His creature every morning
(7:18), searching after his iniquity (10:6), and, instead of forgiving
his sin (7:21), snatches at him stormily (9:17)—how He, being
infinitely superior to man, thinks it good to reject the work of His
hands (10:3). And, in spite of this, Job knows that the friends, who
side with God (13:8), do not contend for the true God. He has
recognized before this the true God as the near and intimate God.
Now he only experiences Him through suffering and contradiction,
but even in this way he does experience God. What Satan designed
for him and his wife in the prologue, recommended to him, more
exactly—that he should "bless" God, dismiss Him, and die in the
comfort of his soul—was for him quite impossible. When in his last
long utterance he swears the purification oath, he says: "As God
liveth, who hath taken away my right" (27:2). God lives, and He
bends the right. From the burden of this double, yet single, matter,
Job is able to take away nothing; he cannot lighten his death. He
can only ask to be confronted with God. "Oh that I had one to hear
me!" (31:35)—men do not hear his words, only God can be his
hearer. As his motive he declares that he wants to reason with the
deity (13:3); he knows he will carry his point (13:18).

In the last instance, however, he merely means by this that God
will again become present to him. "Oh that I knew where I might
find Him!" (23:3). Job struggles against the remoteness of God,
against the deity who rages and *is silent*, rages and "hides His
face," that is to say, against the deity who has changed for him
from a nearby person into a sinister power. And even if He draw
near to him again only in death, he will again "see" God (19:26)
as His "witness" (16:19) against God Himself, he will see Him
as the avenger of his blood (19:25) which must not be covered
by the earth until it is avenged (16:18) by God on God. The absurd
duality of a truth known to man and a reality sent by God must
be swallowed up somewhere, sometime, in a unity of God's presence. How will it take place? Job does not know this, nor does he
understand it; he only believes in it. We may certainly say that
Job "appeals from God to God,"[5] but we cannot say that he
rouses himself against a God "who contradicts His own innermost
nature,"[6] and seeks a God who will conduct Himself toward him
"as the requital dogma demands."

By such an interpretation the sense of the problem is upset.
Job cannot renounce justice, but he does not hope to find it when
God will find again "His inner nature" and "His subjection to the
norm," but only when God will appear to him again. Job believes
now, as later Deutero-Isaiah (Isa. 45:15) did under the influence
of Isaiah (8:17), in "a God that hides Himself." This hiding, the
eclipse of the divine light, is the source of his abysmal despair.
And the abyss is bridged the moment man "sees," is permitted to
see again, and this becomes a new foundation. It has been rightly
said[7] that Job is more deeply rooted in the primitive Israelite view
of life than his dogmatic friends. There is no true life for him but
that of a firmly established covenant between God and man;
formerly he lived in this covenant and received his righteousness
from it, but now God has disturbed it. It is the dread of the faithful
"remnant" in the hour of the people's catastrophe that here finds
its personal expression. But this dread is suggestive of the terror
that struck Isaiah as he stood on the threshold of the cruel mission
laid upon him (Isa. 6:9 f.). His words "How long?" (6:11)
are echoed in Job's complaint. How long will God hide His face?
When shall we be allowed to see Him again? Deutero-Isaiah expresses (40:27) the despairing complaint of the faithful remnant
which thinks that because God hides Himself, Israel's "way" also
"is hid" from Him, and He pays no more attention to it; and the
prophet promises that not only Israel but all flesh shall see Him
(40:5).

The fourth view of God is that expressed in the speech of God
Himself. The extant text is apparently a late revision, as is the
case with many other sections of this book, and we cannot restore
the original text. But there is no doubt that the speech is intended
for more than the mere demonstration of the mysterious character
of God's rule in nature to a greater and more comprehensive extent
than had already been done by the friends and Job himself; for
more than the mere explanation to Job: "Thou canst not understand the secret of any thing or being in the world, how much less
the secret of man's fate." It is also intended to do more than teach
by examples taken from the world of nature about the "strange
and wonderful" character of the acts of God, which contradict
the whole of teleological wisdom, and point to the "playful riddle
of the eternal creative power" as to an "inexpressible positive

value."[8] The poet does not let his God disregard the fact that
it is a matter of *justice*. The speech declares in the ears of man,
struggling for justice, another justice than his own, a divine
justice. Not *the* divine justice, which remains hidden, but *a* divine
justice, namely that manifest in creation. The creation of the world
is justice, not a recompensing and compensating justice, but a
distributing, a giving justice. God the creator bestows upon each
what belongs to him, upon each thing and being, insofar as He
allows it to become entirely itself. Not only for the sea (Job 38:10),
but for every thing and being God "breaks" in the hour of creation
"His boundary"; that is to say, He cuts the dimension of this
thing or being out of "all," giving it its fixed measure, the limit
appropriate to this gift. Israel's ancient belief in creation, which
matured slowly in its formulations, has here reached its com-
pletion. [...]

The creation itself already means communication between
creator and creature. The just creator gives to all His creatures
His boundary, so that each may become fully itself. Designedly
man is lacking in this presentation of heaven and earth, in which
man is shown the justice that is greater than his, and is shown that
he with his justice, which intends to give to everyone what is due to
him, is called only to emulate the divine justice, which gives to
everyone what he is. In face of such divine teaching as this, it
would be indeed impossible for the sufferer to do aught else than
put "his hand upon his mouth" (40:4), and to confess (42:3) that
he had erred in speaking of things inconceivable to him. And
nothing else could have come of it except this recognition—if he
had heard only a voice "from the whirlwind" (38:1; 40:6). But the
voice is the voice of *Him who answers,* the voice of Him that "heard"
(31:35), and appeared so as to be "found" by him (23:3). In vain
Job had tried to penetrate to God through the divine remoteness;
now God draws near to him. No more does God hide Himself—
only the storm cloud of His sublimity still shrouds Him—and Job's
eye "sees" Him (42:5). The absolute power is for human personality's sake become personality. God offers Himself to the sufferer
who, in the depth of his despair, keeps to God with his refractory
complaint; He offers Himself to him as an answer. It is true, "the
overcoming of the riddle of suffering can only come from the
domain of revelation,"[9] but it is not the revelation in general that

is here decisive, but the particular revelation to the individual:
the revelation as an *answer* to the individual sufferer concerning
the question of his suffering, the self-limitation of God to a person,
answering a person.

The *way* of this poem leads from the first view to the fourth.
The God of the first view, the God of the legend borrowed by the
poet, works on the basis of "enticement"; the second, the God of
the friends, works on the basis of purposes apparent to us, purposes
of punishment or, especially in the speeches of Elihu (which are
probably a later addition), of purification and education; the third,
the God of the protesting Job, works against every reason and
purpose; and the fourth, the God of revelation, works from His
godhead, in which every reason and purpose held by man is at
once abolished and fulfilled. It is clear that this God, who answers
from the whirlwind, is different from the God of the prologue; the
declaration about the secret of divine action would be turned into
a mockery if the fact of that "wager" were put over against it.
But even the speeches of the friends and of Job cannot be har-
monized with it. Presumably the poet, who frequently shows himself to be a master of irony, left the prologue, which seems
completely opposed to his intention, unchanged in content in order
to establish the foundation for the multiplicity of views that
follows. But in truth the view of the prologue is meant to be
ironical and unreal; the view of the friends is only logically "true"
and demonstrates to us that man must not subject God to the
rules of logic. Job's view is real, and therefore, so to speak, the
negative of truth; and the view of the voice speaking from the
whirlwind is the supralogical truth of reality. God justifies Job:
he has spoken "rightly" (42:7), unlike the friends. And as the
poet often uses words of the prologue as motive words in different
senses, so also here he makes God call Job as there by the name
of His "servant," and repeat it by way of emphasis four times.
Here this epithet appears in its true light. Job, the faithful rebel,
like Abraham, Moses, David, and Isaiah, stands in the succession
of men so designated by God, a succession that leads to Deutero-
Isaiah's "servant of yhvh," whose suffering especially links him
with Job.

"And my servant Job shall pray for you"—with these words
God sends the friends home (42:8). It is the same phrase as that

in which yhvh in the story of Abraham (Gen. 20:7) certifies the patriarch, that he is His *navi*. It will be found that in all the pre-exilic passages, in which the word is used in the sense of inter-cession (and this apparently was its first meaning), it is only used of men called prophets. The significance of Job's intercession is emphasized by the epilogue (which, apart from the matter of the prayer, the poet apparently left as it was), in that the turning point in Job's history, the "restoration" (Job 42:10) and first of all his healing, begins the moment he prays "for his friends." This saying is the last of the reminiscences of prophetic life and lan-guage found in this book. As if to stress this connection, Job's first complaint begins (3:3 ff.) with the cursing of his birth, reminding us of Jeremiah's words (Jer. 20:14 ff.), and the first utterance of the friends is poured out in figures of speech taken from the pro-phetic world (Job 4:12 ff.), the last of which (4:16) modifies the peculiar form of revelation of Elijah's story (I Kings 19:12). Job's recollection of divine intimacy, of "the converse of God upon his tent" (Job 29:4), is expressed in language derived from Jeremiah (Jer. 23:18, 22), and his quest, which reaches fulfillment, to "see" God, touches the prophetic experience which only on Mount Sinai were non-prophets allowed to share (Exod. 24:10, 17). Jere-miah's historical figure, that of the suffering prophet, apparently inspired the poet to compose his poem of the man of suffering, who by his suffering attained the vision of God, and in all his revolt was God's witness on earth (cf. Isa. 43:12; 44:8), as God was his witness in heaven.

YEHEZKEL KAUFMANN :
JOB THE RIGHTEOUS MAN AND JOB THE SAGE

The chief contribution to biblical scholarship by the Jerusalem scholar Yehezkel Kaufmann (1889–1963) lies in his multivolumed Hebrew work, *History of the Israelite Faith*. In it the author reassesses the conventional view of the origins of Israelite monotheism that interpreted Israelite religion as an outgrowth of the pagan milieu of the ancient Near East. Examining the biblical sources, Kaufmann rejects the conventional view and arrives at the notion of

an organically, internally developed Israelite religion, the rise of which marked
the fall of paganism in Israel. He reads the book of Job as offering one "aspect
of the popular religion": the conflict between piety and "wisdom," which he
sees resolved in our book. Kaufmann's work has been abridged and translated
into English by Moshe Greenberg (*The Religion of Israel* [Chicago, 1960]);
the selection that follows is taken from this edition.

Two elements have combined to form the book of Job: the
prose framework (1–2; 42:7–17) and the poetic cycle of dialogues
(3–42:6). The legend of Job's trial at the instance of Satan is
surely early. The story belongs, with the stories of the Flood,
Sodom and Gomorrah, and Jonah, to the ancient moralistic literature of Israel. Job is a righteous non-Israelite, a hero of popular legend mentioned together with Noah and Daniel in Ezekiel
14:14 ff. The Wisdom author of the book of Job utilized this early
story for his own purposes. Hence, there are two elements in the
book, one legendary, the other sapiential.

The Job of the legend is a righteous man, not a sage. The
problem of the legend is to what extent a righteous man can withstand trials. It also teaches that suffering may aim only at testing
men. Job's successful resistance is put forward as a model for all.

Passing to the poetic dialogue, we enter the realm of wisdom.
Job, like his companions, is now a sage who speaks in parables
and figures. The problem of the dialogue is a speculative one—
how to interpret the fate of Job in the light of the wisdom dogma
of just retribution. The question involves more than the suffering
of the righteous; it is whether there is at all a moral order in the
world. In the course of the dialogue Job eventually denies the
existence of the moral order. Apparently, then, there is a contradiction between the legend and the wisdom chapters. The Job of
the legend stands the test and does not sin with his lips, whereas
in the dialogue he accuses God. However, if we bear in mind the
two levels on which the book moves, the conflict disappears.

The issue of the legend is the character of Job, not his world
view. Satan claims that Job will "bless" God—that is, come to hate
Him, and no longer be "blameless and upright and God-fearing"
(1:1). And, in fact, his wife does urge him to "bless God and die"
(2:9), but Job withstands all trials and remains righteous. He does
no less in the dialogue. To the very end, he speaks as a profoundly

moral and religious man. He is not cynical; he does not curse God; nor does he draw impious conclusions from his accusations. Throughout the argument he remains God-fearing and good. Even in despair, he prays, exalts God, yearns for Him and puts his trust in Him. He even threatens his companions with divine judgment for having spoken falsely about God (13:7 ff.). A dual personality thus appears: Job the righteous man of the legend, and his twin, Job the sage. The sage, notwithstanding his blameless heart, cannot escape the conclusions to which he is led by his mind. The tragic conflict between heart and mind climaxes the troubles that have come upon him. With wonderful subtlety the poet lets Job the sage finish the work of Satan and deal Job the righteous man the final blow: to deprive him of his dearest treasure, faith in divine justice. This lost, all is lost. Yet even out of the depths of his anguish, what does he cry?

> By the life of God, who has deprived me of justice,
> And Shaddai, who has embittered my life!
> As long as my breath is in me,
> And the spirit of God is in my nostrils,
> My lips shall not speak wrong, nor my tongue utter deceit.
> Far be it from me to justify you,
> Till I die I shall not deny my innocence,
> I hold to my righteousness and will not let go!   (27:2ff.)

His final word is his great oath. Though his world has collapsed, he clings to the one value that is left him, his righteousness. That has become an intrinsic value, without hope of any reward. Thus the poet raises Job to the bleak summit of righteousness bereft of hope, bereft of faith in divine justice.

Job is portrayed as righteous out of love of God alone. He challenges God only because he considers it a moral duty to speak the truth before Him. To the end, then, Job the sage, like Job the righteous man, remains firm in his moral character. His friends, however, follow an easier path. Armed with the conventional clichés of wisdom, they acquit themselves with these empty phrases. That is why God ultimately rebukes Eliphaz and his friends for not having spoken rightly concerning Job (42:7).

Only gradually does Job arrive at the repudiation of the moral order. All his arguments take their departure from the primary conviction of his righteousness. He knows with an immediate, unshakable knowledge that he is innocent; that is his Archimedean point. He has feared God and loved goodness all his life, and continues to do so now. He does not deny that he has sinned, but what man born of woman is blameless? His sins are failures and weaknesses; they are not enough to make him "wicked." He argues repeatedly the injustice of an almighty God holding to account so weak a creature as man for petty moral failures.

Step by step, he passes from his own case to generalized observations. In his second response to Zophar (chapter 21) and his third response to Eliphaz (chapter 24), he asserts that not only does God fail to distinguish the righteous from the wicked, He fails wholly to requite men. The wicked man prospers and goes unpunished. The idea that righteousness is rewarded in the end is wrong; the wicked crushes the good man, despoiling and killing him with impunity. Job has reached the climax of his denials. Distress has opened his eyes to see what he was blind to before: the absence of a moral providence in the world. This is the shattering conclusion to which he is led.

Job's companions have but one argument: wisdom teaches the infallible truth that there is just retribution. Job must have sinned to deserve his misery; if he does not know what his sin is, God in His wisdom does. To the companions, everything is quite plain: Job has suffered, *ergo* he is wicked. This they repeat with endless variations from beginning to end. Only in Job's responses can a development in the argument be discerned.

At the end of the discussion between Job and his friends, a new speaker, Elihu, comes upon the scene. Elihu is not mentioned in the narrative, because he was not a figure of the ancient legend. But the Elihu chapters are nonetheless an organic part of the book. They are a transition from the final charges of Job to the manifestation of YHWH. Elihu is an additional figure, apparently a reflex of the poet himself. He begins with the last point reached by Job, the repudiation of a moral providence. He does not argue, like the three companions, that Job's suffering was caused by his wickedness. For him the issue is not the personal one of Job, but the terrible conclusion that Job has reached.

Through the many obscurities in the text, it is possible to discern in Elihu's chapters a certain direction, and even a certain form. Elihu argues for divine providence from evidence that even Job must allow. He calls on the testimony of events that befall nations and men, and on the evidence of the ordering of the world. Three examples of the former and three of the latter are adduced alternatively. Of happenings to men, he adduces: (1) the providential promptings to repentance, in the form of dreams or sickness, which rescue man from divine doom (33:14–33); (2) the sudden collapse of tyrants which can be ascribed only to God, and explained only as punishment for their tyranny (34:16–37); (3) a continuation of (1), mentioning other sufferings by which God rouses man to repent of sin and be saved from punishment (36:2–21). From the order of the world, he adduces: (1) First, God's perpetual maintenance of the cosmos; can God, who in His kindness maintains the world perpetually, be indifferent to it? Creation itself speaks against the denial of providence (34:13–15). (2) Next Elihu points to the moral consciousness of man as evidence of God's love; through this alone is he elevated above the brutes. Can a God who implanted in man moral consciousness be Himself indifferent to moral demands? Job's very sense of moral outrage is an outcome of God's goodness (chapter 35). (3) The last of Elihu's arguments is chapter 28 (to which 36:22–37:24 are an introduction), an argument from man's wisdom and fear of God. Man's wisdom "searches out to the furthest bound"; "his eye sees every precious thing" (28:3, 10). This too testifies to God's grace and His concern for man. Yet God has given man only human wisdom, and if that is not enough to penetrate even the secrets of nature, how much less ought it to pass judgment on the gracious God. For although God has kept divine, cosmic wisdom from man, He has endowed him, in its stead, with a unique and precious gift, the fear of God. This again is a sign of grace and a token of divine solicitude. Thus human wisdom leads us to the final conclusion: the recognition of God's graciousness and of man's nothingness in the face of God's wisdom. Therefore it subjects itself to the fear of God, and its expression—the moral law—as the end of all wisdom and understanding. Wisdom and the fear of God are the supreme evidences of the divine providence and concern that Job has too rashly denied.

There follows immediately the final, conclusive evidence of God's graciousness to man: yhwh speaks to Job out of the whirlwind. In a series of vivid pictures, the thought that Elihu has already stressed is repeated. How can man presume to judge God if the world, which is merely His handiwork, is filled with mysteries he cannot fathom. Once again, Job's special case is not dealt with. The foundations of the moral universe are at stake; God's providence has been impugned. In view of this, the special plight of Job falls into the background.

Is the whole answer, then, that God's ways are hidden from man? Surely the poet desired to say more. It is noteworthy that in these final chapters wisdom and legendary elements commingle. God's words are sapiential, but their framework is a legend: God speaks in a daytime theophany out of the storm. Is this not the embodiment in legend of wisdom's maxim, "He has said to man: Behold, the fear of the Lord, that is wisdom" (28:28)? In the theophany and the discourse with man, God's ultimate grace shines forth, the grace of revelation. This is His supreme favor. Not what He said, but His very manifestation is the last, decisive argument. "I had heard of Thee only a report, but now my eye beholds Thee, therefore I despise myself and repent in dust and ashes." These are Job's last words (42:5 f.). If the almighty God has consented to reveal Himself to mortal man and instruct him, what further room is there to question His providence and His concern for the world?

God's answer is the beginning of Job's restoration. In itself, it restored his last and severest loss, his faith in God's providence. God's reproach of the companions next restores his honor and good repute, which were lost consequent to his afflictions. Lastly, God restores his material possessions which were the first to perish.

The answer of the book of Job is, then, religious to its very core. It comes from the realm of revelation, not wisdom; this is the distinctive Israelite feature of the book. A tragic conflict broke out between the righteous man and the sage in Job. The righteous man believed in the existence of God; the sage does not argue with this belief, but seeks to separate God from the idea of morality and justice. God exists, but His rule is not moral. This separation is rejected by the book; the idea of God necessarily includes the moral idea. The Israelite sage contends with God, but in the end, he, like the righteous man, "lives by his faith" (Hab. 2:4).

LEON ROTH : JOB AND JONAH

An authority on Descartes, Spinoza, and Maimonides, Leon Roth (1896–1963), who served as Professor of Philosophy at the Hebrew University, Jerusalem, left his interpretation of Judaic beliefs in *Judaism: A Portrait* (London, 1960). And "since Judaism is the prototype of the monotheistic religions," he wished "to offer material for reflection on the nature of religion in general." Written in a non-technical, informal, personal style, Professor Roth's work demonstrates a scholar's disciplined mind harmoniously combined with the passion of a man of faith and an Englishman's subtle wit. The passage here reprinted is from chapter 16 ("The Jews and Judaism").

When the Psalmist calls on his soul to praise God, he knows what kind of God it is who deserves praise. God is not man, whose breath goes forth and who then returns to the particular parcel of earth he happens to be in. He is the creator who made heaven and earth and sea and all that in them is; and He cares for His creation:

> He executeth judgment for the oppressed;
> He giveth food to the hungry;
> The Lord looseth the prisoners;
> The Lord preserveth the strangers;
> He upholdeth the fatherless and widow;
> But the way of the wicked He turneth upside down.
> (Ps. 146:7 ff.)

It is a simple faith, but at its heart lies the affirmation of one unique center of authority which calls man to account. It is this God who "shall reign for ever," who is (or is to be?) "thy God, O Zion, unto all generations" (Ps. 146:10).

We may pursue the thought in two books of the Hebrew Bible, that of the prophet Jonah and the book of Job.

The book of Jonah is the *reductio ad absurdum* of topographical religion. Jonah assumes that he can escape God by the normal human device of going away and leaving no address. God accepts the challenge and provides Jonah with a floating lodging, but for all that keeps Jonah under His eye; and just as God needs no postal address in order to find Jonah, so Jonah soon discovers that a fixed residence is not required in order to find God. It was when his soul fainted *within* him that he remembered the Lord (Jonah 2:8).

Jonah returns to duty in a country which is not "his." There he makes a second and even more difficult discovery. God's ways are not men's ways. Not only is He not confined to a special geographical area. He is not bothered by the supposed requirements of logic either. His interest is in moral growth; and moral growth means unpredictable change, not predictable permanence. Jonah complains that this puts an end to his career as a scientist, and it were better for him to give up and die. Science means to predict exactly what is going to be, and Jonah is prepared to do that; but if men are allowed the right to moral change and are even encouraged to change, no science of human behavior is possible.

God takes up the point and talks to him as one intelligent being to another. He says in effect that the important thing in human behavior is not biological growth (up one day and down the next like the vegetable world exemplified in the gourd of chapter 4) but the moral business of learning to give up violence and ill-doing. If a choice has to be made between predictive science and human improvement, it is the science that has to be foregone. Human behavior is not a matter for factual accountancy. It is to be weighed according to the measure of pity it displays.

The book culminates with the lesson to be drawn from creation. The creator of all fact does not allow fact to be supreme. As the source of existence, He is *responsible for* existence. *Because* He creates He has not only knowledge but compassion. And His compassion extends beyond man. It covers the whole sentient world:

> And the Lord said, "Thou hast had pity on the gourd, for which thou hast not labored, neither madest it grow; which came up in a night, and perished in a night: and should not I have pity on Nineveh, that great city, wherein are more than sixscore thousand persons that cannot discern between their right hand and their left hand, and also much cattle?" (Jonah 4:10 f.).

The book of Job deals with a challenge similar to that posed to the egocentric Jonah, but on a larger and more magnificent scale. Jonah had a country to flee from and was assigned a country to work in. Job's only "witness" is "in heaven." Since a human being must be situated at some point of space, he is put in the Land of Uz (wherever that may be). But the significance of the setting is that geography is irrelevant; and when at the end of the drama the God of heaven comes to reply to Job, it is in no particular country: it is from the whirlwind.

As in Jonah, the ultimate secret is seen to lie in the fact of creation. But creation now outsteps not only humankind; it outsteps the sentient world too. It covers the mountain goats and the eagles, the war horse and the ostrich, but also and primarily the sea and the stars, the winds and the frost and the hail. Its rain falls to satisfy the waste and desolate ground and to cause the tender grass to spring forth. The greensward too is the work of God; so is the desert where there is no man.

The instructive thing is that Job declares himself convinced. He is silenced and lays his hand upon his mouth: "I had heard of Thee before but by the hearing of the ear; but now mine eye seeth Thee" (42:5). It is often asked what he became convinced by, and what it is that he became convinced of; but the answer is surely that whereas there had been *brought before* him the wonders of the creation, what he *saw* was the far greater wonder, the wonder of the creator. He does *not* say: "Mine eye seeth *behemoth* and *leviathan*." He says: "Mine eye seeth *Thee*." He had an immediate apprehension of the unity that lies behind the variety and majesty of the world, the unity in which power, authority, goodness, and wisdom meet together in cosmic creativity. Job was justly proud of his integrity. He had seen God as his enemy. He had challenged God to justify His rule of the world. God retorts by showing Job that the world is an even stranger affair than Job had imagined, but strange as it is, it yet has meaning. [...]

Jonah, like Jeremiah, was a prophet to the world at large. Job is man as such. Jonah says he serves the God of heaven and earth who created the seas and dry land, and he is made to live up to his profession. Job demonstrates, to the incredulity of the powers of heaven itself, that it is not external circumstance that makes a man. Neither Jonah nor Job, the lesson of the whale and of the whirlwind, is, as has been so often imagined, primitive or naïve. They are both works of advanced reflection. They are masterpieces of irony, and irony springs from a body of settled opinion so deeply embedded in the popular mind as to serve as a permanent background for thought. Irony dares to suggest that received opinion, however deeply embedded and widely spread, may be wrong.

The book of Job turns on the question of the nature of religion: can man serve God for nought? The test is made *in corpore vili*. Job is put on the operating table and examined. When Job says, "Though He slay me, yet will I trust in Him" (13:15), he vindicates both himself and God.

The book of Jonah depicts the bearers of God's oracles: their recalcitrance, their suffering, their doubts. They flee, or are made to flee, from country to country, yet they cannot escape the Word.

As God is found everywhere, so man can live anywhere. He can survive even the inside of a whale. And just as God can put man there, so from there can man seek for God, and so too can God find man.

ROBERT GORDIS :
THE TEMPTATION OF JOB—
TRADITION VERSUS
EXPERIENCE IN RELIGION

Robert Gordis (born 1908), American Bible scholar and rabbi, Professor at the Jewish Theological Seminary, New York, has for many years dedicated himself to a study of Job. His "All Men's Book—A New Introduction to Job" appeared in *The Menorah Journal,* Winter, 1947. His definitive presentation of the subject is *The Book of God and Man: A Study of Job* (Chicago and London, 1965). The essay here reprinted, "The Temptation of Job—Tradition versus Experience in Religion" (*Judaism,* IV [1955]), presents a summary of the author's views.

In the first sections of the essay, Gordis points to the book of Job's concern with "the conflict between the accepted tradition of the group [i.e., the biblical doctrine of retribution and divine justice] and the personal experience of the individual," i.e., Job's innocent suffering. It deals with "the tragic paradox of evil in God's world," which Israel's lawgiver, prophet, historian, and sage had attempted to resolve. One possible approach was to understand divine justice as manifesting itself in the group, the nation (rather than in the personal destiny of the individual), or in the survival of the "Saving Remnant" within the nation, or in the life of the "Suffering Servant," God's witness and teacher to the nations, or in the hope for the Messianic era that will "restore the scales of justice to the true balance" in Israel and in the world.

To wait patiently for the triumph of God's retribution was relatively easy, so long as the nation was the unit under consideration, for God has eternity at His command, and nations are long-lived. This is particularly true of Israel. In Ben Sira's words:

> The life of man is but a few days,
> But the life of Jeshurun, days without number. (37:25)

Yet, from the beginning, the individual played a part in the religious consciousness. His hope and desires, his fears and frustrations, could not be submerged wholly in the destiny of the nation. The people might prosper and a man might be miserable; the status of society might be critical, yet the individual could find life tolerable. The Law of God demanded obedience from the individual; was it unfair to expect that righteousness or sinfulness would receive their reward or punishment in the life of the individual as well? Imperceptibly, the problem emerged in the days of the First Temple. Isaiah had taken the simplest course by reaffirming the traditional doctrine and applying it to the individual:

> Say ye of the righteous, that it shall be well with him;
> For they shall eat the fruit of their doings.
> Woe unto the wicked; it shall be ill with him;
> For the work of his hands shall be done to him. (3:10 f.)

As inexorable doom began descending on the nation, and the small Judean state saw its life-blood ebbing away, the mere reiteration of conventional ideas was not enough. Now there was no comfort or compensation in collective retribution. Moreover, since the individual was now the unit and the scale of judgment, the counsel of long-range patience was pathetically irrelevant, for man flowers but a brief instant. The prophets Jeremiah and Ezekiel whose tragic destiny it was to foretell and to witness the destruction of the Temple and the Babylonian exile, agonized over the prosperity of the wicked and the suffering of the righteous:

> Right wouldest Thou be, O Lord,
> Were I to contend with Thee,
> Yet will I reason with Thee:
> Wherefore doth the way of the wicked prosper?
> Wherefore are all the traitors secure?   (Jer. 12:1)

Both prophets protested energetically against the popular doctrine enshrined in a folk saying: "The fathers have eaten sour grapes, and the children's teeth are set on edge" (Jer. 31:29; Ezek. 18:2). Ezekiel, in particular, emphasized the doctrine of individual responsibility and individual retribution. He was content to bolster ethical living without formulating a complete theodicy. Other men of faith, psalmists and poets, urged obedience to God's will, buttressed by the faith that righteousness would soon triumph in the life of the individual:

> For His anger is but for a moment,
> His favor is for a life-time;
> Weeping may tarry for the night,
> But joy cometh in the morning.   (Ps. 30:6)

> The Lord is good unto them that wait for Him,
> To the soul that seeketh Him.
> It is good that a man should quietly wait
> For the salvation of the Lord.   (Lam. 3:25 f.)

Thus, biblical religion, resting on the cornerstone of faith in a just and powerful God, met all challenges and held fast to its faith that justice prevails in God's world. On this faith every generation in Israel had been nurtured, drawing from it the motive for obedience to God's law, the strength to bear affliction, and the patience to await the hour of vindication.

Job, too, had always accepted this body of religious teaching as the truth. Then came the crisis, catastrophe following catastrophe, leaving the temple of his existence a mass of rubble. We who have read the tale of the wager between God and Satan in the prologue know that Job's misery and degradation is part of a cosmic experiment to discover whether man is capable of serving the ideal for its own sake, without the hope of reward. Job has no such inkling—for him, *the accepted religious convictions of a lifetime are now contradicted by his personal experience,* by his unshakable knowledge that he is no sinner, certainly not sinful enough to deserve such a succession of blows upon his defenseless head.

Of Job's inner travail the friends are unaware. Eliphaz, the oldest and the wisest of the three, proceeds to remind Job of the truths by which he has lived. It is noteworthy that the author, whose sympathies are clearly on Job's side, nevertheless gives the fullest and fairest presentation of the conventional theology. Divine justice does prevail in the world, the apparent contradictions in the world of reality notwithstanding. In the first instance, the process of retribution takes time, and so Job must have patience. The righteous are never destroyed, while the wicked, or at least their children, are ultimately punished. Eliphaz then describes a vision from on high which disclosed to him the truth that all men are imperfect, so that not even the righteous may justly complain if he suffers. God is not responsible for sin, for it is a human creation (5:6 f.). Moreover, suffering is a discipline—and hence a mark of God's love (5:17). Ultimately, the righteous are saved and find peace and contentment.

In his later speeches, Eliphaz will emphasize the familiar doctrine of God's visiting the sins of the fathers upon the children, and will extend it. For by the side of this "vertical responsibility" linking all the generations through time, there is "horizontal responsibility" in space, uniting all men in a given generation. Thus, the entire people is visited by a plague because of King David's sin (II Sam. 24:11 ff.). On the other hand, it is this interdependence of mankind that makes it possible for the saint, by his presence, to redeem his sinful contemporaries, as when Abraham sought to save Sodom for the sake of a righteous minority. Accordingly, Eliphaz promises Job that, if he repents and makes his peace with God, he will be able to intercede with Him for sinners and save them:

> Thou wilt then issue a decree, and
>   it will be fulfilled for thee,
> And upon thy ways, light will shine.
> When men are brought low, thou wilt say, "Rise up!"

And the humble will be saved.
Even the guilty will escape punishment
Escaping through the cleanness of
    thy hands.   (Job 22:28–30)

Job has scarcely heard, let alone been persuaded by, Eliphaz's arguments or by the considerably more heated and less illuminating speeches of the other friends. He has no theory to propose as a substitute, merely his consciousness that he is suffering without cause. He does not claim to be perfect, but insists he is not a willful sinner. Against the conventional ideas he sets the testimony of his own experience, which he will not deny, whatever the consequences. As the round of debate continues, Job's fury mounts, as does the helpless wrath of his friends. For his attacks upon their disloyalty, his pathetic description of his physical pain and mental anguish, his indignant rejection of their deeply held faith, serve all the more to convince them that he is a sinner. For do not arrogance and the assumption of innocence by man, with the implied right and capacity to pass judgment on God, constitute the height of impiety?

Bildad paints a picture of the destruction of the wicked and the ultimate restoration of the righteous, and he hymns the power of God. Job dismisses this as irrelevant, for he does not deny God's power; it is His justice that he calls into question. Zophar, the youngest and least discreet of the friends, summons Job to repent of his secret sins.

With bitter irony, Job turns again upon his friends, who, in their security and ease, can afford to indulge in artificial arguments far removed from the painful realities of life. In a passage long misunderstood, he parodies their speeches on the greatness of God and concludes that their defense of God, dishonest and biased as it is, will not likely win His favor.

As the first cycle ends, Job has been fortified in his conviction that he is right. What he experiences existentially cannot be refuted theoretically; it must be taken into account in any conception of reality.

Job is aware of the contention that morality depends upon faith in divine justice. Denying the latter, how can he maintain the former? Job is driven to a desperate expedient, which is to prove one of the great liberating ideas in religion: he cuts the nexus between virtue and reward. Honest men will tremble at his undeserved suffering, but will not on that account be deterred from righteousness:

> Upright men are astonished at this,
> And the innocent stirreth up himself against the godless.
> Yet the righteous holdeth on his way,
> And he that hath clean hands waxeth stronger and
>   stronger.   (17:8 f.)

The Mishnah[1] quite correctly contends that Job served God from love and not from fear. God's ways still remain to be justified, but, in the interim, man's ways must be just.

In the succeeding cycles, Eliphaz adds a supplement to the traditional position. He emphasizes that there is more to the punishment of the wicked than his ultimate destruction, whether in his own person or in that of his offspring. During the very period of his ostensible prosperity he lives in trepidation, never knowing when the blow will fall. Otherwise, the same ideas are reiterated, but with greater vehemence. The conventional theodicy, maintained by the friends, has exhausted itself.

The full meaning of Job's existential tragedy begins to disclose itself. Increasingly, Job has become convinced, not merely that the friends have maligned him, but that they have traduced God. In the first cycle, Job has ventured a hope that some impartial arbiter might decide between him and God:

> For He is not a man, as I am, that I should answer Him,
> That we should come together in judgment.
> Would that there were an arbiter between us,
> That might lay his hand upon us both,
> Were he to take His rod away from me,
> And not let His terror make me afraid;
> I should speak and not fear,
> For I am not so with myself.   (9:32–35)

As the friends proceed to attack Job's integrity with less and less restraint, the contact between Job and them all but disappears. Their conception of God is meaningless for him. He proceeds to discover a new faith, forged in the crucible of his undeserved suffering, as unshakable as his experience of his own innocence— behind the cruel reality of suffering, a just order must exist in the world. He can find no sympathy or understanding among his erst- while friends; then there must be, there would be, a witness on his behalf later:

> O earth, cover not my blood,
> And let my cry have no resting-place.
> Even now, behold, my Witness is in heaven,
> And He that testifies for me is on high.
> Are my intercessors to be my Friends?
> Unto God does my eye pour out tears!
> For He would prove a man right
>   even when he contends with God
> As between one man and his fellow!   (16:18–21)

As the debate reaches a crescendo of fury, Job attains a cre- scendo of faith. The longing he first expressed for an arbiter has become a conviction of a witness ready to speak on his behalf. Now he reaches the peak of faith. In a moment of mystic ecstasy, he sees his vindication through a redeemer, who will act to avenge his suffering. The term he uses, go-el, means a kinsman, a blood- avenger, who, in earlier Hebrew law, was duty bound to see that justice was done to his aggrieved brother.

The inherent difficulties of communicating a mystic vision are aggravated by textual problems in the famous passage, which, we believe, should be rendered as follows:

> Oh that my words were now written!
> Oh that they were inscribed in a book!
> That with an iron pen and lead
> They were graven in the rock for ever!
> But as for me, I know that my Redeemer liveth!
> Though He be the last to arise upon earth.
> For from within my skin, this has been marked,
> And from my flesh do I see God,
> Whom I see for myself,
> My own eyes behold, not another's!

But the momentary vision of God arising to redeem him fades; Job cannot hold the ecstasy—

My reins are consumed with longing within me.
(19:23–27)

Similarly, the modern saint Rabbi Abraham Isaac Kook has sought to describe the ecstasy of the experience of "the nearness of God," which extends beyond "the walls of deed, logic, ethics, and laws." But exaltation is followed by depression, as the mystic sinks back "into the gray and tasteless world of conflict, contradiction, and doubt."

Job, however, in spite of his experience, is no mystic, who can find peace in the beatific vision. Even after the ecstasy has faded, he demands vindication. Only if God appears to him and answers will he know that his suffering is not meaningless, that it counts for something in the universe. In his last speech, which sets forth his code of conduct, he closes with a plea:

> Would that I had someone to hear me,
> Lo, this is my desire, that God answer me
> And that I had the indictment my foe has written,
> I would surely carry it on my shoulder
> And bind it as a crown for myself!
> I would announce to him the number of my steps,
> Like a prince would I confront him!   (31:35–37)

Who is this arbiter, this witness, this redeemer to whom Job looks for salvation and comfort? Job's refuge is the God of righteousness, who lives and rules the world behind the sway of the God of power. The dichotomy never becomes a dualism; for the Hebrew author, as for his hero, these two aspects merge as one. In the end, the two aspects of the divine are reunited when the God of reality not only ignores the defenses of the friends in His speeches, but castigates them, "for ye have not spoken the truth about me as has my servant Job" (42:7), so that Job must intercede for them. God's power and God's righteousness, the attribute of justice and the attribute of mercy, are one in Him; it is only to man's limited and imperfect gaze that they seem distinct, if not contradictory.

Centuries later, the medieval Hebrew poet Solomon Ibn Gabirol, in his *Royal Crown*, echoed the heartbeat of Job in his affliction, but like him retained his faith in the One Living God of the universe:

> Therefore though Thou shouldst slay me,
>   yet will I trust in Thee.
> For if Thou shouldst pursue my iniquity,
> I will flee from Thee to Thyself,
> And I will shelter myself from Thy wrath in Thy shadow,
> And to the skirts of Thy mercies I will lay hold,
> Until Thou hast had mercy on me,
> And I will not let Thee go till Thou hast blessed me.

The later poet Immanuel of Rome rephrased the same thought:

> I shall flee for help, from Thee to Thee,
> And cover myself with Thy wings in the day of trouble
> And from Thy wrath flee to Thy shadow.

Job's final speech is no longer addressed to his friends. Like his opening lament (chapter 3), his closing confession of innocence (chapter 31) is a soliloquy.

There now appears a brash young character named Elihu, of whom, we are to assume, the dignified elders have previously taken no notice. He has overheard the debate and feels impelled to inject himself into the discussion. [. . .]

The differences between the Elihu chapters and the rest of the book, which are fewer than is generally alleged, may perhaps be explained by the assumption that they were added by our author at a later period in his career. The creation of a masterpiece like Job might well have been a lifetime undertaking. [. . .]

It is noteworthy that Elihu is at least as antagonistic to the friends as he is to Job. Actually, he denies the truth of both positions. The friends have maintained that God is just and that, therefore, suffering is both the penalty and the proof of sin. Job has countered by insisting that his suffering is not the result of sin, and, therefore, he charges God with injustice. Elihu denies the conclusions of both sides by injecting a virtually new idea, adumbrated in another form in Deutero-Isaiah and referred to in one verse by Eliphaz.[2] Elihu declares that God is just, and yet suffering may rightly come to the innocent, as a discipline and a warning. Job has contended that God avoids contact with man. On the contrary, Elihu insists, God does communicate with man through dreams and visions, and when these fail, through illness and suffering.

This recognition of the uses of pain is the kind of mature insight that would come to a man through years of experience. For life teaches, at every hand, how insufferable are those who have never suffered and that frustration and sorrow are men's passport to fellowship and sympathy with their brothers.

The author of Job would thus wish to express this observation. Yet suffering as a discipline is certainly not the whole truth regarding the problem of evil. How could the idea be given its proper weight? Obviously the doctrine could not be placed in the mouth of Job, who denies that there is any justice in suffering. Nor could it be presented by the friends, for the author wishes to negate their standpoint, as we have seen. Finally, were this idea included in the subsequent God-speeches, it would weaken the force of the principal answer. By creating the character of Elihu, who opposes the attitude of the friends as well as that of Job, the author is able to express this secondary idea, giving it due place in his world view.

Elihu's words end as a storm is seen rising in the east. The Lord Himself appears in the whirlwind and speaks to Job. The argument of the friends that Job must be a sinner is treated with the silence it deserves. Nowhere does God refer to Job's alleged misdoings. Instead, the entire problem is raised to another dimension. Can Job comprehend, let alone govern, the universe that he weighs and finds wanting? Earth and sea, cloud and darkness and dawn, snow and hail, rain and thunder, snow and ice, and the stars above —all these wonders are beyond Job. Nor do these exhaust God's power. With a vividness born of deep love and careful observation, the poet pictures the beasts, remote from man, yet precious to their Maker. The lion and the mountain goat, the wild ass and the buffalo, the ostrich, the horse, and the hawk, all testify to the glory of God. For all their variety, these creatures have one element in common—they are not under the sway of man, or even intended for his use. Even the ponderous hippopotamus and the fearsome crocodile, far from conventionally beautiful, reveal the creative power of God and His joy in the world. Moreover, God declares, were Job able to destroy evil in the world, even He would be prepared to relinquish His throne to him—a moving acknowledgment by God that the world order is not perfect!

Job is not overwhelmed, as is often alleged, by God's physical power. For that had failed to cow Job into silence during the earlier debate with the friends. It is the essential truth of God's position that impels Job to submit. His surrender, however, is still a victory, for his wish has been granted:

> I had heard of Thee by the hearing of the ear;
> But now mine eye has seen Thee;
> Wherefore I abhor my words, and repent,
> Seeing I am dust and ashes.   (42:5 f.)

Job's triumph lies in the fact that God speaks to him and does not ignore him. The confrontation of God is Job's vindication.

But that is not all. In rebelling against tradition because of his experience, Job has enriched tradition. For religious truth, like all truth, can grow only through the evidence derived from the experience of life. To use the language of the hour, Job's protest is existential, but it contributes to a deeper essential religion. It compels a reconsideration of the conventional theology, which the author incidentally does not reject out of hand; he merely regards it as inadequate. The author's positive ideas—one major, the other minor—are stated in the two closing sections of the book.

The minor thought is expressed by Elihu, who stresses that suffering frequently serves as a source of moral discipline and is thus a spur to high ethical attainment.

The principal idea is reserved for the God-speeches, where the implications, in accordance with widespread Semitic usage, are at least as important as their explicit content.

The vivid and joyous description of nature in these chapters testifies that nature is more than a mystery; it is a cosmos, a thing of beauty. The force of the analogy is not lost upon Job. Just as there is order and harmony in the natural world, so there is order and meaning in the moral sphere. Man cannot fathom the meaning of the natural order, yet he is aware of its beauty and harmony. Similarly, if he cannot expect to comprehend the moral order, he must believe that there is rationality and justice within it. As Kant pointed out, if it is arrogant to defend God, it is even more arrogant to assail Him. After all legitimate explanations of suffering are taken into account, a mystery still remains. Any view of the universe that fully explains it is, on that very account, untrue. The analogy of the natural order gives the believer in God the grounds for facing the mystery with a courage born of faith in the essential rightness of things. What cannot be comprehended through reason must be embraced in love. For the author of Job, as for Judaism always, God is one and indivisible. As nature is instinct with morality, so the moral order is rooted in the natural world.

One other significant contribution to religion emerges from the book of Job. For the poet, the harmony of the universe is important not only as an idea but as an experience, not only logically but esthetically. When man steeps himself in the beauty of the world, his troubles grow petty, not because they are unreal, but because they dissolve within the larger plan, like the tiny dabs of oil in a masterpiece of painting. The beauty of the world becomes an anodyne to man's suffering.

The author of Job is not merely a great artist and poet. He is too deep a religious thinker to believe that any neatly articulated system of man can comprehend the beauty and the tragedy of existence. Yet he is too great an intellect to abdicate the use of reason and reflection in pondering the mystery of evil and comprehending as much of it as we can. He would endorse the unemotional words of the third-century sage Yannai: "It is not in our power to understand the suffering of the righteous or the well-being of the wicked."[3] There is a residuum of the unknown in the world, but we have good grounds for holding fast to the faith that harmony and beauty pervade God's world. The mystery is also a miracle.

When Job found that the tradition of the past was contradicted by his personal experience, he resisted the temptation to submit to the platitudes of the past. Because of his unswerving allegiance to the truth, he refused to echo accepted truths, however respectable and ancient their source. His steadfastness and agony found their reward—for out of his suffering emerged a deeper vision of the Eternal and His ways.

MARGARETE SUSMAN : GOD THE CREATOR

Margarete Susman (1874–1966), German-Jewish essayist and poet, wrote *Das Buch Hiob und das Schicksal des jüdischen Volkes* (The Book of Job and the Destiny of the Jewish People) (1946), in which Job appears as the prototype of Israel's tragic history among the nations, but also a symbol of the nations themselves. This passionately written book may be considered to be Susman's most mature work. The reflection on Job here reprinted is the introductory part to an essay on Franz Kafka that appeared in *Gestalten und Kreise* (Personalities and Groups) (Zurich, 1954); the English version was published in *The Jewish Frontier* (September, 1956).

Susman reads the drama of Job as a prefiguration of the fate of the Jewish people in exile. Like Job, Israel demands that God act with absolute justice, and because of this claim, her life, again like Job, has been one incessant controversy with God. In the modern period the ancient argument continues in a new version: a version in which God is altogether silent and man alone speaks. Susman interprets the work of Franz Kafka as typifying this new phase. Here "God has fallen silent, and nothing remains but the sheer nihilism of a world created by man and abandoned by God." At the heart of the surrealist world depicted by Kafka is the Joban problem of suffering and guilt; their interconnection seems completely unintelligible. Divine and human justice no longer refer to one another. God is concealed—"and yet it is He alone of whom every book, every line of Kafka speaks. He is the real subject of all of Kafka's thoughts and figures." "No work bears more clearly the traits of Job's ancient dispute with God than Kafka's work."

Since the earliest times and down to this day Israel has not ceased to quarrel with God, to take man's part in his dispute with God for His justice. This is the reverse side of life under the law that presupposes God's unconditional justice. And this demand for the unconditional purity of God's justice is intransigent precisely to the degree that God's demand on man is seen and accepted without conditions. Since God is inapproachably far and above man, human demands on Him are fired with all the passion and the sorrow of man's impotence. Yet, when Jeremiah quarrels with God, when he cries, "Wherefore doth the way of the wicked prosper? Wherefore are all they secure that deal very treacherously? But Thou, O Lord, knowest me; Thou seest me and triest my heart toward Thee" (Jer. 12:1, 3); when he threatens to break under the burden of his mission, he always knows *why* he suffers. He knows that his suffering is part of his mission; he knows that God knows his heart, that He has chosen him from his mother's womb; that God had intended him to suffer because He had chosen him to take on himself the backsliding and the guilt of his people, to suffer for them. Jeremiah's God is just.

Not so Job's God. For Job, too, God is infinitely distant and omnipotent. His thoughts are not our thoughts and His ways are not our ways. But Job is all alone vis-à-vis this God. Neither his people nor humanity support him, and he does not support them; he argues only on his own behalf. His dispute is only between God and himself. He, this driven leaf, this dry stubble, this tiny, ephemeral, mortal being, abandoned by the whole world, is also unmistakably the one who confronts the infinitely distant God, who dares to lift his voice—the breath of a moment—in anguish and accusation against the Eternal One.

His friends cannot understand his discussion with God; they see and hear it only from the outside, and they speak of Job and of God "like the common people" do, from the outside, not getting to the heart of the matter, in generalities. They speak of God's justice in the abstract, of the general connection between guilt and suffering. But Job has fallen out of "life in general," he has crashed into the abyss of radical aloneness. Nothing has remained of him but the pure burning core of his personal suffering: a question put straight to God. Because for us suffering is, in all eternity, only *my* suffering. There is no such thing as the suffering of another; as such it simply cannot be lived. Compassion is empty and vain as long as I have not taken upon myself the other's suffering and made it my own. This is what Job's friends failed to do, and for that reason they spoke neither of the real suffering nor of the real God, and God said of them, "for ye have not spoken of me the thing that is right, as my servant Job hath" (42:7). Job, on the other hand, spoke out of *his own* suffering to *his own* God—to Him, of whom he said, "I shall see Him, and my eyes shall see Him and no stranger" (19:27).

But he never reaches God, so near to him and so very much his own, because God is also immeasurably distant and absolutely unintelligible. The abysmal archfright of the book of Job is the sudden knowledge that the voice of God does not respond to the voice of any one single man, that the voice of man cannot reach God and God's voice cannot reach man, that the fate of the individual—my fate, my life (and that's the only one I have)—drowns before God in life's universe, without justice or help.

What Job demands of God is neither solace nor suspension of his suffering, but God's justice and only that. But God is far too great and far too powerful, far too distant from man to grant this demand. "Oh that I knew where I might find Him! That I might come even to His seat!"(23:3). Thus Job struggles for God's nearness, he calls and adjures Him again and again, begging Him to listen to the voice of poor, drowning man, begs Him to let Himself be found by man, not to deny man his accounting, though His ways are secret past human searching. God, whom he trusts, has made a pact against him with the devil and has surrendered His suffering servant to the seducer, has struck him almost unto death and then passed over and away from him without pity, going His majestic and unintelligible ways. God to whom he calls out, "Wilt Thou harass a driven leaf? And wilt Thou pursue the dry stubble?" (13:25). He who takes Job so seriously that He "remembers him every morning and tries him every moment" (7:18), this same God turns a deaf ear to his cries and does not hear him. And still Job cannot cease to search for His justice because he feels that God's punishment which he is experiencing is meant for him and yet cannot be meant for him.

Above all, Job knows himself innocent. He repeats it again and again. He finds no guilt in his personal life. He finds no reason within himself for the divine punishment. And God does not answer him. Still, not for a moment does he doubt that his suffering is a punishment ordained by God. That is why, in seeking God's justice, he cannot leave off searching for his own guilt. Finally, when the ceaseless search brings to light the hidden guilt of his existence, it turns out he cannot be blamed for this guilt which is not his own, but the guilt implicit in being a man, which finds its expression in Job's question, "Who can bring a clean thing out of an unclean?" (14:4).

No man is pure before God. Everything human is judged a priori by God's unconditionality. That is also the reason why His judgment passes over the individual to whom it applies. Justice can be applied only to the individual, though it is not meant for the individual. Divine and human justice are not congruent; they are, in truth, not mutually intelligible. And it is this fearful insight into the futility of personal innocence that permeates the entire book of Job. God does not penetrate to the point of personal innocence, because every one of us is far too deeply enmeshed in universal guilt, judged *ab initio* before God by the mere fact of being a man.

Indeed, the ultimate hopelessness of personal innocence is best revealed by the fact that the punishment for universal guilt must be applied in all its severity and impact precisely to the man who is personally innocent. For the man who is personally guilty experiences—supposing he does experience it—God's punishment for his own guilt. But only the man who is personally without guilt can experience the punishment for the universal human guilt, which does not reach the man guilty in his own life because the punishment for his personal sins interposes itself between him and the experience of universal guilt and punishment. Thus God's anger confronts the innocent without any mediation.

The very lack of measure in Job's misfortunes testifies to the immediacy of God's anger. And it is only for the innocent that this anger is nothing but anger. For the guilty it is justice—but for the innocent it is fright, pure and simple; a case for doubting divine justice. Uncomprehending, questioning, adjuring, man stands before his God whose features he no longer recognizes in this unintelligible anger. And yet he feels himself thrust by the violence of this anger before God's face; with an immediacy and a sense of reality far surpassing that of the man punished for his personal sin, he experiences in just this unintelligibility and injustice of the divine law that it is God's law. The law that is intelligible and conceivable is man's law; God's law is absolutely beyond man's grasp.

And Job, who is pressed down beneath the incomprehensibility of the divine sentence with every thought, with every thread of his torn soul, who in his suffering is compressed into one single burning question to God, is the symbol that only he who suffers without guilt can experience the wrath of God, unattainably far and fearfully near. Like a man consumed by fire Job cries: "Have pity upon me, have pity upon me, O ye my friends, for the hand of God hath touched me" (19:21). This certainty that it is God who touched

him, and just him, is always with Job, even in his deepest quarrel
with God. Only this certainty can explain his unceasing human
question which, in itself, is the mark of God's touch.

When God finally answers him, it is not by inclining close to
him, nor by giving him any kind of intelligible answer, but rather
by posing a counterquestion to Job. God reveals to him the greatness and the power of His creation. He Himself, the creator of
the world, passes in the thunder of His omnipotence before Job's
eyes and puts him in his place by asking him the devastating question: "Where wast thou when I laid the foundations of the earth?
Have the gates of death been revealed unto thee? Or hast thou
seen the gates of the shadow of death? Canst thou bind the chains
of the Pleiades or loose the bands of Orion?" (38:4, 17, 31). But in
the moment when God reveals to him the immeasurable distance
between creature and creator, between the Eternal and the ephemeral human being, when Job, who till then has seen these things
only with human eyes, can now see them, so to speak, from God's
point of view—in that wondrous moment Job recognizes again *his*
God.

Precisely in and through the creation God has become pure
Thou for infinitesimal man, called by God and again bypassed
by Him, the *Thou* which in its omnipotence yields up the answer
by not yielding it. *Thou, Thou,* the *Thou* who hast done the immeasurable deed, Thou hast created all this which encloses me,
Thou needest give no answer to the driven leaf, to the dry stubble
because I am Thine. I belong to Thee, I am enclosed in Thy creation, ordered in Thy law. I understand who I am because I see
who Thou art. "I had heard of Thee by the hearing of the ear, but
now mine eye seeth Thee" (42:5). Thus, in perceiving its creator,
the flying leaf, the dry stubble has become something else. This
primordial salvation vis-à-vis the primordial fright in the book of
Job consists in the recognition that from the moment when man
"sees" God as the creator he no longer drowns without rights in
life's universe but is received into God's creation and that, as creature, he may worship the creator. Only in pure worship does he
experience God as pure *Thou*.

Job's trial is completed; his question is silenced at the very
moment when God's creation has become the answer to the question of his own innermost existence. This is not accomplished by

Job's understanding of the order of creation and the rôle his own
suffering plays in it—on the contrary, he does not understand, and
that is his answer. He does not want to understand; there is nothing
for him to understand; in humility he has accepted his own place
in God's creation and in doing so has said yes to his own suffering.

Job, who in his suffering was delivered by God to his tempter,
prefigures in his fate the sorrowful fate of the Jewish people in
exile. Like Job the Jews accepted their suffering as something decreed by God. But they do not simply accept it, they want to
understand. They want to understand God for whose sake they
suffer. Like Job they demand that God whose bidding and law
they have accepted be absolutely just. Here is the reason why
life for the Jews in their exile is one long litigation, an incessant
quarrel with God. They have done their best, they have opted for
Him and have remained loyal. For his sake they remained doubly
homeless. Since the destruction of the Temple and the journey into
exile, they have recognized no country but the one on which the
Temple stood, and for the sake of the Temple they have remained
homeless. And they have accepted homelessness on earth in a far
deeper sense still by resisting the god who (bodily) appeared in
history and by cleaving unconditionally and in purity to the in-
visible God.

Acting therefore on the belief that they have done everything
for their God, Israel, like Job, unceasingly asks for the connection
between human suffering and guilt, which is as much as saying
they ask for divine justice. The very fact that they suffer, and
suffer for reasons unknown, forces the Jews in exile to a theodicy;
that is to say, it imposes upon them again and again the attempt
to justify God and to explain suffering and guilt and their connection. There is not one great achievement of Judaism in exile that
at bottom is not a theodicy.

But under the pressure of historic necessity this theodicy changes
its design. Increasingly it is influenced by contact and the mutual
confrontation with the world. This process begins early and continues into the ghetto and beyond it. Hasidism, this last great
flame burning at the very heart of the ghetto, feeding upon everything that was dim and dark in the ghetto and converting it into
light, is the last Jewish theodicy couched in explicitly religious

terms. It is the last to be openly centered on the revealed God. A deep and immeasurable chasm divides this world from ours.

Only after the dissolution of the ghetto in the West and its internal slackening in the East does Jewish destiny begin to assume the shape in which we know it today. Only here, in the modern world, do we recognize that the suffering and the abandonment of the Jew was not exhausted by his twofold homelessness and the acceptance of suffering for the sake of God. A new factor has been added. Since the ghettos have been dissolved, the Jews have come to share without mediation the fate of the occidental world, and their homelessness, already twice compounded, has received its final and completing portion of isolation. God, for whose sake they have accepted all this, cannot be found any longer, because for the occidental world—of which the Jew is now an integral part— the revealed God whom the Jew has accepted has become, in a manner unimaginable till now, the *Deus absconditus,* the absent God, the God who simply can no longer be found. This absence is far more catastrophic for the Jew than for the Christian. The Christian, after all, keeps this world in which the divine has once appeared for him and which is forever after filled for him with its glow. But when the Jew has lost his God, he has lost everything. The reverse of Abraham's unconditional sacrificial readiness is the absolute desolation of the Jew when God abandons him.

Thus, the isolation and the abandonment of the Jew in exile has been completed with his assimilation into the occidental world. But the dispute with God cannot cease even now. The Jew cannot remain silent when God hides Himself now as He hid Himself before Job. Because, just as He evaded Job in his personal fate, so He evades the modern Jew in his universal fate. For this reason the process against God must assume a new shape; it must start anew and in a new version: a version in which God is all silence and man alone speaks. And yet, though His name is never mentioned, only He is addressed.

HANS EHRENBERG :

ELIHU THE THEOLOGIAN

"The breakdown of the rich and pious Job in the Bible has come to pass anew in the breakdown of our rich and pious bourgeois society." Such is the contention of the German Protestant theologian and philosopher Hans Ehrenberg (1883–1958). This view and the notion that our time has become "ripe for Job" (*Hiob-reif*) underlies his five dialogues *Hiob der Existentialist* (Job the Existentialist) (Heidelberg, 1952). The fifth dialogue, in a translation by Harry Zohn, is given below. Other works by Ehrenberg include *Fichte*, 1923, *Luthertum* (Lutheranism), 1947, and *Goethe der Mensch* (Goethe the Man), 1949.

[ELIHU appears]

ELIHU: What do you want from me after these thousands of years, Job? When I spoke to you, you had no answer for me. And yet I spoke only for your sake!

JOB: How many were silent then! But I am greatly in your debt. That is quite true.

ELIHU: And now you have something to say to me?

JOB: I should think so. But it would be better if first you spoke your piece for the three of us once more. Two thousand years ago you were an anachronism, but today . . . ? Now your time has come!

ELIHU: Could be. But tell me, why?

JOB: Very simple. All I need to do is to mention your title.

ELIHU: My title? I don't understand.

JOB: I call you "the theologian." One of today's professors of theology, a white sheep among all the black ones, has called you "the advocate of God." Almost no one else has any knowledge of you. To most people you are an interloper who indulges in textual criticism.

ELIHU: A new category: an interloper indulging in textual criticism! But I do like this "advocate of God." It flatters me and compensates me for many things. But are there any Elihus today?

JOB: Oh yes, lots of them, including a few great ones.

ELIHU: In those days I saw a void, an ineluctable void.

JOB: But you didn't have this word for it yet.

ELIHU: No, that would have been asking too much. Well, then: I saw the void, the empty space, threateningly close in on me like an open maw, and I did not flee or evade it.

JOB: Did *I* evade it?

ELIHU: No, but you were in the thick of it and there was no evading it. You weren't able to see the emptiness because you were too close to it.

JOB: Then you did not speak as a human being nor as a fellow man or comforter, you did not even fulfill the function of the three friends? So you spoke—I cannot put it any other way—in God's stead, didn't you?

ELIHU: I made the world respectable; I adapted myself to the situation and made a system of theology out of it. I wasn't really speaking to you, even though I was addressing you.

JOB: What *were* you doing, then?

ELIHU: Strange though it may sound, I was speaking from inside you.

JOB: I see. Just as in giving a real sermon we are not supposed to talk about the Word, but to be its voice.

ELIHU: I am not a preacher.

JOB: But you are a theologian, and in those days you did preach.

ELIHU: Then call me a lay theologian. That is your technical term, isn't it?

JOB: That's the best kind of theologian! And you are a dialectic lay theologian, aren't you?

ELIHU: I am not too familiar with your special terms. I am still so used to being an anachronism that I haven't been able to keep up with your concepts.

Job: I thought you knew more about them than our professional theologians. But, by all means, do speak in your own words.

Elihu: As you wish. You see, I realized that the discussion had got hopelessly out of hand. In the end it was so messed up that no one can find his way around the last parts of the dispute between you and the three friends. The reason for this confusion, as I saw it, was not any incompetence of those taking part in the conversation, but the fact that both sides—if I may put it that way—had failed to formulate the subject correctly. They desired a theoretical decision in a practical matter that had come to a head. You wanted to reach a decision with concepts like God, justice, innocence, guilt, suffering, and so forth, and that simply can't be done.

Job: I sensed this myself, and I always resisted engaging in a theological dispute.

Elihu: You weren't the chief debater; the three friends were. That's why I chided them. "Also against his three friends was his wrath kindled, because they had found no answer, and yet had condemned Job" (32:3). Yes, I was angry, theologically angry. I wanted to have you straightened out. I wasn't angry with you, but I did want to give you a piece of my mind.

Job: I am still willing to listen to you; it will do me a lot of good. I am grateful to you for remarking that your aims were different from those of the friends.

Elihu: It will be best if I give a brief résumé, using key phrases, of what I said in several speeches then. The first such phrase is "God is too great for man" (33:12). God is quite different. The second: "The spirit of God hath made me" (33:4). [To Job:] "Why hast thou striven against Him? Seeing that He will not answer any of his words. For God speaketh in one way, yea in two, though man perceiveth it not" (33:13 f.). And something else: "For I am full of words; the spirit within me constraineth me. Behold, mine inwards are as wine which hath no vent; like new wine-skins which are ready to burst. I will speak, that I may find relief; I will open my lips and answer. Let me not, I pray you, respect any man's person; neither will I give flattering titles unto any man. For I know not to give flattering titles; else would my Maker soon take me away" (32:18–22). And in this spirit, Job, I held out my hand to you which was "also formed out of the clay; its pressure shall not be heavy upon thee, and my terror shall not make thee afraid" (33:6 f.).

JOB: I suppose that many are afraid.

ELIHU: I can't help that. Do the three of you now understand why at that time I called out to the friends: "Behold, there was none that convinced Job, or that answered his words!" (32:12).

READER: What was your point of departure? What was your goal? What was your main argument?

ELIHU: You are the youngest here, and yet you ask such old-fashioned questions. I can satisfy you only if you hear my words simultaneously.

MAN: More easily said than done!

ELIHU: I stood in a different place. Where, you ask me. Where God placed me! That's what gave me the authority; that's why I gave no apologetics, no theodicy! My approach was quite matter of fact, for God's cause was to be presented. There were two positions, and I was authorized to be in both. The first was between Job and the friends. I had been waiting—"and shall I wait?" (32:16) —and I had to say of them: "They are amazed, they answer no more; words are departed from them" (32:15). That's why I jumped into the breach.

JOB: We can certainly concede that Elihu was authorized to enter the conversation; I have no doubt of that. But what about your other authorization, Elihu, to participate in the conversation with God, considering that you were an anachronism in it?

ELIHU: I was careful. My speeches were constructed according to a plan. At first I spoke about the situation of the conversation; then of my call to contribute something to the conversation; and my final subject was what you, Job, would like to hear about again. Here it is: There are no postulates for God, no premises for any statements we have to make, and are able to make, about God. God is always "first hand." He is not subject to any concept. Nor does He express Himself in such a way that one could speak about Him in any manner but on the basis of His own Word. The following is in keeping with this: "If He set His heart upon man, if He gather unto Himself his spirit and his breath; all flesh shall perish together, and man shall return unto dust" (34:14 f.). Mark this: God is God precisely because He is God-for-us. God's situation and ours always coincide—as ordained by God. This is the meaning of Luther's struggle against metaphysics—a struggle that has been little understood and is discussed again today, although it is abused superdialectically. Here is another of my key phrases: "I have found a reconciliation, so that He may open people's ears" (33:24, 16). This may not be expressed in your words of today, but it *is* thought in terms of your present-day ideas. God and His Word, then. Things are clearing up even among Catholics. I know a little bit about them, for I used my long leisure time to orient myself ecumenically, to avoid being late as once I was early. God and His Word, then! But when and how? "In a dream, a nocturnal vision . . . in pain . . . in sickness . . . in the help toward redemption," for the preceding phrase went like this: "I have found a reconciliation, so that He may open people's ears." And the final key words are: "For the ear trieth words, as the palate tasteth food. Let us choose for us that which is right; let us know among ourselves what is good" (34:3 f.). But this is only stammering; therefore we should always say: "For hath any said unto God: 'I have borne chastisement, though I offend not; that which I see not teach Thou me; if I have done iniquity, I will do it no more'?" (34:31 f.).

MAN: That is how we learned it in confirmation class, too: penance and forgiveness!

JOB: The message! It took me a long time to grasp it.

ELIHU: The message!! at whose bottom God redeems my soul . . . "and my life sees the light" (33:28).

JOB: I had always found the God that is silent, the God of judgment. Now you, Elihu, have proclaimed that the God of judgment is Himself the merciful God. It is invariably a tiny shift of emphasis that brings everything about. You, too, showed me the right way, but differently from the friends; I was able to listen to *you*. All you desired was that I really be "tested to the end."

READER: You really did not evade this test to the bitter end.

MAN: The Stuttgart Jubilee Edition of the Bible has this to say about Elihu's wish in its concise commentary to the text: "Truly an uncharitable desire on the part of Elihu!"

ELIHU: That's priceless!

READER: This is what the official church is like.

JOB: It's good to have something to laugh about.

ELIHU: There is a good text for a sermon among my speeches:

"Just wait awhile! I will show you; for I have something more to say on God's behalf." Always on God's behalf! I also tell you: "There is judgment wherever He is." Therefore wait but a little while longer! For "He, my Maker, giveth songs in the night" (35: 10); let us convey these songs of praise to the community. [Raising his voice:] "I have asked you what God is." I have asked you quite differently from those who "cry out by reason of the multitude of oppressions and cry for help by reason of the arm of the mighty" (35:9). Just wait; then you will know where God is. Thou—so I speak to God—Thou art great and unknown. Although Thou art close to us, God, Thou "doest loftily in Thy power; who is a teacher like unto Thee?" (36:22). Ye hear Him when He speaks His Word, and "He hath allured thee out of distress into a broad place, where there is no straitness; and that which is set on thy table is full of fatness . . . He delivereth the afflicted by His affliction, and openeth their ear by tribulation" (36:16, 15). This is GOD! Help as salvation, help through hearing!

JOB and MAN: Indeed, this is God!

READER: For *you* this is God! But what is to become of the world? What is He to the world? Today, Marxists and capitalists join together in asking: what about God's government on earth after two thousand years of futile Christianity? What about the peace which we are supposed to owe to Him? They all desire a better world in which He will champion the cause of the godless so that their rights are preserved. They ought to have included you, Job, in their better world.

JOB: Yes, they all want a world without suffering, without death, without war, without cruelty, without evil! If they get such a world, they are even ready to believe in God!

READER: When you come right down to it, people dream of a better world and leave the world the way it is!

ELIHU: The world shall not remain unchanged. It is better . . .

JOB: . . . if it is allowed to change.

READER: That's hairsplitting!

ELIHU: Don't you unleash the forces of judgment! Don't ever play providence! Never start a preventive war! And don't keep God from improving His world!

READER: Is that what we are doing?

ELIHU: Yes, it is! We keep stepping between ourselves and the God who wants to help, between the people and the godhead. I have said: "Behold, He spreadeth His light upon it; and He covereth the depths of the sea. For by these He judgeth the peoples; He giveth food in abundance" (36:30 f.). Did you hear that? The message! For faith! "Theological Existence Today!"[1]

READER: That man will break through walls.

MAN: How remote all this is! But it is slowly getting closer.

JOB: How close it all is! But it is slowly, slowly moving up to heaven.

READER: This is the first time that a theologian hasn't bored me to death. I'm really listening to him.

ELIHU: But don't disregard this: If someone speaks, he is swallowed up, and "He sealeth up the hand of every man, that all men may know what He can do" (37:7).

READER: We're not babies, are we, that can be lulled to sleep by God. If the church can show us Christianity the way it really is, then . . . well, then I ought to be able to go along. Until such time I accuse the church, don't even take it seriously.

ELIHU: Shall we become joyful together? "He prayeth unto God, and He is favorable unto him; so that he seeth His face with joy" (33:26).

JOB: You speak in God's place, but you also pay the price for it. But watch out that in your insecurity you don't secure yourself again, considering that you have renounced all security. Now I can understand you and absorb you; at that time I couldn't. You are not a professor or a prophet, not a Jewish sage, no evangelist, no philosopher or scholar; you truly are the advocate of God, plain and simple. You say such a beautiful thing about clouds: "Whether it be for correction, or for His earth, or for mercy, that He cause them to come" (37:13). You do not speak to man as an ideal or on the basis of his actions; you say this about him: "He prayeth unto God, and He is favorable unto him; so that he seeth His face with joy." The gospel that the sinner will be taken into life has been in good hands with you.

READER: But how can there be a church for your God? In the house of the father the voice of the elder brother is bound to prevail, as in Gide's *Prodigal Son.*

ELIHU: Let us assume that this is so. And then? Does the father no longer exist? Isn't the last word really his? But you must never expect a final answer to such a question!

JOB: Your appearance among us has clarified many things that we would never have fully understood by ourselves. Don't ever turn into a *deus ex machina!* The professional theologians have much to apologize for to the Elihus of all times, but for the time being God is going to put you on ice again.

MAN: We have an indescribable but human God!

READER: I don't mind an interlude with such a theologian if he really recognizes only man, without any privileges, and has no use for any gilded saints, academic gowns, religious geniuses, or powerful priests.

ELIHU: All of you have challenged God, especially Job himself—so have the friends, through their propriety, and so have you, Man and Reader, despite your smartness. Have *I* done it, too?

READER: Not enough, and for that very reason you have—you, too—somehow.

ELIHU: "About God is terrible majesty. The Almighty, whom we cannot find out, is excellent in power, yet to judgment and plenteous justice He doeth no violence" (37:23).

READER: Is someone outside the door now?

ELIHU: May I leave? Have I done my duty?

JOB: You are dismissed, with my enormous gratitude. We shall never forget you; but we shall not summon you another time.

ELIHU: I wouldn't come again anyway.

READER: A mathematical problem that will never be solved! But is that still necessary?

[ELIHU's ghost disappears.]

JEAN DANIÉLOU :

JOB: THE MYSTERY OF MAN AND OF GOD

Jean Daniélou (born 1905), French Catholic scholar in the field of Early Christianity, presents Job as one of the "holy pagans of the Old Testament." In a short book by that name (translated from the French by Felix Faber [London, New York, Toronto, 1957]), he proffers examples of "saints" mentioned in the Bible but standing outside the covenant of Abraham. They are the priests of the "cosmic religion" (a term Daniélou prefers to "natural religion"), common to all men, a religion in which God reveals Himself to the Gentile world by means of human conscience. These saints "typify the mysterious advent of Christ into the pagan world." In addition to Job, they are Abel, Enoch, Daniel, Noah, Melchizedek, Lot, and the Queen of Sheba.

Job is an ancient Idumean patriarch, alien to the race and religion of Israel. The earliest reference made to him in the Bible is in Ezekiel (14:14 and 20) where he is associated with Noah and Daniel. This is in character, for Noah and Daniel are also alien to Israel. The Hebrew book of Ecclesiasticus also makes mention of him (49:9). But, above all, a later Jewish writer, making use perhaps of ancient Idumean traditions, devoted to him one of the most beautiful books of the Old Testament.

Job, a pagan, is presented to us as a model of righteousness and piety. The Jewish writer who composed the book of Job was well aware of it. Already Ezekiel had spoken of his justice (14:14). In the New Testament, the Epistle of James extols his patience and proclaims him blessed. And Pope St. Gregory the Great, in the beautiful spiritual commentary he made on the book of Job, does not hesitate to proclaim the sanctity of this pagan: "It is not without reason that the life of a just pagan (*gentilis*) is offered to us as a model. Our Savior, coming for the redemption of Jews and Gentiles, willed to be foretold by the voice of Jews and Gentiles."[1]

Moreover, the liturgical tradition gives evidence of the veneration paid to St. Job. Etheria, writing at the end of the fourth century, testifies to this veneration in Idumea, as also to that paid to Lot in Moab and to Melchizedek in Samaria: "I wished to go to the land of Hus to visit the tomb of Saint Job in order to pray there."[2] She informs us that he was also venerated in Hauran, in the north of Palestine. Mention is made of Job in the ancient prayer for the recommendation of a soul, as being a model of those whom God has delivered. The Roman Martyrology celebrates his feast on May 10, the Greeks and Copts on the 6th of the same month. Holy Scripture and tradition are thus of one mind in seeing in the ancient Idumean a saint of the pagan world.

Job is, in the first place, a personification of justice or righteousness within the sphere of the cosmic religion, and he is in some sense its ideal expression. This righteousness bears relation to the cosmic covenant. God made promise to be faithful in be-

stowing the good things of nature; He pledged Himself to give
the rain that ensures the fruitfulness of the seasons and to per-
petuate life in animals and men. But He establishes a bond between
men's righteousness and the cosmic order. He requires them to
render Him worship and to observe His laws: "Flesh with blood
you shall not eat . . . whosoever shall shed man's blood, his blood
shall be shed, for man was made to the image of God" (Gen.
9:5, 6).

Job is the perfect pattern of this covenant. He is the model of
the just man: "That man was simple and upright, and fearing God
and avoiding evil" (Job 1:1). [Edouard-Paul] Dhorme observes
that these different words express the various aspects of virtue:
simplicity (or integrity) refers to a man's duties toward himself,
uprightness to his duties toward his neighbor, fear to his duties
toward God.[3] He watches over his family and, after the feastings
in which his sons and daughters take part, he gathers them together and purifies them (1:5). He offers holocausts to God in
reparation for their sins (1:5). His charity goes out to the orphan
and the widow (29:12–15). He is "the father of the poor" (29:16)
and the terror of the unjust. He was "clad with justice . . . as with
a robe" (29:14).

In return, God was pleased to load Job with temporal blessings. The first of these was fruitfulness of offspring; he had seven
sons and three daughters. He possessed great herds: seven thousand sheep, three thousand camels, five hundred yoke of oxen.
He was a rich man. He was "great among all the people of the
east" (1:3). He was also a man of standing. He enjoyed a great
authority among his fellows. When he went forth to the gate of the
city and they prepared a seat for him in the street, the young men
saw him and hid themselves and the old men rose up (29:7–8).
When he had spoken, none dared add to his words (29:22). He
was loaded not only with riches but with honors, and his success
seemed like a testimonial from God to his virtue.

This should suffice to justify our making Job the pagan parallel
of the Hebrew patriarchs, upon whom also the blessings of the
earth were showered. But the object of the history of Job, as received no doubt by the sacred writer from the Idumean tradition,
is to approach another problem. For so far there is no certainty

that Job was truly a righteous man. Did he truly love God for
Himself or for the good things he had received from Him? Was
his religion without ulterior motive? Maybe he was unduly attached
to his human happiness, to his family life, to the riches he possessed, to the esteem he enjoyed. More subtly still, perhaps he
found a certain complacency in his very righteousness and in the
privileges it earned him. That was precisely what Satan thought,
not believing in Job's sincerity. He queried our own thesis, namely,
that there are saints in the pagan world.

That is why it was necessary that Job's righteousness be tested,
and the essential theme, a new one, of the book of Job is this testing of righteousness. In order to discover whether Job loved God
for Himself or for what he received from God, he must be deprived
of these good things, and this is what God allows Satan to do. It
is important to note that it is a matter of permission. The law of the
cosmic covenant, the temporal reward of virtue, is not abrogated,
but only suspended. The proof of this is that Job will later recover
his family, his herds, and his good name. This is the primary
meaning, at least, of what happened, the one we shall deal with
first of all.

Here, then, is Job, once loaded with possessions, now a dere-
lict. Everything he possessed has been taken away from him. Fire
has consumed his sheep, the Chaldeans have stolen his camels, his
children have been crushed to death. By a worse humiliation he
is stricken with a repulsive leprosy, making him an object of loath-
ing, to add to the suffering it inflicted on him. The esteem he had
enjoyed disappears with his prosperity. Those who saw in his
success a blessing from God, now, quite logically, see in his down-
fall a divine condemnation and probe him to find out why. He
becomes the laughingstock of the young men, who make songs
about him and spit in his face (30:9–10).

But the trial does not shake his righteousness. He does not hurl
any curse at God, as his wife suggests (2:9). His integrity remains
unshaken. He will accept unhappiness from God just as he had
received happiness; "If we have received good things at the hand
of God, why should we not receive evil?" (2:10). Thus the spon-
taneity of his love is made evident. He is bound to God for Himself and not for what he receives from Him. His love is without

ulterior motive; his righteousness is sincere; his fidelity in his un-happiness proves his fidelity in his happiness. Moreover, it is proved that true righteousness is possible within the order of the cosmic covenant and of temporal reward. Job's trial does not brand as false the virtue that finds its recompense here below, but on the contrary bears witness to its possibility.[4]

What we have seen so far of Job's history belongs to its primitive elements, which the Jewish author obtained from the Idumean tradition and which are to be found mainly in the epilogue and prologue of the book. But upon this elementary theme the Hebrew author has developed another, the one that occupies the discourses of Job's friends and constitutes a debate upon the mystery of suffering. In this development we have an initial exposition of the depth of meaning underlying the primitive theme. But the person of Job still definitely remains in the author's mind as that of a pagan, and the problem of suffering is set at the level of natural religion.

This is apparent from the fact that God is there represented as manifesting His power on a cosmic level (38–39), and not in the historical order. Still more, although the work is a relatively late one, the problem of suffering is placed in the setting of the cosmic revelation, without any of the profundities brought to bear upon it by the Mosaic revelation as seen in texts which are, nevertheless, more ancient, like those about the Servant of Yahweh in Isaiah or in Psalms 49 and 53. No allusion is made to recompense in the hereafter, a doctrine well known to Judaism, nevertheless, at the time when the author was writing. This definitely establishes his desire to set the problem in relation to mankind before the Mosaic revelation, and thus in a pagan environment.

The first point to be made by the author is the insupportable character of suffering. The cries it wrings from Job are among the most vehement ever uttered. Against this suffering he protests with his whole being. He will have no truck with it. There is no trace of resignation in him, either. The picture of "Job the Patient" is a later elaboration; nothing could be less patient than the true Job. He bears witness to the existence of suffering and can do no other. Nothing can give him ease. Words of consolation seem to him like derision. Only one course is possible in the face of it, either to fight it or to give way to it. Thus, it appears as an absolute, outside all discussion; and that is why the discourses of Job's friends seem derisory. Suffering brings into the heart something of the very mystery of existence.

This is all the more striking in the case of Job because it is a question of the suffering of a righteous man. This suffering is therefore not susceptible of any explanation; it is wholly divorced from reasoning; it derives from existence and not from logic. It appears as a pure paradox, as the outcome of an irrational world. But at the same time it brings us to the reality of existence; it lays bare the roots of being. By depriving Job of everything that is not essential, suffering makes him the pattern of sheer humanity. It takes away from his righteousness everything that might possibly disguise it; it loosens it from every compromise with happiness.

While Job's suffering leads into the mystery of man, it leads at the same time into the mystery of God. For, granted that Job does not acknowledge himself responsible for his unhappiness, neither does he blame God for it. That would again be to reduce suffering to the discursive level. But in this context the argumentation is not that of Job's friends, but his wife's. In her view, nothing remains but for Job to curse God; and her position is a logical one, just as theirs is. It is the same standpoint as that which leads so many nowadays to revolt. If God exists, they say, it is not possible that truly good people should be unhappy; that is contrary to all justice. But, as Job sees it, there does exist a God who is just, and yet there do exist truly good people who suffer; and that is admittedly not patient of explanation. But in these circumstances what has to be rejected is not God, but any attempt to explain. That means quite simply that it is no more possible to make God a subject of argument than it is to do this with man. Because God is just and man is righteous, and yet suffering exists, the only thing is to admit that God is a mystery and man is a mystery.

Job's suffering reveals the mystery of man, because it does away with the pretension on man's part to claim any right. In a most radical way it prevents him from regarding his relations with God as a form of commutative justice. And thus, by stripping him of all pretension, it brings to light his natural creature condition, that is to say his basic poverty of being, which takes away from him the right to lay claim to anything since he possesses nothing

except as a wholly gratuitous gift. That is why Job, in his poverty
and abjectness, expresses the very essence of humanity while in
his riches and goods he hides it.

At the same time Job's sufferings reveal the mystery of God in
terms of his sovereign freedom. From the moment he no longer
possesses anything from God, Job is no longer suspect of turning
to Him on the grounds of having it. As far as that is concerned, he
could only protest against God. But the adoration he continues to
offer Him has no other object than God Himself. It is the recognition of His overriding omnipotence manifested by His sovereign
freedom in creation. It is this sovereignty that God claims in the
striking passage in chapter 38:

> Where wast thou when I laid the foundations of the earth?
> Tell me, if thou hast understanding,
> Upon what are its bases grounded?
> Or who laid the corner stone thereof,
> When the morning stars praised me together,
> And all the sons of God made a joyful melody?   (38:4–7)

It can be seen here how the biblical author has transformed the
figure of Job. He is no longer the just man obviously approved by
God, but the just man afflicted with suffering. The former represents a confirmation of the cosmic revelation; the latter marks the
end of it. The just man afflicted with suffering presents an inexplicable mystery, if it is viewed within the limits of the cosmic
revelation; the latter must either be denied or passed by, for it is
impossible to stop there. But even so, the author of the book of Job
has no wish to pursue the question any further. He remains faithful to his purpose of describing for us a pagan saint. But he has
plumbed this sanctity to its depths in pursuing it to its extreme
limits where nothing remains possible but sheer abandonment of
total darkness, the heroic profession of faith, the stark testimony of
adoration.

We shall find ourselves involved in a fresh development of the
figure of Job when we come to its interpretation by the Judeo-
Hellenistic world. While the Jewish author had given it a theological significance—that of man face to face with mystery—the
Greek authors tended rather to underline its moral character and

to show Job as the model of endurance, of suffering accepted with patience. This is, in truth, to change entirely the figurative significance of Job, for, as we have observed, in the view of the Jewish author patience is not his outstanding quality. We can see here a change of perspective, where there is less concern to deal with metaphysical problems than to propose edifying examples. This is characteristic of the Haggadah of Judaism which was to be revived by the Christians.

This change was already in evidence with the Greek translation of the Old Testament. The Jew of Alexandria who translated the book of Job introduced basic modifications. He wanted not merely to translate, but to effect a transition from one mental attitude to another. Thus he gives a more scientific and less animistic trend to his descriptions of nature: "The stars sang" becomes "the stars were born" (38:7). Hebrew expressions are changed: *sheol* becomes Hades or even Tartarus; jackals become sirens. A mythological tinge is introduced. The realistic description of the crocodile with sharp potsherds under his belly is turned into the mythical description of the dragon, "all the gold of the sea" under his belly. This Hellenization shows itself also in the character of Job. [...] Violent expressions are moderated. Where the Hebrew has: "God causes the just and the impious to perish equally," the Greek translates: "Anger destroys the great and powerful" (9:22). Where the Hebrew has: "Peace reigns under the tent of the robbers," the Greek puts the contrary: "Let no wicked one think he will remain unpunished" (12:6). It is noteworthy that, parallel with this changing of the character of Job, the Greek translator introduces into the text the idea of reward in the hereafter. It is no longer a question of scandal by reason of the happiness of evil men and the suffering of the righteous, but only of the patience of the righteous man who knows that he will receive recompense while the evil man will be punished. We come back to the doctrine of reward, but now raised to the level of reward in the hereafter.

It is precisely under this aspect that Job is shown to us in the Epistle of James. The passage concerned is about patience: "Be patient therefore, brethren, until the coming of the Lord" (5:7); and Job is the perfect model of this patience: "Take, my brethren, for an example of suffering evil, of labor and patience, the prophets who spoke in the name of the Lord. Behold we account them blessed who have endured. You have heard of the patience of Job and you have seen the end [received by him] of the Lord, that the Lord is merciful and compassionate" (5:10–11).

It will be noted that Job is numbered among the blessed. The New Testament bears witness to his sanctity. But this sanctity is not the heroism of faith; it is the patience with which trials are endured, because it is known they are but for a time. It is not a question of stoical patience, of pure resignation bearing witness to greatness of soul. It is patience linked with hope, founded on the certainty of the happiness promised by Christ; and this certainty gives strength to endure the trials of earthly life. That is a new picture of Job, bound up with faith in eternal life.

This is the aspect under which the Christians, following the Epistle of James, were to exalt "blessed Job." Thus Tertullian in his *Treatise on Patience*: "Blessed is that man who exhausted all manner of patience against the assaults of the demon" (14). In the *Apostolic Constitutions* it is put even more explicitly: "Accept undisturbed the misfortunes which come to thee and bear contradictions without vexation, knowing that recompense will be given thee by God, as it was given to Job and Lazarus" (VII, 8, 7). And Gregory the Great, in his wonderful *Moralia super Job*, placed Job among the Gentile saints as worthy of imitation in that respect: "Abel came to exhibit innocence, Enoch to give a lesson in integrity of morals, Noah to teach perseverance in hope, Job to exhibit patience in the midst of trials" (Preface).

Thus, at each successive step in revelation the figure of the ancient Idumean appears in a different light. His trial served for a touchstone as to the possibility of sanctity under a regime of temporal reward. Later, it expressed the anguish of souls faced with the failure of temporal reward, with the apparent injustice of this world, and exemplified the possibility of complete transcendence over it. When finally the gleam of hope in a future life had begun to shine over mankind, it became for the ancient Hellenists the pattern of patience enduring the ills of this life in the knowledge that it would lead to the possession of the good things of the life to come.

A last point must be added. The Christians not only saw in Job an ideal of virtue; they thought of him as a figure of the Christ who was to come. Already in the fourth century the then bishop of Verona, Zeno, established a parallel between Job and Christ. Job, rich in the goods of this earth and reduced to poverty, prefigures Christ, "leaving for love of us the goods of heaven and making himself poor to make us rich" (*Tract.*, 11, 15). Job's temptation prefigures our Lord's. Job covered with ulcers represents Christ who "by taking flesh takes upon himself the blemishes of all humanity." Job is insulted by his friends and Jesus by the priests. Job upon his dunghill represents Christ in the midst of the aftermath of sin. It is noteworthy that Zeno underlines especially the parallel between Job's abjection and the *kenosis* of Christ; it is the Incarnation even more than the Passion that he emphasizes in the comparison. Gregory the Great speaks in the same strain: "It was necessary therefore that the blessed Job, who foretold the greatest of the mysteries, the Incarnation, should prefigure by his life him whom he described in words" (*Moralia*, Preface). This is far-reaching. The comparison between Job and Christ bears not only upon some particular aspect, such as temptation, patience, suffering. It bears upon the human condition as such in terms of suffering, that is to say, as a question mark. It goes further than merely to prefigure Judaism; it touches humanity as a whole. When Jesus, stripped of his garments, covered with bruises, encompassed with shame, stands before the judgment seat of Pilate, the Roman judge, it is not Isaac or Moses or David that is recalled to mind. He transcends the prefiguration of Judaism. Pilate is right in saying: "Ecce homo." He is mankind itself reduced to the nakedness of its tragic condition; and Job was its most perfect prefiguration.

Thus there is a real and mysterious link between Job and Jesus. Job is the question, Jesus the answer. [C. G.] Jung wrote an *Answer to Job* that is an answer to stark transcendence. He sees this answer in Mary, who made human the divine. But the true answer was first of all Jesus. Jesus is the immediate answer to Job because he shares his suffering and is the only one to do so. Suffering encloses a man in solitude, puts him outside communion with his fellow men. Between Job and his friends an abyss was cleft. They regarded him with astonishment as a strange being, as the sudden appearance of the unprecedented in the midst of the very ordinary, as one marked with a sacred sign. But they could no longer get to him. Only Jesus could cross this abyss, descend into the abyss of misery, plunge into the deepest hell. And it is only because he has first shared the suffering of everyone who suffers that in him and by him every man who suffers can find communion with other men.

Jesus is furthermore the answer to Job because he gives a meaning to suffering. Not that he explains it, for it does not come within the sphere of explanation. But he puts it into the world of the supernatural. Suffering is the means whereby the righteous man may be reunited with the sinner. It exists in a sinful universe. But the suffering of the righteous shatters the logic of suffering and sin. It allows suffering to exist where sin does not exist; and because it is bound up with sin, by this very fact it allows the righteous man to take the load of sin upon himself and so destroy sin. It allows the righteous man to enter into communion with sinners. Thus Jesus unveils the hidden meaning of Job's suffering, a suffering which remained a mystery to Job himself.

Finally, Jesus is the answer to Job because he does away with his suffering. Suffering cannot be accepted any more than it can be explained. If love can cause someone to take suffering upon himself, it is the love therein alone that is lovable, and its final purpose is to do away with suffering. The book of Job is in fine a book of hope. The Septuagint did well to make the dawn of resurrection rise above the suffering of the righteous Idumean. But this resurrection finds its justification in Christ alone. He took suffering upon himself in order to do away with suffering. More still, he descended into the lower region to reach the very root of evil, so that those who had been grafted thereon might be freed from evil. Thus the resurrection of Christ is the supreme answer to the heartrending cry of Job, and justified his protestation.

The character of Job is one of those that lead most deeply into the mystery of the human soul. This explains the attraction he has never ceased to have for thinking men. Gregory the Great saw him as the model of the soul caught up in the ways of contemplation. In our own days [L.] Chestov has contrasted him with Hegel as one who faces reason with the absurd. Jung makes him the criterion of sheer transcendence. [A.] Feuillet has used him to illustrate the enigma of suffering. So the multiplicity of interpretations continues to spread around the mysterious Idumean. He appears at the confines of the cosmic covenant, as one in whom man becomes aware of his own enigmatic character and of his powerlessness to know himself. He is witness to the fact that man is a mystery; and thus he prepares the way for him in whom this mystery will be unveiled, for, as Pascal has said, against Socrates, we do not know ourselves except by Jesus Christ.

ERNEST RENAN : THE CRY OF THE SOUL

Ernest Renan (1823–92), French historian of religion, philosopher, and writer, is best known for his *La Vie de Jésus* (1863); the controversy about the book brought about his removal for several years from his professorial chair at the Collège de France. His *Life of Jesus* was followed by *Histoire des Origines du Christianisme* (7 vols.; 1863–83) and *Histoire du Peuple d'Israël* (5 vols.; 1887–93). Born a Catholic, Renan grew more and more skeptical of dogmatism and increasingly dedicated to scholarly pursuit and motivated by an optimistic faith in humanity's progress. In his thinking the community of man is continually engaged in the mission of evolving a God of justice. He accepted Kant's distinction between pure reason and practical reason, man's rational and his moral nature.

Among biblical books Renan was closest to the prophets, whom he considered to be founders of the religion of humanity, and to Ecclesiastes, which he called the only amiable book written by a Jew; its skepticism, irony, and urbane wisdom fitted his own temperament. His *Le Livre de Job* (1859) offered a French translation of the book, complemented by a study of the age and character of the poem. His explication of Job is a good example of his imaginative, analytical acumen and his brilliant style. Summarizing his probing into the meaning of the book (which he attributes to an "old patriarch of Idumea"), he says: "The march of the world is enveloped in darkness, but it tends toward God."

In order to comprehend the poem of Job, it is not sufficient to fix its date; it must be restored by means of the sentiment of the race that created it, and of which it is the most perfect expression. Nowhere do the aridity, the austerity, and the grandeur that characterized the original works of the Semitic race show themselves more nakedly. In this strange book there is not a moment in which one feels vibrate the fine and delicate touches which make the grand poetic creations of Greece and of India so perfect an imitation of nature. In it entire sides of the human soul are in default; a kind of grandiose stiffness gives to the poem a hard aspect, which resembles a tone of brass. But never has the position, so eminently poetical, of man in this world, his mysterious struggle against an inimical power which he sees not, his alternatives justified equally by submission and revolt, inspired so eloquent a plaint. The grandeur of human nature consists in a contradiction which has struck all sages and has been the fruitful mother of all elevated thought and of all noble philosophy: on the one hand, conscience declaring right and duty to be supreme realities; on the other, the experiences of every day inflicting upon these profound aspirations inexplicable contradictions. Hence that sublime lamentation which has endured since the beginning of the world, and which to the end of time shall bear toward heaven the protestations of the moral man.

The poem of Job is the most sublime expression of that cry of the soul. In it blasphemy approximates the hymn, or rather is itself a hymn, since it is only an appeal to God against the lacunae conscience finds in the work of God. The pride of the nomad, his religion—at once cold, severe, and far removed from all devotion—his haughty personality, can alone explain that singular mixture of exalted faith and of audacious obstinacy.

The imagination of the Semitic peoples never goes beyond the narrow circle which has traced around it the exclusive preoccupation of the divine grandeur. God and man, face to face with one another in the heart of the desert, is the summary and, as we say in our day, the formula of all their poetics. The Semites[1] are ignorant of the species of poesy founded upon the development of action—the epic, the drama—and the species of speculation based upon the experimental or rational method—philosophy or science. Their poesy is the song; their philosophy is the parable.[2] The period rendered their style defective, just as reasoning did their thoughts. With them enthusiasm, as well as reflection, found expression in vivid and concise details, in which we must not look for anything approximating the oratorical numbers of the Greeks and Latins. The poem of Job is unquestionably the most ancient masterpiece of that rhetoric of which the Qur'ān is, on the contrary, the example the nearest approaching to ours. We must renounce all comparison between processes so far removed from our liking and the grave, closely-knit texture of classical works. Action and the regular progression of thought, which are the soul of Greek compositions, are wanting here completely. But a vividness of imagination, a force of concentrated passion, to which there is nothing that can be compared, fly off, if I may so speak, in millions of sparks and make of each line a discourse or a complete philosophic theme.

Above all, it is the manner in which the author of the book of Job conducts his argument that astonishes us and betrays most unmistakably the characteristics of his race. Abstract relations, in the Semitic languages, can be expressed only with the greatest difficulty. The difficulty Hebrew presents in the statement of the most simple argument is quite surprising. The form of the dialogue which, in the hands of Socrates, was for the Greek mind so admirable an instrument of precision, is never used in the former to conceal the defects of a rigorous method. From one end of the poem to the other, the question in dispute is not advanced a single step. There is not a trace of that, though often subtle, yet always singularly importunate *dialectic*, the model of which is presented to us in the dialogues of Plato and in the Sutras of Buddhism. The author, like all Semites, has no conception of the beauties of composition which result from a severe discipline of the mind. He proceeds by vivid intuitions, not by inductions. An insoluble problem is proposed; an immense exercise of thought is expended in order to resolve it. God must in the end appear, not as in the classic drama to unravel the enigma, but, by the employment of even more brilliant instances, to demonstrate its unfathomable depth.

Far be it from us to think of demanding from these books of antiquity the qualities we find in the most insignificant of ours. If they strike us as being the revelation of another world, if they convey to our souls that profound emotion which carries with it the first and innocent expression of all great thought—is not that enough to explain the admiration of ages, and to justify the enthusiasm that has decreed to them the application of sacred? One circumstance, however, transforms the defect of method which offends the logician in the book of Job into a sublime beauty. If the question was one accessible to the human mind, it would shock one to see the rules of scientific investigation so grossly violated. But the question that the author poses to himself is precisely that which every thinker asks himself, without being able to answer it: embarrassments, uneasiness, that fashion of turning over in every sense the fatal obstacle without finding in it the issue, contains much more philosophy than the trenchant scholastic, who pretends to impose silence on the doubts raised by reason in rejoinders of apparent perspicacity.

Contradiction in such matters is an evidence of truth, for the little that has been revealed to man in regard to the plan of the universe is reduced to a few curves and projections, the fundamental law of which is not clearly understood and which extends into depths of infinity. To maintain in the presence of both the eternal aspirations of the heart, the affirmations of the moral sentiment, the protests of conscience, the testimony of reality—this is wisdom. The general sentiment of the book of Job is therefore one of perfect truth. It is the grandest lesson that has been given to intemperate dogmatism, and to the pretensions of the superficial mind which has become imbued with theology; it is in a sense the highest result of all philosophy, for it signifies that man has but veiled his face in the presence of the infinite problem that the government of the world opens to his meditations. The hypocritical pietism of Eliphaz and the bold intuitions of Job are equally at a loss to explain such an enigma; God Himself has been careful not to reveal the secret, and, instead of explaining the universe to man, He has contented Himself with showing what a small place man occupies in the universe.

The complete absence of the scientific instinct is one of the features that characterize the Semitic peoples. The investigation of causes is in their eyes either a vain occupation, of which they soon grow weary (Ecclesiastes 1–3), or an impiety, a usurpation of the rights of God (Job 38–41). Hence it is that the Jewish mind, though powerful by its very simplicity and persistence, has produced so few great philosophic speculations. Monotheism, in holding man under the continual thought of his impotence, and above all by excluding metaphysics and mythology, excluded by the same stroke all theology the least refined. The theory of the first principles of the universe (forces, ideas, etc.) is, in its way, a sort of polytheism, and it would be possible to demonstrate that metaphysics was only developed from the bosom of religions that were imitations proceeding from the Semitic race, and contrary to the spirit of those religions.

The system of the world, as set forth in the book of Job, is one

of the simplest. God, creator of the universe and universal agent
of the universe, has put life into all beings by breathing on them,
and produced directly the whole phenomena of nature. Around are
ranged as a court the sons of God, beings holy and pure, among
whom, however, there has stolen in a jealous detractor of the universe, who denies the existence of disinterested virtue and persecutes the good. For the rest, there is no speculation in regard to
celestial beings; a single metaphor more coherent than the others
and giving scope to a rich development (chapter 28) was pregnant
of the future: I speak of that pompous description of Wisdom, regarded as a primordial, having a distinct personality from that of
divinity and serving as an assessor to it. Such is the true Semitic
foundation upon which the theories of the Word some centuries
later became grafted.

Nature, in such a system, could only be conceived as absolutely
inanimate. In place of the living nature which spoke so powerfully
to the imagination of the ancestors of the Indo-European race, here
it is God who made all, in pursuance of a plan conceived by Himself alone. Some lively images, such as "the first-born from the dead,
the king of terrors" (38:13 f.),[3] recall at first glance the personifications of Greece and of India: one fancies one is reading the
Vedas in seeing Aurora (38:13 f.) seizing the four corners of the
earth in order to chase the wicked, and to change the face of the
world as the seal changes the *terra sigillata* (fine clay).[4] But all
this did not bear fruit. With the Aryans these attributes of Aurora
had become an act or an adventure of a goddess. Then in time,
ceasing to be understood, there were produced some whimsical
stories in which the caprice of the poets had changed. It had, as I
suppose, been related that *shahar* (Aurora) was a vigorous young
woman, who one day encountered brigands dividing their booty
on a carpet, seized the four corners of it, and killed them. People
then sought for in this narrative, which was interpreted with indefinite latitude, matter for dramas, allegories, and literary compositions of every kind.

Among the Hebrews these bold figures never went beyond the
metaphor. God promptly extinguished in their germ these fantastic
creations, which, nevertheless, proceeded in multitudes from a language full of life, fructified by an imagination that was not confined by dogma. When one has closely penetrated the genius of

these primitive Aryan languages, one finds that each sentence embraces a myth, and that each element of exterior nature was inevitably destined to become for the peoples that spoke them a divinity. Meteorological phenomena especially, which play so capital a part in the primitive religions because in this order of phenomena the immediate cause of them completely escapes observation, were a fruitful source of divine beings. There is nothing resembling this in the book of Job. The clouds, and all that is above them, are the dwelling place and the special domain of one single being which thence governs everything. They are His reservoirs, His arsenals, the pavilions in which He resides.[5] Thence He regulates the storms and makes use of them at His good pleasure for purposes of recompense or of chastisement. The thunderstorm, in particular, has always been regarded as a theophany; it signals the descent of God upon the earth: the roll of thunder is the voice of God; lightning is His luminary; electric flashes are the shafts darted by His hands.

It is useless to mention that we would have to seek quite vainly in that antique poem for a trace of the grand Grecian idea, which was born in Ionia and destined to become in modern times the basis of all philosophy: we mean the idea of the laws of nature. In the former the miracle is everything; everything breathes that facile admiration (the joyous gift of infancy) which peoples the world with marvels and enchantments. Thales and Heraclitus, one or two centuries after the book of Job, would have smiled at the artless questions by which Jehovah thought to reduce to silence the aspirations of man to know the laws of the world. Nowhere more than here is the diversity of the Aryan and the Semitic genius to be more keenly felt; the former was predestined by its primitive conception of nature and by the very form of its language to polytheism, mythology, metaphysics, and physics, while the latter was condemned never to go beyond the barren and grandiose simplicity of monotheism. Even in our own day the Muslim possesses no clearer ideas of the laws of nature than did the author of the book of Job; and the principal motive of reprobation the sincere believers in Islam raise against European science is that the latter ignores the power of God, by reducing the government of the universe to a play of forces that are susceptible of being calculated.

Thus, between the cosmogonies founded upon abstract principles and the scientific physics of the Greeks and of modern nations, the theory of the world contained in the book of Job is the most complete form of the order of nature rigorously deduced from monotheism. There can be no science of the world as long as the world is governed by the individual will of a capricious and impenetrable sovereign. From this point of view, ignorance is a cult and curiosity a wicked attempt: even in the presence of a mystery that assails and ruins him, man attributes in a special manner the character of grandeur to that which is inexplicable; all phenomena whose cause is hidden, all beings whose end cannot be perceived, are to man a humiliation and a motive for glorifying God. Greece saw the divine in that which was harmonious and evident; the Semite saw God in that which was monstrous and obscure. The deformed *leviathan* (40:25–32) is the most beautiful hymn to the Eternal. The animal, with its hidden instincts, is constantly contrasted with man, and is even preferred to him; for it is more directly under the dependence of the divine spirit which acts in it without it, while reflective reason and freedom are in some way a larceny committed upon God.

The theory of the moral world, which is made use of as a basis in the book of Job, is not less innocent. Man is in perpetual and direct relations with the divinity: he sometimes beholds it, but only to die. At other times the divinity speaks with him in dreams and in visions. Again it warns him by the ordinary events in life. The difference between the good and the bad is the result of a path which God has traced and which He reveals to man. God, in like manner, recompenses the good and punishes the bad. Again, man dies when his time has come, and descends into hell without his perceiving it. The wicked, on the contrary, die before their time. All violent deaths, all prolonged and cruel sickness, were thus regarded as punishments for concealed wickedness. The dictionary itself is strongly opposed to that which another doctrine prides itself in. The words crime, chastisement, pain, suffering, injustice, evil are, in Hebrew, almost identical, and the translator, who has struggled at almost every step against the difficulties that surround such words as *shav, aven, amal*, understands better than anyone else the impossibility the Hebrew mind had in arriving (with such a confusion in words) at a distinction that we regard as the principle of all morality.

Such is the system that I shall denominate patriarchal, and upon which the book of Job depends. We perceive at the very outset the objections to which such a system must lend itself the moment that reflection becomes the least exacting, and is no longer satisfied with the naïve explanations of the early ages. Some of the impious, at the epoch of the book of Job, were already bold enough to say, like the Epicurean, that God interfered little in the affairs of this world, and that "He walked up and down upon the vault of heaven." Above all, an insurmountable objection resulted from the spectacle presented by society. The old theory, that each is treated by God here below according to his deserts, might have been sustainable in that noble and venerable antiquity which the aged Samuel essayed vainly to defend against the new requirements that were every day springing up from all parts (see I Sam. 8).

In this Eden of the patriarchal life, in which nobleness, wealth, and power were inseparable, the theory of the friends of Job was applied almost rigorously. But this theory, which possessed some reality in an aristocracy of honest men, such as was the primitive society of the Semite nomads, became more and more insupportable in proportion as the Semitic world, up till now very pure, in the environs of Palestine, drifted into the ways of profane civilization, and which happened about the year 1000 before our era. We see then the wicked prosperous, tyrants recompensed, brigands conveyed with honors to the tomb, the just despoiled and reduced to beg for their bread. The nomad, remaining faithful to his patriarchal ideas, was not deserving of the fatal injustices which were brought in the train of a complicated civilization whose extent and aim he did not comprehend. The cry of the poor, which before had not been heard—for the poor only existed among the inferior races to which was hardly accorded the name of man[6]—began to resound everywhere in accents full of eloquence and passion.

We can conceive the perplexity of the ancient sages in the presence of an inexplicable phenomenon which henceforth presented itself every day. The Semitic mind until now had been bounded by a theory as to the destiny of man of marvelous simplicity. Man, after death, descended to *sheol*, a subterranean abode which is often difficult to distinguish from the tomb and where the dead preserved a vague existence, analogous to the *manes* of Greek and Latin antiquity, and especially to that of the Shades of the *Odyssey*. The doctrine of the immortality of the soul, which might

have offered an immediate and easy solution to the perplexities
we are speaking of, had not for once been mooted, at least in the
philosophic and moral sense we give to it; the resurrection of the
body was only entertained in the most indecisive manner. Death
did not call forth any idea of sadness, when the hour came when
a man should rejoin his fathers and when he left behind him numerous children. In this respect no difference existed between the
Hebrews and the other peoples of remote antiquity. The narrow
horizon that bounded life left no room for our uneasy aspirations
and our thirst for the infinite. But the mind of everyone was
troubled when catastrophes such as that of Job were recounted in
the text, up till then free from such stumbling blocks. The whole
of the old philosophy of the fathers was upset; the sages of Teman,
whose leading precept—that man received here below his recompense or his punishment—was entertained by backward minds, in
the presence of such misfortunes could only weep in silence for a
space of seven days and seven nights.

The book of Job is the expression of the incurable trouble that
seized the conscience at the epoch when the old patriarchal theory,
based exclusively upon the promises of the terrestrial life, became
insufficient. The author perceives the weakness of this theory; he
is, with good reason, shocked at the crying injustice that an artificial interpretation of the decrees of providence brings with it; but
he can discover no outlet from the closed circle from which man
can only free himself by a bold appeal to the future. His attempts
to shake off the ancient prejudices of the race are powerless, or
only land him in perpetual contradictions. Some partisans of the
old theory, constrained by the evidence of facts, avowed that man
is not always punished during his life; but they also maintained
that his sins are visited upon his children, who, according to the
patriarchal ideas in regard to the solidarity of the tribe, are in some
sort himself. The author does not accept this idea; for, as such a
punishment might be efficacious, it was imperative that the guilty
should be sought out. But in *sheol* nothing is known of what takes
place on earth.

At times Job seems to lift the veil from his future beliefs; he
hopes that God will assign him a place by himself in *sheol* where he
may rest in peace until he shall return to life. He knows that he
will be justified, and, the lively intuition of the justice of the future

carrying him beyond, he declares that in his flesh he shall see God (19:26). But these flashes are always followed by the most profound darkness. The old patriarchal conception returns and presses upon him with its whole weight; the spectacle of the misery of man, the tardy destruction of nature, that horrible indiscriminateness of death which strikes down without distinction the just and the wicked, the happy man and the unfortunate, brought him back to the verge of despair. In the epilogue he falls back again, purely and simply, into the theory that for a moment he has essayed to surpass. Job is avenged; his fortune is restored to him twofold; he dies old and full of days.

It must be said that the Jewish mind left to itself has never completely broken through that fatal circle. The poem of Job is not the only monument into which inquietude and embarrassment have entered—the inevitable consequences of the imperfection of Jewish ideas as to the final end. Two psalms, the thirty-seventh and the seventy-third, express with much vivacity a thought greatly analogous to that of the book of Job: the jealousy and indignation of the good in beholding the success of the wicked. An entire book, the date of which is uncertain—Kohelet, or Ecclesiastes—revolves in the same circle of contradictions, yet seems much further from a moral solution. The author of the book of Job found a solution of his doubts in a pure and simple return to the precepts of the ancient sages. Ecclesiastes is much more deeply tainted by skepticism. He ends in a sort of epicurism, fatalism, and a disgust for great things. But this was in the destiny of Israel only a temporary accident, the result of a few isolated thinkers. The destiny of Israel did not solve the problem of the individual soul, but boldly laid down the problem of humanity. Moreover, the doubts of Ecclesiastes and of Job preoccupied the people only at the moments when it had no very clear perception of its duties. There is no trace of such a doubt among the prophets. We find it only among the sages, who were almost strangers to the great theocratic spirit and to the universal mission of Israel.

At the very periods in which the Jews imposed their thoughts on the world, can we say that it was through philosophic immortality that they consoled man, and raised him to the heroism of the martyr? Certainly not. Resurrection was to them not individual revenge against the injustices of the present life, but revolution which should substitute for the brutal powers that be, the reign of a celestial and pacific Jerusalem. It was the hope of a final overthrow that should herald the advent of the Kingdom of God upon the earth, by which Christianity has conquered the world.[7] In this, nascent Christianity really continued the tradition of Israel. The Utopia of Israel did not consist in creating a world to make compensation and reparation to the latter, but to change the conditions of the latter. It was when this grandiose dream had vanished before the obstinate prolongation of the old world, and when the immediate renewal of the universe could not be expected until millennia later, that people transferred to personal judgment and to the destinies of the individual soul that which hitherto had been understood as a total and immediate renovation of humanity.

Certainly, at first sight, it seems inexplicable that men of the world who were the most imbued with the sacred fire of their work—a David, an Elijah, an Isaiah, a Jeremiah—had not, in regard to the future of man, the system of ideas that we are accustomed to consider as the basis of all religious belief. But it was in this very thing that the grandeur of Israel manifested itself. Israel has done better than to invent for the gratification of its imagination a distinct system of future rewards and pains; she has discovered the true solution for great souls; she has resolutely cut the knot she could not unravel. She has cut it by action, by the obstinate pursuit of her idea, and by the most unbounded ambition that has ever possessed the hearts of a people. There are problems that cannot be solved, but which can be passed over. That of the destiny of humanity belongs to this class. The former would destroy whatever impeded it. It alone has succeeded in discovering the secret of life which can quench inward sadness, dispense with hopes, silence those enervating doubts that attach only to feeble souls and to degenerate epochs. What matters recompense when the work is so engaging that it embraces within itself the promises of eternity?

Three thousand years have passed over the problem agitated by the sages of Idumea, and, in spite of the progress of the philosophic method, we cannot say that it has advanced a step toward solution. Regarded from the point of view of individual recompenses and chastisements, this world will continue to be a subject of eternal disputation, and God will always give the direct lie to the maladroit apologists who would defend providence upon that desperate basis. The sorrow the Psalmist experienced in "witnessing the peace of sinners" (Ps. 73:3), the anger of Job against the prosperity of the impious are sentiments justified in all times. But that which neither the Psalmist nor Job could comprehend, that which the succession of schools, the mixture of races, a long education of the moral sense could alone reveal, we have learned; beyond this chimerical justice that the superficial common sense of all ages has sought to discover in the government of the universe we perceive laws and direction much more exalted, without the knowledge of which human affairs would only seem a tissue of iniquities.

The future of the individual man has not become more clear, and perhaps it is best that an eternal veil should cover the verities which are of no value save where they are the fruit of a pure heart. But a word that neither Job nor his friends uttered has acquired a sublime meaning and value; that word is duty, which, with its incalculable philosophic consequences, is imposed upon all, resolves all doubts, conciliates all opposition, and serves as a basis for re-edifying that which reason destroys or allows to crumble away. Thanks to this neither equivocal nor obscure revelation, we affirm that he who shall choose the good will be the true sage. The latter shall be immortal, for his works will live, if definitive justice be a résumé of the divine work that has been accomplished by humanity. Humanity made the divine as the spider weaves his web; the march of the world is enveloped in darkness, but it tends toward God. While the foolish or frivolous wicked man shall wholly perish, in the sense that he shall leave nothing behind in the general result of the labor of his species, the man devoted to the good and the beautiful shall participate in the immutability of that which he loved. Who is he that sees today as much as the obscure Galilean who, eighteen hundred years ago, threw into the world the glaive that divides us and the words that unite us? The works of the man of genius and of the man of probity thus alone escape the universal decay, for they alone are computed in the sum of things acquired, and their fruits go on increasing, even when ungrateful humanity has forgotten them. There is nothing lost; that which makes for the good of the most unknown of virtuous men counts more in the eternal balance than the most insolent triumphs of error and of evil. Whatever form he gives to his beliefs, whatever symbol he employs to invest his affirmations of the future, the just man has thus the right to say with the old patriarch of Idumea, "Yes, I know that my redeemer liveth, and that he shall appear at the latter day upon the earth" (19:25).

H. H. ROWLEY : THE INTELLECTUAL VERSUS THE SPIRITUAL SOLUTION

One of the most versatile scholars in the field of ancient thought and institutions is H. H. Rowley (born 1890), for many years professor of Semitic languages and literature in the University of Manchester, England. His studies encompass biblical Israel (*The Growth of the Old Testament* [1950]; *The Faith of Israel* [1956]), the apocalyptic literature (*The Relevance of Apocalyptic* [1944]), the Dead Sea scrolls (*The Zadokite Fragments* [1952]), comparative religion (*Prophecy and Religion in Ancient China and Israel* [1956]), and Eastern thought (*Submission in Suffering* [1951]). In a number of places in his works Professor Rowley refers to the problem of Job. The passage here reprinted appears in *From Moses to Qumran: Studies in the Old Testament* (London, 1963).

The author of our book was concerned less with theology than with religion. So far as any theological or philosophical explanation of the mystery of suffering is concerned, he has none to offer.[1] The reader is told the explanation in Job's case, but that was necessary in order to establish that Job was really an innocent sufferer. Neither Job nor his friends can deduce the reason, and when God speaks from the whirlwind to Job He does not disclose it. Had He done so, the book would immediately have lost its meaning for those who suffer. For men must suffer in the dark, and a Job who was not left in the dark would have no message for others. It is true that God spoke to Job from heaven, whereas no such voice comes to us. But the voice brought no new revelation of truth, but merely reminded Job of what he could have perceived for himself. It merely reminded him of the unfathomable wonders of creation, and made him realize that there are mysteries beyond human penetration.

To say this is not to suggest that theology and philosophy are futile disciplines. There are secrets of nature that man cannot penetrate; but this does not mean that scientists ought not to investigate nature. There are mysteries of experience that neither theology nor philosophy can fully elucidate; but this does not mean that the human spirit should not wrestle with the problems. But what the book of Job says is that there is something more fundamental than the intellectual solution of life's mysteries. The author has a message for the spirit rather than for the intellect. He is no academic writer addressing himself to the select few profound thinkers. He knows that intellectual giants are few, but that all men have a spirit, and that all may suffer. When one is suffering it may be good to understand the cause; but it is better to be sustained to endure.

We may pause to note that the cause of Job's suffering was more than the Satan's insinuation against him. He was suffering to vindicate more than himself. He was vindicating God's trust in him. He was not so much abandoned by God as supremely honored by God. The author does not, of course, suggest that this is always the reason for undeserved suffering. He is not so foolish as to imply that a single cause covers all cases, and, so far from wishing the reader to deduce that this is always the case, he wishes to make it plain that the actual cause in any given case cannot be deduced by man. The cause or reason for the suffering is hidden in the heart of God. In the case of Job it was not unworthy of God—or of Job. It was the expression of God's confidence in him, and by his very suffering he was serving God. Yet Job could never know this. To the reader, then, the author is saying that when suffering comes undeserved, while he can never guess its explanation, he may face it with trust that, if he could know the cause, he too might find that he was serving God and was honored in his very agony.

I have said that there is an inner conflict in the mind of Job. While he repudiates the view of the friends that his suffering proves his sin, he yet has the ever lurking feeling that this ought to be so. He cannot wholly extricate himself from their ideas, and therefore he cannot extricate himself from the consequence of those ideas.

Where suffering is believed to be the effect of sin, it is the evidence of a man's isolation from God, since sin is isolation from God.

At the beginning of the Bible we find that when Adam sinned he was thrust out from the Garden of Eden. But before he was thrust out and the angel set to guard the gate, Adam had hidden himself from God. He was conscious that his sin had come between him and God and had erected a barrier. Here in this early story, which we so easily characterize as primitive and childish, there is a profound perception of the nature of sin. It separates man from God. If, then, suffering is thought to be the evidence of sin, it is by the same token the evidence that the sufferer is cut off from God. And this is what Job feels, despite all his protests. He still tries to cling to God, and appeals to the God he has known; but he feels he cannot get at God, and all his appeals are but carried away on the wind.

By insisting that there is such a thing as innocent suffering, the author of Job is bringing a message of the first importance to the sufferer. The hardest part of his suffering need not be the feeling that he is deserted by God, or the fear that all men will regard him as cast out from God's presence. If his suffering is innocent it may not spell isolation from God, and when he most needs the sustaining presence of God he may still have it. Here is a religious message of great significance, and it is by his religious message, which matches the magnificence of his literary gift, that the author of our book created his masterpiece.

It is this that is brought out in the closing verses of the poetical portion of the book, in which Job bows himself in submission before God. "I had heard of Thee with the hearing of the ear," he cries, "but now mine eye seeth Thee; wherefore I repent and abhor myself in dust and ashes" (42:5 f.). He does not repent of any sin that had brought his trial upon him. On that issue he is vindicated as against the friends. He repents of the charges he has brought against God, and of the doubts he has entertained. More significant is his recognition that, with all the loss and the pain he had suffered, he had gained something even from his agony. In his prosperity he thought he had known God. Now he realizes that compared with his former knowledge his present knowledge is as the joy of seeing compared with a mere rumor. All his past experience of God was as nothing compared with the

experience he had now found. He therefore no longer cries out to
God to be delivered from his suffering. He rests in God even in
his pain.[2]

This is not to explain the meaning of suffering. It is to declare
to the reader that even such bitter agony as Job endured may be
turned to spiritual profit if he finds God in it. This is to be distinguished from the thought of the Elihu speeches. Elihu supposed
that the suffering itself was disciplinary. Here is no thought that
the suffering is itself enriching. Rather is it that the fellowship of
God is enriching, and that that fellowship may be found in adversity no less than in prosperity.

Many writers have suggested that the failure of the book to
solve the problem of suffering is to be set in contrast to the Christian message.[3] It is supposed that for a fuller answer to the problem
it was necessary to wait until a better doctrine of the afterlife had
been attained than Job knew. There are many passages in which
the book of Job shows no advance on the thought of the afterlife
that the author's contemporaries cherished. *Sheol* is thought of as
a place where good and bad alike go, where man is shut off from
God and in ignorance of the fortunes of his family, and where he
is conscious only of his misery.[4] It is true that Job longs for death,
and speaks of *sheol* as something to be desired, in comparison with
his present misery.[5] But that is only his eloquent way of indicating
the depth of his misery, and not his way of suggesting that after
death any existence that was desirable in itself was to be hoped
for. In one familiar passage he has been supposed to attain a faith
in a more worthwhile afterlife. As translated in the Authorized
Version, the passage runs: "I know that my redeemer liveth, and
that He shall stand at the latter day upon the earth; and though
after my skin worms destroy this body, yet in my flesh shall I see
God: whom I shall see for myself, and mine eyes shall behold, and
not another" (19:25–27). In fact this is one of the most cryptic
passages in the book, and both text and interpretation are far from
sure. [. . .]

While it must be agreed that the words are ambiguous, I think
it is possible that the author is here reaching out after something
more satisfying than the dreary doctrine of *sheol* reflected elsewhere in his book. But he has not securely grasped it. Here is no
clear faith in a worthwhile afterlife, but at best the belief that

God will one day vindicate him and that he will be conscious of that vindication. Yet, having said this, I would return to say that no faith in an afterlife can touch the problem with which the book of Job is concerned. The problem of suffering is as real a problem today as it was in the days of our author, and Christian theology is as impotent as Jewish to solve it.[6] It is sometimes thought that the faith that beyond this life there is another, where the injustices and inequalities of this life may be rectified, offers an answer to the problem. In truth it offers none. When the wicked is seen to prosper, it may be possible to find some comfort in the thought of what lies before him in the next world—though this is not a very exalted comfort. When the pious is seen to suffer, it may be possible to find some comfort in the thought of the bliss that awaits him hereafter. But this can offer no possible explanation of his present sufferings. The book of Job is far more profound in its message that here and now the pious sufferer has no reason to envy the prosperous wicked. The wicked may have his prosperity, but the pious may have God; and in God he has far more than the other. The inequalities of life belong to man's outer lot; but this is immaterial to his spiritual life.

This is already apparent in the story of Joseph, told in the most ancient document of the Pentateuch. "The Lord was with Joseph" (Gen. 39:2, 21), and therefore he could face alternate adversity and prosperity in serenity of spirit. And when we come to the New Testament we find that it cannot advance upon this. St. Paul was a Pharisee before he became a Christian, and as a Pharisee he already believed in the resurrection (Acts 22:3; 24:21). He continued to hold that belief after he became a Christian. But it brought him no relevant message in suffering. He suffered from some acute malady that brought him agonizing pain—so agonizing that at times he cried out to be delivered from it. He does not appear to have found any consolation in thinking of the next world. He says: "Concerning this thing I cried unto the Lord thrice, that it might depart from me. And He hath said unto me, my grace is sufficient for thee: for my power is made perfect in weakness. Most gladly therefore," cries Paul, "will I rather glory in my weaknesses, that the power of Christ may rest upon me" (II Cor. 12:8 ff.). Here we see that Paul ceases to cry out for deliverance from his suffering, but finds enrichment in his suffering, so that he comes to rejoice in the suffering itself because it has brought him a new experience of the grace of God. This is fundamentally the same as we have found in the book of Job. It falls far short of an intellectual solution of the problem of suffering. But it achieves the spiritual miracle of the wresting of profit from the suffering through the enrichment of the fellowship of God. It was in this that the author of the book of Job was interested and to this that he leads the reader.

LEONHARD RAGAZ :
GOD HIMSELF IS THE ANSWER

One of the most remarkable modern applications of religious thought to practice is that of the Swiss Protestant theologian Leonhard Ragaz (1868– 1945); he withdrew from a comfortable professorship in Zurich in 1921 to devote himself wholly to those most in need of help and to the international peace movement. A prolific writer, he wrote *Das Evangelium und der soziale Kampf der Gegenwart* (The Gospel and the Social Struggle Today) (1906), *Sozialismus und Gewalt* (Socialism and Power) (1919), *Christentum und Judentum* (Christianity and Judaism) (1927). The chapter on Job, here reprinted (in a translation by Harry Zohn), is a section in a multivolume work, *Die Bibel: Eine Deutung* (The Bible: An Interpretation) (Zurich, 1947–50).

The ballad that we call the book of Job probably goes back to a late period. We know neither its author nor its place of origin nor details about how it came into being. It is fitting that this should be so. For, despite its close connection with the people of Israel and their God, its theme is in a very special way a universally human and eternal one. In the history of man's struggle for God, this poem stands out like a solitary mountain peak.

To reproduce and interpret this work is just as impossible and unnecessary as in the case of the book of Psalms. The details of this work will be self-explanatory to the thoughtful reader. But we must say a few words about the overall meaning and thus about the significance and value of this component of the Bible.

What we may call the most important value of the poetic drama is this: the problem of God's justice can here be discussed down to its roots; man is allowed to express his doubts in a way that cannot be surpassed and even exceeds what the book of Psalms achieves in this area; man is allowed to appear as the accuser of God, and in such a way that God Himself not only permits but favors it and severely censures those who take Job to task and condemn him for it.

This again takes us into the realm of an unparalleled freedom in the relationship between man and God—a realm that neither paganism nor Christianity has dared to claim. This too is redemption; the permission to speak out is liberation; being permitted to ask a question is tantamount to receiving an answer. You would not ask me unless you already had the answer! Again we may say: Doubt, which is usually something proscribed, is sanctioned here. God wishes to be asked. We may also say: Prometheus and the Titans are redeemed by being overcome only now, in this freedom of the sons of God.

The second magnificent feature of this book is connected with this. God Himself rejects all false apologias; He will have none of that justification of His dominion which His unauthorized pious advocates repeatedly feel obliged to make, a justification that reaches its philosophical zenith in the *Théodicée* of Leibniz. Such a defense of God by men usually is petty, presumptuous, and full of untruths, and convinces only those who want to be convinced at any price. It is, basically, an insult to God.

At this point it may be well to speak of another element which, as it were, reappears in the Bible along with Job: the rôle played in it by Satan, the author of the evil that besets Job, who is nevertheless the servant of God and must not do anything without His permission, who appears before His throne among the "sons of God." Only now does the opposing power which we encountered on the first pages of the Bible appear in the personification that will henceforth assume such importance and be at the very center in the New Testament. The great antithesis comes to a head here, simplifying the problem of God's justice on the one hand and complicating it on the other.

But what is the solution of the problem? What is God's answer? It is powerful, at once crushing and uplifting, and, as far as it goes, of eternal validity: it is God Himself. This means that God does not involve Himself with arguments for and against His dominion, but lets Himself be seen. His answer consists in His manifesting His greatness in powerful speech and creative deeds. This, rather than the arguments of God's defenders, causes Job to grow silent and beg God's forgiveness. He has been afforded no insight into the enigmas that have tormented him, but he has seen God Himself. "I have heard of Thee but by hearsay [from theological works and apologias, pious phrases, and the like], but now mine eye has seen Thee! Therefore I despise my words and repent in sackcloth and ashes" (42:5 f.).

This is the core of the ballad, everything else being but the outer shell. It is an insight similar to the one conveyed by Psalm 73. Jacob's fight with God is fought anew. "I have seen God face to face and have remained alive" (Gen. 32:31). It is also the answer of Isaiah 40:21–31. It is the eternally valid answer. Arguing back and forth about God's government does not help one to overcome doubts; only God Himself can. It is a matter of penetrating to Him through the ranks of God's accusers and defenders, including the pious consolers. And God wishes that this be done. It is also the innermost meaning of sorrow that one be brought to that point. God lets Himself be asked, and thus lets Himself be found. And He Himself is the answer. In individual cases it is possible to struggle with difficult, unsolved problems and yet know that God lives, being not only consoled by this knowledge, but joyously getting a new lease on life. The end of the story of Job is a symbol of this.

It is an eternally valid answer, but not the ultimate one. There is an error in the way that Job has posed the problem, and thus in the solution as well.

Job shares with the Psalms the false premise that there is much doubting of God's justice and much defense of it, that the world as it is—nature and history, including the fate of the individual—directly constitutes the work and the will of God. This is not the innermost meaning of the Bible. To be sure, it knows God's creation, not only the one act but a continuing creation, and recognizes it as "very good," but it also knows about the Fall and the destruction that flowed from it. It knows even more than Job did about the opposing power. It expects the solution of the problem of God's justice to come from redemption by Christ; it expects it from God's and man's deeds, which, following the example of Christ, make manifest the works of God through the struggle with evil and the enigma inherent in it. [. . .]

ROBERT LOWTH : OF THE POEM OF JOB

Robert Lowth (1710–87), English theologian, is a pioneer in modern biblical studies. As professor of poetry at Oxford University (1741–50), he devoted his research to biblical poetry. He discovered the rhythm and the parallelism (vaguely noticed before) as the art form of the Hebrew poem, its imagery, metaphors, and allegories, and opened the door to an aesthetic appreciation of this body of writing, applying to it aspects of comparative literature. His *De Sacra Poesi Hebraeorum* (1753) became the basis for all future work in the field. In 1773 appeared a treatise by Anton A. H. Lichtenstein, *Num liber Jobi cum Odyssea Homeri comparari possit?* J. G. Herder, whose work on Hebrew poetry appeared in 1782–83, acknowledged his indebtedness to the English master. From 1766 to 1777 Lowth served first as Bishop of Oxford, then as Bishop of London.

In the chapter that follows, Lecture XXXIII of his *magnum opus* (one of three lectures devoted to Job), Lowth examines the poetic form of the book of Job: Is it a drama in the strict Aristotelian sense? Obviously not, since plot and action are missing. To prove his point, Lowth invites comparison with Sophocles' *Oedipus Rex* and *Oedipus at Colonus*. But, in view of the book's form and arrangement, he confirms its claim for "first place among the poetical compositions of the Hebrews."

When I undertook the present investigation, my principal object was to enable us to form some definite opinion concerning the poem of Job, and to assign it its proper place among the compositions of the Hebrew poets. This will possibly appear to some a superfluous and idle undertaking, as the point seems long since to have been finally determined, the majority of the critics having decidedly adjudged it to belong to the dramatic class. Since, however, the term *dramatic*, as I formerly had reason to remark, is in itself extremely ambiguous, the present disquisition will not be confined within the limits of a single question; for the first object of inquiry will necessarily be, what idea is affixed to the appellation by those critics who term the book of Job a dramatic poem? And after we have determined this point (if it be possible to determine it, for they do not seem willing to be explicit), we may then with safety proceed to inquire whether, pursuant to that idea, the piece be justly entitled to this appellation.

A poem is called dramatic either in consequence of its form— the form I mean of a perfect dialogue, which is sustained entirely by the characters or personages without the intervention of the poet (and this was the definition adopted by the ancient critics), or else, according to the more modern acceptation of the word, in consequence of a plot or fable being represented in it. If those who account the book of Job dramatic adhere to the former definition, I have little inclination to litigate the point; and indeed the object of the controversy would scarcely be worth the labor; though a critic, if disposed to be scrupulously exact, might insist that the work, upon the whole, is by no means a perfect dialogue, but consists of a mixture of the narrative and colloquial style; for the historical part, which is all composed in the person of the writer himself, is certainly to be accounted a part of the work itself, considered as a whole. Since, however, on the other hand, the historical or narrative part is all evidently written in prose, and seems to me to be substituted merely in the place of an argument or comment for the purpose of explaining the rest, and certainly does not constitute any part of the poem; since, moreover, those short sentences which serve to introduce the different speeches contain very little more than the names—I am willing to allow that the structure or form of this poem is on the whole dramatic. But this concession will, I fear, scarcely satisfy the critics in question, for they speak of the regular order and conduct of the piece, and of the dramatic catastrophe; they assert that the interposition of the deity is a necessary part of the machinery of the fable; they even enumerate the acts and scenes, and use the very same language in all respects as if they spoke of a Greek tragedy; insomuch that when they term the poem of Job dramatic, they seem to speak of that species of drama which was cultivated and improved in the theater of Athens. It appears, therefore, a fair object of inquiry, whether the poem of

Job be possessed of the peculiar properties of the Greek drama, and may with reason and justice be classed with the theatrical productions of that people.

We have already agreed that the greater and more perfect drama is peculiarly distinguished from the lesser and more common species, inasmuch as it retains not only the dramatic form, or the perfect dialogue, but also exhibits some entire action, fable, or plot. And this is perfectly agreeable to the definition of Aristotle; for, although he points out many parts or constituents in the composition of a tragedy, he assigns the first place to the plot or fable. This he says is the beginning, this the end, this is the most important part, the very soul of a tragedy, without which it is utterly undeserving of the name, and indeed cannot properly be said to exist. A plot or fable is the representation of an action or event, or of a series of events or incidents tending all to one point, which are detailed with a view to a particular object or conclusion. A tragedy, says the same author, is not a representation of men, but of actions, a picture of life, of prosperity and adversity; in other words, the business of the poem is not merely to exhibit manners only, nor does the most perfect representation of manners constitute a tragedy: for, in reality, a tragedy may exist with little or no display of manners or character; its business is to exhibit life and action, or some regular train of actions and events, on which depends the felicity or infelicity of the persons concerned. For human happiness or prosperity consists in action; and action is not a quality, but is the end of man. According to our manners, we are denominated good or bad; but we are happy or unhappy, prosperous or unsuccessful, according to actions or events. Poets therefore do not form a plot or action merely for the sake of imitating manners or character; but manners and character are added to the plot, and, for the sake of it, are chiefly attended to. Thus far he has accurately drawn the line between the representation of action and that of manners. He adds, moreover, that unity is essential to a regular plot or action, and that it must be complete in itself, and of a proper length. But to comprehend more perfectly the nature of a plot or fable, it must be observed that there are two principal species, for they are either complete or simple. The former contains some unexpected vicissitude of fortune, such as the recognition of a person at first unknown, the recovery of a lost child, or a sudden change in the situation of the parties, or perhaps both. The latter contains nothing of the kind, but proceeds in one uniform and equal tenor. In every plot or fable, however, be it ever so simple, and though it contain nothing of the wonderful or unexpected, there is always a perplexity or embarrassment, as also a regular solution or catastrophe; the latter must proceed from the former, and indeed must depend upon it; which cannot be the case, unless there be a certain order or connection in the incidents and events that inclines them toward the same end, and combines them all in one termination.

On fairly considering these circumstances, I have no hesitation in affirming that the poem of Job contains no plot or action whatever, not even of the most simple kind: it uniformly exhibits one constant state of things, not the smallest change of fortune taking place from the beginning to the end; and it contains merely a representation of those manners, passions, and sentiments that might actually be expected in such a situation. Job is represented as reduced from the summit of human prosperity to a condition the most miserable and afflicted; and the sentiments of both Job and his friends are exactly such as the occasion dictates. For here a new temptation falls upon him, by which the constancy of Job is put to the severest trial; and this circumstance it is that constitutes the principal subject of the poem. Job had, we find, endured the most grievous calamities, the loss of his wealth, the deprivation of his children, and the miserable union of poverty and disease, with so much fortitude, and with so just a confidence in his own integrity, that nothing could be extorted from him in the least inconsistent with the strictest reverence for the Divine Being: he is now put to the proof, whether, after enduring all this with firmness and resignation, he can with equal patience endure to have his innocence and virtue (in which perhaps he had placed too much confidence) indirectly questioned, and even in plain terms arraigned. Job, now sinking under the weight of his misery, laments his condition with more vehemence than before. His friends reprove his impatience, and drop some dark insinuations to the apparent disparagement of his virtue and integrity, by entering into very copious declamation concerning the justice of God in proportioning His visitations to the crimes of men. Job is still more violently agitated, and his friends accuse him with less reserve. He appeals to God, and expostulates with some degree of freedom. They urge and press him in the very heat of his passion, and, by still more malignant accusations, excite his indignation and his confidence, which were already too vehement. Elihu interposes as an arbiter of the controversy; he reproves the severe spirit of his friends, as well as the presumption of Job, who trusted too much in his own righteousness. Job receives his admonitions with mildness and temper, and, being rendered more sedate by his expostulation, makes no reply, though the other appears frequently to expect it. When the Almighty, however, condescends to set before him his rashness, frailty, and ignorance, he submits in perfect humility, and with sincere repentance. Here the temptation of Job concludes, in the course of which there was great reason to apprehend he would be totally vanquished; at the same time the poem necessarily terminates, the state of things still remaining without any change or vicissitude whatever. The poem indeed contains a great variety of sentiment, excellent representations of manners and character, remarkable efforts of passion, much important controversy; but no change of fortune, no novelty of incident, no plot, no action.

If indeed we rightly consider, we shall, I dare believe, find that the very nature of the subject excludes even the possibility of a plot or action. From that state of settled and unvarying misery in which Job is involved arises the doubt of his integrity, and those insinuations and criminations which serve to exasperate him, and by which he is stimulated to expostulate with God and to glory in his own righteousness. It was proper, therefore, that, by a continuance of the same state and condition, he should be recalled to a humble spirit, and to a proper reverence for the Almighty Providence; for it would have been altogether contrary to what is called poetical justice if he had been restored to prosperity previous to his submission and penitence. The repentance of Job, however, we find concludes the poem. Nor was it at all necessary that the question concerning the divine justice should be resolved in the body of the work, either by the fortunate issue of the affairs of Job, or even by the explication of the divine intentions: this, in fact, was not the primary object, nor does it at all constitute the subject of the poem, but is subservient, or in a manner an appendage to it. The disputation that takes place upon this topic is no more than an instrument of temptation, and is introduced in order to explain the inmost sentiments of Job, and to lay open the latent pride that existed in his soul. The Almighty, therefore, when He addresses Job, pays little regard to this point; nor indeed was it necessary, for neither the nature nor the object of the poem required a defense of the divine providence, but merely a reprehension of the overconfidence of Job.

If, indeed, we suppose any change to have taken place in the state of affairs, the nature and subject of the poem will also be changed. If we connect with the poetical part either the former or the latter part of the history, or both, the subject will then be the display of a perfect example of patience in enduring the severest outward calamities, and at length receiving an ample reward at the hands of the Almighty; from this, however, the universal tenor of the poem will be found greatly to differ. It will be found to exhibit rather the impatience of Job in bearing the reproaches and abuse of his pretended friends. And this appears to lead to the true object of the poem, for Job is irritated—he indulges his passion, he speaks too confidently of his own righteousness, and in too irreverent a style concerning the justice of God; in the end, he is converted by the admonitions of Elihu, and the reproofs of his omnipotent creator. The true object of the poem appears therefore to be to demonstrate the necessity of humility, of trust in God, and of the profoundest reverence for the divine decrees, even in the holiest and most exalted characters.

Should it be objected that I have contended with a scrupulous perverseness concerning the meaning of a word, and should it, after all, be affirmed that this very temptation of Job, this dispute itself, possesses in some degree the form or appearance of an action, I am content to submit the trial to another issue, and to be judged by a fair investigation of the practice of the Greek poets upon similar occasions. There is no necessity to remind this assembly with how much art and design the fable or plot of the *Oedipus Tyrannus* of Sophocles appears to have been constructed; with what powers of imagination and judgment the process of the drama is conducted;

and in what manner, by a regular succession of events arising naturally from each other, the horrid secret is developed, which, as soon as disclosed, precipitates the hero of the tragedy from the summit of human happiness into the lowest depths of misery and ruin. Let us only suppose Sophocles to have treated the same subject in a different manner, and to have formed a poem on that part of the story alone which is comprised in the last act. Here Oedipus would be indeed exhibited as an object of the most tender compassion; here would be a spacious field for the display of the most interesting and tragical affections. The fatal catastrophe would be deplored; the blindness, disgrace, exile of the hero would enhance the distress of the scene; and to the bitterness of present calamity would be added the still more bitter remembrance of the past. The poet might copiously display the sorrow and commiseration of his daughters, his detestation of himself, and of all that belong to him; and more copiously, of those who had preserved him when exposed, who had supported and educated him. All these topics the poet has slightly touched upon in these lines:

> O curst Cithaeron! why didst thou receive me?
> Or, when thou didst, how couldst thou not destroy me?

The succeeding passages are also extremely pathetic. These would easily admit of amplification, and, when the ardor of grief was a little abated, he might have added his vindication of himself, his asseverations of his innocence, his plea of ignorance and fatal necessity, and his impassioned exclamations against fortune and the gods. From all this might be constructed a poem, great, splendid, copious, diversified; and the subject would also furnish a topic of disputation not unlike that of Job. It might also assume in some measure the dramatic form: the same characters that appear in the tragedy might be introduced; it might possess the exact proportions and all the requisites of a drama, fable alone excepted, which indeed constitutes the very essence of a dramatic poem, and without which all other qualities are of no avail, for the Greeks would have called such a production a monody, or elegiac dialogue, or anything but a tragedy.

This opinion receives still further confirmation from the example and authority of Sophocles himself in another instance. For, when he again introduces the same Oedipus upon the stage in another tragedy, though the groundwork of the piece be nearly that which we have been describing, the conduct of it is totally different. This piece is called *Oedipus Coloneus*. The plot or fable is quite simple, on which account it is a fairer object of comparison with the poem of Job than any the plot of which is more complex. Oedipus is introduced blind, exiled, and oppressed with misery: none of these circumstances above mentioned have escaped the poet, such as the lamentation of his misery, the passionate exclamations against fate and the gods, and the vindication of his innocence. These, however, do not form the basis of the poem; they are introduced merely as circumstances which afford matter of amplification, and which seem to flow from that elegant plot or action he has invented. Oedipus, led by his daughter, arrives at Colonus, there to die and be interred according to the admonitions of the oracle; for upon these circumstances the victory of the Athenians over the Thebans was made to depend. The place being accounted sacred, the Athenians are unwilling to receive him, but Theseus affords him refuge and protection. Another of his daughters is introduced, who informs him of the discord between her brothers; also that Creon is coming, with an intention of bringing him back to his own country in pursuance of a decree of the Thebans. After this, Creon arrives: he endeavors to persuade Oedipus to return to Thebes, and, on his refusal, attempts to make use of violence. Theseus protects Oedipus, and in the meantime Polynices arrives, with a view of bringing over his father to his party in the war against the Thebans, this being the only condition on which he was to hope for victory. Oedipus refuses, and execrates his son in the severest terms. In conclusion, the answer of the oracle being communicated to Theseus, Oedipus dies, and is secretly buried there. In this manner is constructed a regular, perfect, and important action or plot, all the parts of which are connected together in one design, and tend exactly to the same conclusion, and in which are involved the fates of both Thebes and Athens. The manners, passions, characters, and sentiments serve to adorn, but not to support, the fable. Without any striking representation of these, the plot or action would still remain, and would of itself sustain the tragedy; but if the action be removed, though all the rest remain, it is evident that the tragedy is totally annihilated.

From these observations it will, I think, be evident, that the poem of Job cannot properly be brought into comparison either with the *Oedipus* of Sophocles or with any other of the Greek tragedies. It will be evident, I think, that this poem ought not to be accounted of the same kind; nor can it possibly be classed with them, unless the whole nature and form of either the Greek or the Hebrew poem be changed, or unless the plot or action be taken from the one or added to the other: for without this great essential no poem can indeed be accounted a perfect drama.

But though I have urged thus much against its claim to that title, let it not be understood that I wish to derogate from its merits. That censure will rather apply to those who, by criticizing it according to foreign and improper rules, would make that composition appear lame and imperfect which, on the contrary, is in its kind most beautiful and perfect. If indeed the extreme antiquity of this poem, the obscurity and the difficulty that necessarily ensue from that circumstance, be considered, and if allowance be made for the total want of plot and action, we shall have cause to wonder at the elegance and interest we find in its form, conduct, and economy. The arrangement is perfectly regular, and every part is admirably adapted to its end and design. The antiquary and the critic, who has been at the pains to trace the history of the Grecian drama from its first weak and imperfect efforts, and has carefully observed its tardy progress to perfection, will scarcely, I think, without astonishment, contemplate a poem produced so many ages before, so elegant in its design, so regular in its structure, so animated, so affecting, so near to the true dramatic model; while, on the contrary, the united wisdom of Greece, after ages of study, was not able to produce anything approaching to perfection in this walk of poetry before the time of Aeschylus. But however this be—whatever rank may be assigned to Job in a comparison with the poets of Greece, to whom we must at least allow the merit of art and method—among the Hebrews it must certainly be allowed, in this respect, to be unrivalled. It is of little consequence whether it be esteemed a didactic or an ethic, a pathetic or dramatic, poem; only let it be assigned a distinct and conspicuous station in the highest rank of the Hebrew poetry.

J. G. HERDER : GOD AND NATURE IN THE BOOK OF JOB

Johann Gottfried Herder (1744–1803), German interpreter of literature and religion, student of Kant (1762–64), friend of J. G. Hamann, intellectually related to Lessing and Winckelmann, was early in life attracted by the Old Testament, its prose tales, historic accounts, prophetic addresses, its poetry and hymns. He translated parts of this literature and planned a German rendition of the entire work. In the process of translation, he attempted to penetrate the spirit of ancient Hebrew writing. In 1774 appeared his *Die älteste Urkunde des Menschengeschlechts* (The Earliest Document of the Human Race), an interpretation of the first chapters of Genesis; in 1782 and 1783 he published the first two parts of *Vom Geiste der Ebräischen Poesie* (*The Spirit of Hebrew Poetry*); a third, concluding, part was planned but not executed.

Averse to narrow theological, dogmatic, or shallow rationalist approaches to the Bible, Herder wished to read the Scriptures in the spirit in which they were composed. In his view, the Hebrew Bible, in itself only remnants of a vaster body of writings, is part and parcel of world literature—and of world history. It is due to Herder's work that the Bible—divinely inspired as he considered it to be—was removed from the sphere of theology and religious institution to the realm of humanist, literary, aesthetic creativity. He emphasizes the linguistic basis of this literature (the preponderance of the verbal form), its form (the parallelism of poetic lines), the brilliance and richness of its imagery, its ideas, and, among them, the purposeful design of the cosmos and the rôle of nature and its wonders, all of them pointing to "a parallelism of heaven and earth."

In the book of Job, Herder finds an outstanding example of poetic cosmology, that is, in addition, a work in praise of a man who, in suffering, stands firm in his fear of God. In Herder's view, Job is the oldest of biblical writings.

The chapter that follows, Dialogue IV of *Vom Geiste*, analyzes the description of God as judge of the stars, the creator of the world, the stiller of the tempest; elucidates the pictures of nature; and examines the poetry of nature in general and "the influence of the poetry of nature on the feelings." Some of the passages quoted from Job are not fully cited but indicated by reference.

When Euthyphron inquired for his friend, he found him reading the book of Job.

ALCIPHRON: You see how your scholar is employed, and it is hardly necessary to say that I am reading this book with delight.

I cannot yet indeed accustom myself to the long speeches, the tedious complaints and claims to innocency, and still less the vindications of providence, which cannot themselves be vindicated. Of the guiding thread of the dialogue, I yet know nothing. But the descriptions of nature in it, the sublime and yet simple account of the attributes of God, and His government of the world, elevate the soul. If you are inclined to listen, then, I will (as these people say) open the treasures of my heart, and read a few passages to you. I leave it to you afterwards to set me in the right way in regard to the plan, the antiquity and author of the book.

EUTHYPHRON: It is a very proper course for you to begin in that way of selecting particular passages. To read the work continuously is for us perhaps too strong meat. We are accustomed to prefer brevity in the dialogue, and a more obvious sequence of ideas than we find here. The Orientals in their social intercourse heard each other quietly through, and were even fond of prolonged discourses, especially in verse. They are pearls from the depths of the ocean, loosely arranged, but precious: treasures of knowledge and wisdom in sayings of the olden times.

ALCIPHRON: But of what time? One must be surprised to find here so much intelligence, and furnished so abundantly with unperverted impressions and ideas of nature; and yet again there are other ideas so poor, so childlike.

EUTHYPHRON: Pass over, if you please, the consideration of time and authorship, and confine yourself to the work, as it is, in its poverty and its richness. Beyond all contradiction the book is from very ancient times, and I take it up whenever I venture to decipher its thoughts, with a species of reverence. My thoughts are carried to distant countries and remote ages, the ruins of the great revolutions that have taken place as well in matters of taste, as in the governments of the world. I listen to a voice that comes to me from a distance, perhaps of three or four thousand years, and instead of sitting in judgment on the book, or bringing it to the test of my own times, I say to myself in the words of the book itself,

> We are of yesterday, and know nothing,
> Our life on earth is but a shadow.
> The fathers, they shall teach and tell us.
> They give us the language of their hearts.   (8:9 f.)

Proceed then with its beautiful descriptions of God and nature.
My ear is open, and listens with attention to the ideas of the most
ancient of the infant world.

ALCIPHRON:

> Power and its terrors are His,
> He is arbiter in the heights of heaven.
> Are not his Hosts without number,
> And His light prevails over all?
> Shall man then be just before God?
> One born of woman be pure?
> Behold even the moon abides not with its tent,
> The stars are not pure in His eyes.
> And shall man, who is a worm, be pure?
> A child of earth, a worm!   (25:2–6)

EUTHYPHRON: A sublime representation of God, the supreme
judge of heaven! the arbiter among the stars and angels. His glit-
tering hosts are numberless, His splendor obscures them all; His
lights, His purity, the truth and justice of His judicial decree put
them to silence. The moon with its tent disappears, the stars are
impure in His sight. Then from these bright eminences we glance
at man, and ask,

> Shall man, who is a worm, be pure?
> A child of earth, a worm!   (25:6)

ALCIPHRON: Your explanation of the obscure words, "He mak-
eth peace among His heights, over whom doth not His light arise?
The moon pitcheth not her tent before Him," pleases me much. I
see the eastern judge, who decides between angels and stars. How
finely and poetically too is the darkened moon introduced. Its tent
is gone from heaven, it has concealed itself from the presence of its
judge.

EUTHYPHRON: Proceed to the remarks of Job; they are better
still.

ALCIPHRON:

> Whom helpest thou? him who hath no strength?
> Whom dost thou vindicate? whose arm hath no power?
> To whom give counsel? one without wisdom?

Truly much wisdom hast thou taught him!
To whom dost thou give knowledge by words?
And whose breath dost thou breathe?   (26:2 ff.)

EUTHYPHRON: To whom do you suppose this passage to relate?

ALCIPHRON: It seems to me to refer to God. Job means to say that God needs not to be vindicated by him, that his very breath is the breath of God, and that a helpless creature cannot become the defender of his creator.

EUTHYPHRON: Proceed, I shall not again interrupt you.

ALCIPHRON:

The shades are moved from beneath
The abyss, and those that dwell in it.
The realms of darkness are naked before Him,
And uncreated night without a covering.
Over the wasteful deep He spreadeth out the heavens,
He hangeth up the earth upon nothing;
He bindeth up the waters in His clouds,
And the clouds are not rent under them.
He closeth up His throne round about,
He spreadeth the clouds around Him.
He appointeth a boundary for the waters,
To where the light is ended in darkness.
The pillars of heaven tremble,
They are shaken at His reproof.
By His power He scourgeth the sea,
By His wisdom He bindeth its pride.
By His breath He garnisheth the heavens,
His hand seizeth the fleeing serpent,
    Lo these are a part of His ways,
A whisper that we have heard of Him;
But the thunders of His power,
Who can comprehend?   (26:5–14)

EUTHYPHRON: A splendid passage, and, as you are turned poet, I will become your commentator. Job surpasses these opponents in the excellence of his effusions, as much as he has the advantage of them in the result of their contest. He paints only a single representation of the power and majesty of God, but he draws his image from the deepest abyss, and carries his picture to the highest point of sublimity. The realms of nonexistence are spread before the Almighty, the boundless depth of vacancy stretch beneath Him; and as these were conceived, as we have before seen, under the form of a restless ocean, he represents this, the vast realm of ancient night and unborn ages, as appearing before the Almighty, unveiling its wild abyss, and the horrid commotion of its billows. The shades tremble, the shapeless forms of future being are moved with expectation; the abyss, which never before saw the light, is without a covering. Now begins the work of creation. He spreads out the heavens over this dark and boundless deep; He establishes the earth and causes it to rest, and as it were to be suspended over nothingness and vacancy. (For these realms of night and of the shades were supposed to be subterraneous.) Now He arranges the heaven in order, binds up the waters in clouds, and forms for Himself the open expanse; builds and adorns His throne, in the midst of the waters; encloses it around, and spreads the thick clouds as a carpet beneath it. Then He measures and designates the boundaries of the watery heavens to where the light and darkness mingle, that is, to the extremity of the horizon. Next, His power is exhibited in the thunder, and, still more to magnify the effect, in a storm at sea. The waves are represented as rebels, whom He drives before Him, and can in a moment bind in chains. A single breath from Him, and the sea is calm, the heavens clear; His hand meets only with the flying serpent, either, according to an image occurring in other passages (Ps. 74:13; Isa. 27:1), the monsters of the deep in the neighboring seas, as the crocodile, or perhaps the flying and curling waves themselves, which His hand smooths and levels. Either way the picture closes with a stillness as sublime and beautiful as the tumult, with which it commenced, was terrific. And these, says Job, are but a single sound, a small part of His wonders. [. . .] Every morning, as day breaks from the darkness of night, every storm, especially at sea, brings the magnificent picture before us. Have you any other passage?

ALCIPHRON: Take, if you please, the laudatory hymn of the inspired Elihu, immediately preceding the final and magnificent response of the Divine Being.

EUTHYPHRON: Observe however, by the way, that it stands there only as a foil to increase the effect of that response. Much as Elihu thinks, and finely as he speaks, he is still, as he himself says, but new and fermenting wine, that rends and escapes from the bottles. He has splendid images, but directs them to no end; and the finest of them are only amplifications of those which Job and his friends had employed in a more concise form. Hence no answer is returned to him. He prepares the way for the entrance of the Divine Being, and proclaims it without himself being aware of it. In describing a rising tempest in all its phenomena, he paints, without knowing it, the coming of the judge.

ALCIPHRON: I had never remarked this prospective design in the progress of the picture.

EUTHYPHRON: It is, however, as I think, the soul of the whole, without which all that Elihu says would be mere tautology. As the passage is too long to be taken entire, begin at the words "Lo! God is great." I will occasionally alternate with you.

ALCIPHRON:

> Lo, God is mighty in His power,
> Where is a teacher like Him?
> Who shall try his ways?
> And who shall say thou hast erred?
> Consider and praise His doings,
> For all men celebrate them,
> And all men behold them,
> But weak man sees them from far.
>   Lo, God is great, and we know it not,
> The number of His years is unsearchable.
> He draweth up the drops of water,
> Rains are exhaled upwards in vapor;
> The clouds pour them down again,
> They drop upon men abundantly.
>   Who can understand the outspreading of His clouds,
> And the fearful thunderings in His tent?
> Behold, He encompasseth it with lightnings,
> And covereth with floods the depths of the sea.
> By these He executeth judgment upon the people,
> And giveth also their food abundantly.
>   With His hands He holdeth the lightnings,
> And commandeth them where they shall strike.
> He pointeth out to them the wicked;
> The evil-doer is the prey of His wrath.   (36:22–33)

EUTHYPHRON: All these images will occur in a more concise

and beautiful form in the language of God, that follows. The tempest is now rising upon them, and Elihu proceeds—

> Therefore my heart is terrified,
> And leaps from its place with alarm.
> Hear ye! O hear with trembling His voice,
> The word, that goeth out of His mouth.
> It goeth abroad under the whole heaven,
> And His lightning to the ends of the earth.
> Behind Him sound aloud His thunders,
> He uttereth the voice of His majesty,
> And we cannot explore His thunderings.
> God thundereth marvellously with His voice,
> He doeth wonders, which we cannot comprehend.
> He saith to the snow, be thou upon the earth,
> To the dropping shower, and the outpouring of His might;
> So that all men acknowledge His work.   (37:1–7)

ALCIPHRON: In the last words I like better the interpretation—He puts the seal upon the hand of every man, that is, they stand astounded and amazed, feeling that they are powerless—a feeling, that every thunder-shower awakens in us.

EUTHYPHRON: The terrors of the storm are farther described.

> The wild beast fleeth to his cave,
> He cowers himself down in his den.
> Now cometh the whirlwind from the South,
> And from the North cometh the frost;
> The breath of God goeth forth, there is ice,
> And the broad sea is made firm.
> And now His brightness rendeth the clouds,
> His light scattereth the clouds afar.
> They wheel about in their course as He willeth,
> They go to accomplish His commands
> Upon all the face of the earth.   (37:8–12)

We must be Orientals in order to estimate the good effects of rain, and to paint with such careful observation the features and the course of the clouds. It is obviously a present scene that Elihu is describing in what follows (37:14–24).

The consequence of the young pretender's forwardness you perceive is that he shows that to be impossible, which in the face of

his declaration is on the point of taking place. At the moment, when
he is convincing himself that the darkness of the clouds is a perpetual barrier between men and God, and that no mortal shall ever
hear the voice of the Eternal, God appears and speaks—and how
vast the difference between the words of Jehovah and the language
of Elihu! It is but the feeble, prolix babbling of a child, in comparison with the brief and majestic tones of thunder, in which the creator speaks. He disputes not, but produces a succession of living
pictures, surrounds, astonishes, and overwhelms the faculties of Job
with the objects of His inanimate and animated creation.

ALCIPHRON: Jehovah spake to Job from out of the tempest, and
said to him,

> Who is it, that darkeneth the counsels of God
> By words without knowledge?
> Gird up thy loins like a man;
> I will ask thee, teach thou me.
> Where wast thou,
> When I founded the earth?
> Tell me, if thou knowest.
> Who fixed the measure of it? dost thou know?
> Who stretched the line upon it?
> Whereon stand its deep foundations?
> Who laid the corner-stone thereof,
> When the morning stars sang in chorus
> And all the sons of God shouted for joy?   (38:2–7)

EUTHYPHRON: We forget the geology and all the physics of
more modern times, and contemplate these images as the ancient
poetry of nature respecting the earth. Like a house, it has its foundations laid, its dimensions are fixed, and the line is stretched upon
it: and, when its foundations are sunk and its corner-stone is laid
in its place, all the children of God, the morning stars, His elder
offspring, chant a song of joy to the great architect and the glad
welcoming of their younger sister. Next follows the birth of the sea.

ALCIPHRON:

> Who wrapped up the sea in swaddling clothes
> When it broke forth from the mother's womb?
> I gave it the clouds for garments,
> I swathed it in mists and darkness,

> I fixed my decrees upon it,
> And placed them for gates and bars.
> I said thus far shalt thou come, and no farther,
> Here shalt thou dash thy stormy waves.   (38:8–11)

EUTHYPHRON: I do not believe that this object was ever represented under a bolder figure than that by which it is here expressed, of an infant which the creator of the world swathes and clothes with its appropriate garments. It bursts forth from the clefts of the earth, as from the womb of its mother, the ruler and director of all things addresses it as a living being, as a young giant exulting in his subduing power, and with a word the sea is hushed, and obeys Him for ever.

ALCIPHRON:

> Hast thou in thy lifetime commanded the dawn?
> And taught the day-spring to know its place,
> That it seize on the far corners of the earth,
> And scatter the robbers before it?
> Like clay the form of things is changed by it,
> They stand forth, as if clothed with ornament.
> From the wicked their light is taken away,
> Their haughty arm is broken.   (38:12–15)

EUTHYPHRON: It is unfortunate that we cannot more clearly represent the dawn as a watchman, a messenger of the Prince of Heaven, sent to chase away the bands of robbers—how different the office from that which the Western nations assigned to their Aurora! It points us to ancient times of violence, when terror and robbery anticipated the dawn.

ALCIPHRON:

> Hast thou entered into the caverns of the sea?
> Hast thou explored the hollow depths of the abyss?
> Have the gates of death opened for thee?
> And hast thou seen the doors of nonexistence?
> Is thy knowledge as broad as the earth?
> Show me, if thou knowest it all.
> Where dwelleth the light? where is the way to it?
> And the darkness, where is its place?
> That thou mayest reach even the limits thereof.

> For thou knowest the path to its house,
> Thou knowest, for thou wast already born,
> And the number of thy days is great.   (38:16–21)

EUTHYPHRON: Everything here is personified, the light, the darkness, death, and nothingness. These have their palaces with bars and gates, those their houses, their kingdoms and boundaries. The whole is a poetical world and a poetical geography.

ALCIPHRON:

> Hast thou been into the store-house of the snow?
> And seen the treasury of the hail,
> Which I have laid up for the time of need,
> For the day of war and of slaughter?   (38:22 f.)

EUTHYPHRON: A vein of irony runs through the whole passage. God fears the attack of His enemies, and has furnished and secured His vaulted treasury of hail as the armory of war. In the clouds, too, as well as in the abyss, everything breathes of poetry (38:24–30).

Rich and exquisite pictures both of the heavens and the earth! Above, the fountains of light gush forth, and the east wind scatters it over the countries of the earth, the paternal ruler of the heavens traces channels for the rain, and marks out their paths for the clouds. Beneath, the water becomes a rock, and the waves of the sea are chained with ice. Even the rain, the dew, and the hoar-frost have their father and their mother. And then follows one of the most beautiful and sublime views of the universe—

ALCIPHRON:

> Canst thou bind together the brilliant Pleiades?
> Or canst thou loose the bands of Orion?
> Canst thou bring the stars of the Zodiac in their season?
> And lead forth the Bear with her young?
> Knowest thou the laws of the heavens above?
> Or hast thou given a decree to the earth beneath?
> Canst thou lift up thy voice to the clouds,
> And enter into them clothed with floods?
> Canst thou send the lightnings, that they shall go,
> And say to thee, "here are we?"
> Who gave understanding to the flying clouds?
> Or intelligence to the meteors of the air?
> Who by his wisdom hath numbered the drops of rain?

Hath sent down the gentle showers from heaven,
And watered the dust, that it might unite,
And the clods of the earth cleave together?   (38:31–38)

EUTHYPHRON: The description of the so-called inanimate creation is here ended. But in the description no part of creation is
without life. The stars, which joyously usher in the spring, are
bound together in a sisterly union. Orion is a man girded for action, and is the pioneer of winter. The constellations of the zodiac
rise in gradual succession like a wreath encircling the earth. The
Father of the heavens lets the Bear with her young feed around
the north pole; or (in accordance with another mythology and interpretation) the nightly wanderer, a mother of the stars, who is
seeking her lost children, the stars that are no longer visible, is the
object of His consolation (perhaps effected by bringing forth to
her view new stars in place of those that were lost). One who by
night observes the Bear in its course as if feeding with its young
on the fields of the sky, or the zodiac, that, like a girdle with its
beautifully embroidered figures, encompasses the earth, and rises
gradually to view with the revolving seasons, and then reflects upon
the times when the nightly shepherds under an Oriental sky had
these images continually before them and in accordance with the
fancy and feeling that belong to a shepherd's life, ascribed to them
animated being and form—one who does this, I say, will perceive
at once the starry brilliance and beauty of this passage, although,
as to its conciseness and symmetry and the connection of its parts,
it can be but imperfectly translated. It is the same also with the
passage, in which God is represented as giving understanding to
the darkness, to the roving clouds, and meteors. The personifications both of feeling and of form in poetry vanish in another language. Yet all these images, the sending out of the lightnings, and
their reply, the going forth of God among the clouds, His number-
ing of the drops of rain, their gentle but copious descent at His
command, are in the style of the most beautiful descriptive poetry.

ALCIPHRON: You seem to be an admirer of this whole species of
poetry—and yet our critics hold it to be the most barren and inanimate in the whole compass of the art. Some indeed will not even
accord to it the name of poetry, and denominate it a heartless description of things and forms that are indescribable.

EUTHYPHRON: If such be the fact, I agree with all my heart that it does not deserve the name of poetry. Those miserable writers, who describe to us the spring, the rose, the thunder, the ice, and the winter, in a tedious and unaffecting style, are good neither in poetry, nor in prose. The true poetry of nature has something else than a dull description of individual traits, to which in fact it is not principally devoted.

ALCIPHRON: And what has it in the place of it?

EUTHYPHRON: Poetry. It makes the objects of nature to become things of life, and exhibits them in a state of living action. Look at Job. Here the earth is a palace, of which the builder laid the corner-stone while all the children of God shouted for joy at the event. The ocean was born and wrapt in garments, like a child. The dawn is an active agent, and the lightning speaks. The personification is kept up and carried through with consistency, and this gives to poetry its animation. The soul is hurried forward, and feels itself in the midst of the objects described, while it is a witness of their agencies. Tedious descriptions, on the other hand, disjoin them, and paralyze their powers. They exhibit but a tattered dress of words, abstracted and partial shadows of forms, where in true poetry we see actual and living beings.

ALCIPHRON: But who, my friend, could venture to write poetry in the style of the Orientals, to present the ocean as a child in swaddling clothes, the arsenals of snow and hail, and channels for water in the heavens?

EUTHYPHRON: No one should do it. For every language, every nation, every climate has its own measure in matters of taste, and the peculiar sources of its favorite poetry. It shows a lamentable poverty to attempt to borrow from a people so diverse, yet we must adopt the same principles, and create out of the same material. He, to whose eyes and heart nature has no life, to whose apprehension it neither speaks, nor acts, was not born to be its poet. It stands lifeless before him, and it will still be lifeless in his writing.

ALCIPHRON: It follows, then, that the ages of ignorance had great advantages over those in which nature is studied and becomes the object of knowledge. They had poetry—we have only description.

EUTHYPHRON: What call you the ages of ignorance? All sensuous tribes have a knowledge of that nature, to which their poetry relates; nay, they have a more living, and for their purpose a better, knowledge of it than the Linnaean classifier from his bookish arrangement. For a general knowledge of species this method is necessary, but to make it the foundation of poetry would be about as wise as to write it out of Hübner's[1] rhyming dictionary. For myself, I admire those times, when man's knowledge of nature was perhaps less extended, but was a living knowledge, when the eye was rendered discriminating by impassioned feeling, when analogies to what is human struck the view, and awakened feelings of astonishment.

ALCIPHRON: It were to be wished, then, that the times in which those feelings prevailed were again experienced.

EUTHYPHRON: Every age must make its poetry consistent with its ideas of the great system of being, or, if not, must at least be assured of producing a greater effect by its poetical fictions than systematic truth could secure to it. And may not this often be the case? I have no doubt that from the systems of Copernicus and Newton, of Buffon[2] and Priestley,[3] as elevated poetry may be made as from the the most simple and childlike views of nature. But why have we no such poetry? Why is it that the simple, pathetic fables of ancient or unlearned tribes always affect us more than these mathematical, physical, and metaphysical niceties? Is it not because the people of those times wrote poetry with more lively apprehensions, because they conceived ideas of all things, including God Himself, under analogous forms, reduced the universe to the shape of a house, and animated all that it contains with human passions, with love and hatred? The first poet who can do the same in the universe of Buffon and Newton will, if he is so disposed, produce with truer—at least with more comprehensive—ideas the effect which they accomplished with their limited analogies and poetic fables. Would that such a poet were already among us, but so long as that is not the case, let us not turn to ridicule the genuine beauties in the poetry of ancient nations, because they understood not our systems of natural philosophy and metaphysics. Many of their allegories and personifications contain more imaginative power, and more sensuous truth, than voluminous systems—and the power of touching the heart speaks for itself.

ALCIPHRON: This power of producing emotion, however, seems

to me not to belong in so high a degree to the poetry of nature.

EUTHYPHRON: The more gentle and enduring sentiments of poetry at least are produced by it, and more even than by any other. Can there be any more beautiful poetry than God Himself has exhibited to us in the works of creation—poetry, which He spreads fresh and glowing before us with every revolution of days and of seasons? Can the language of poetry accomplish anything more affecting, than with brevity and simplicity to unfold to us in its measure what we are and what we enjoy? We live and have our being in this vast temple of God; our feelings and thoughts, our sufferings and our joys are all from this as their source. A species of poetry that furnishes me with eyes to perceive and contemplate the works of creation and myself, to consider them in their order and relation, and to discover through all the traces of infinite love, wisdom, and power, to shape the whole with the eye of fancy, and in words suited to their purpose—such a poetry is holy and heavenly. What wretch, in the greatest tumult of his passions, in walking under a starry heaven, would not experience imperceptibly and even against his will a soothing influence from the elevating contemplation of its silent, unchangeable, and everlasting splendors. Suppose at such a moment there occurs to his thoughts the simple language of God, "Canst thou bind together the bands of the Pleiades," etc.—is it not as if God Himself addressed the words to him from the starry firmament? Such an effect has the true poetry of nature, the fair interpreter of the nature of God. A hint, a single word, in the spirit of such poetry often suggests to the mind extended scenes; nor does it merely bring their quiet pictures before the eye in their outward lineaments, but brings them home to the sympathies of the heart, especially when the heart of the poet himself is tender and benevolent, and it can hardly fail to be so.

ALCIPHRON: Will the heart of the poet of nature always exhibit this character?

EUTHYPHRON: Of the great and genuine poet undoubtedly— otherwise he may be an acute observer, but could not be a refined and powerful expositor of nature. Poetry that concerns itself with the deeds of men, often in a high degree debasing and criminal, that labors, with lively and affecting apprehensions, in the impure recesses of the heart, and often for no very worthy purpose, may corrupt as well the author as the reader. The poetry of divine things can never do this. It enlarges the heart while it expands the view, renders this serene and contemplative, that energetic, free, and joyous. It awakens a love, an interest, and a sympathy for all that lives. It accustoms the understanding to remark on all occasions the laws of nature, and guides our reason to the right path. This is especially true of the descriptive poetry of the Orientals.

ALCIPHRON: Do you apply the remark to the chapter of Job of which we were speaking?

EUTHYPHRON: Certainly. It would be childish to hunt for the system of physics implied in the individual representations of poetry, or to aim at reconciling it with the system of our own days and thus show that Job had already learned to think like our natural philosophers; yet the leading idea, that the universe is the palace of the Divine Being, where He is Himself the director and disposer, where everything is transacted according to unchangeable and eternal laws, with a providence that continually extends to the minutest concern, with benevolence and judgment—this, I say, we must acknowledge to be great and ennobling. It is set forth, too, by examples, in which everything manifests unity of purpose and subordination to the combined whole. The most wonderful phenomena come before us as the doings of an ever active and provident father of his household. Show me a poem that exhibits our system of physics, our discoveries and opinions respecting the formation of the world, and the changes that it undergoes, under as concise images, as animated personifications, with as suitable expositions, and a plan comprising as much unity and variety for the production of effect. But do not forget the three leading qualities of which I have spoken: animation in the objects for awakening the senses, interpretation of nature for the heart, a plan in the poem, as there is in creation, for the understanding. The last requisite altogether fails in most of our descriptive poets.

ALCIPHRON: You require, I fear, what is impossible. How little plan are we able to comprehend in the scenes of nature? The kingdom of the all-powerful mother of all things is so vast, her progress so slow, her prospective views so endless—

EUTHYPHRON: That therefore a human poem must be so vast, so slow in progress, and so incomprehensible? Let him to whom nature exhibits no plan, no unity of purpose, hold his peace, nor venture to give her expression in the language of poetry. Let him speak for whom she has removed the veil and displayed the true expression of her features. He will discover in all her works connection, order, benevolence, and purpose. His own poetical creation, too, like that creation which inspires his imagination, will be a true *kosmos*, a regular work, with plan, outlines, meaning, and ultimate design, and commend itself to the understanding as a whole, as it does to the heart by its individual thoughts and interpretations of nature, and to the sense by the animation of its objects. In nature, all things are connected, and for the view of man are connected by their relation to what is human. The periods of time, as days and years, have their relation to the age of man. Countries and climates have a principle of unity in the one race of man, ages and worlds in the one eternal cause, one God, one creator. He is the eye of the universe, giving expression to its otherwise boundless void, and combining in a harmonious union the expression of all its multiplied and multiform features. Here we are brought back again to the East, for the Orientals, in their descriptive poetry, however poor or rich it may be judged, secure, first of all, that unity which the understanding demands. In all the various departments of nature they behold the God of the heavens and of the earth. This no Greek, nor Celt, nor Roman has ever done, and how far in this respect is Lucretius behind Job and David!

JOSIAH ROYCE :
THE ONENESS OF GOD WITH THE SUFFERER

Josiah Royce (1855–1916) taught philosophy at Harvard University from 1882 until his death. He represented transcendental idealism, and it is in this perspective that he read the book of Job. God is "not a being other than this world," men are "fragments of the absolute life," and, therefore, man's suffering is a part of God's suffering. Considering the positive forces marshaled to overcome evil and suffering, the latter must be viewed as necessary in the moral economy of the world. Royce sincerely believed that he had dealt with "the central problem of the poem"; in fact, however, he imposed his point of view upon the text. His analysis appeared in *Studies of Good and Evil: A*

Series of Essays upon the Problems of Philosophy and of Life (New York, 1898).

The problem of our book is the personal problem of its hero, Job himself. Discarding, for the first, as of possibly separate authorship, the prologue, the epilogue, and the addresses of Elihu and of the Lord, one may as well come at once to the point of view of Job, as expressed in his speeches to his friends. Here is stated the problem of which none of the later additions in our poem offer any intelligible solution. In the exposition of this problem the original author develops all his poetical skill, and records thoughts that can never grow old. This is the portion of our book that is most frequently quoted and that best expresses the genuine experience of suffering humanity. Here, then, the philosophical as well as the human interest of our poem centers.

Job's world, as he sees it, is organized in a fashion extremely familiar to us all. The main ideas of this cosmology are easy to be reviewed. The very simplicity of the scheme of the universe here involved serves to bring into clearer view the mystery and horror of the problem that besets Job himself. The world, for Job, is the work of a being who, in the very nature of the case, ought to be intelligible (since He is wise), and friendly to the righteous, since, according to tradition, and by virtue of His divine wisdom itself, this God must know the value of a righteous man. But—here is the mystery—this God, as His works get known through our human experiences of evil, appears to us not friendly, but hopelessly foreign and hostile in His plans and His doings. The more, too, we study His ways with man, the less intelligible seems His nature.

Tradition has dwelt upon His righteousness, has called Him merciful, has magnified His love toward His servants, has described His justice in bringing to naught the wicked. One has learned to trust all these things, to conceive God in these terms, and to expect all this righteous government from Him. Moreover, tradition joins with the pious observation of nature in assuring us of the omnipotence of God. Job himself pathetically insists that he never doubts, for an instant, God's power to do whatever in heaven or earth He may please to do. Nothing hinders God. No blind faith thwarts Him.

Sheol is naked before Him. The abyss has no covering. The earth hangs over chaos because He orders it to do so. His power shatters the monsters and pierces the dragons. He can, then, do with evil precisely what He does with Rahab or with the shades, with the clouds or with the light or with the sea, namely, exactly what He chooses. Moreover, since He knows everything, and since the actual value of a righteous man is, for Job, an unquestionable and objective fact, God cannot fail to know this real worth of righteousness in His servants, as well as the real hatefulness and mischief of the wicked. God knows worth, and cannot be blind to it, since it is as real a fact as heaven and earth themselves.

Yet, despite all these unquestioned facts, this God, who can do just what He chooses, "deprives of right" the righteous man, in Job's own case, and "vexes his soul," becomes toward him as a "tyrant," "persecutes" him "with strong hand," "dissolves" him "into storm," makes him a "byword" for outcasts, "casts" him "into the mire," renders him "a brother to jackals," deprives him of the poor joy of his "one day as a hireling," of the little delight that might come to him as a man before he descends hopelessly to the dark world of the shades, "watches over" him by day to oppress, by night to "terrify" him "with dreams and with visions"—in brief, acts as his enemy, "tears" him "in anger," "gnashes upon" him "with His teeth." All these are the expressions of Job himself. On the other hand, as with equal wonder and horror the righteous Job reports, God on occasion does just the reverse of all this to the notoriously and deliberately wicked, who "grow old," "wax mighty in power," "see their offspring established" and their homes "secure from fear." If one turns from this view of God's especially unjust dealings with righteous and with wicked individuals to a general survey of His providential government of the world, one sees vast processes going on, as ingenious as they are merciless, as full of hints of a majestic wisdom as they are of indifference to every individual right (14:18 ff.).   •

Here is a mere outline of the divine government as Job sees it. To express himself thus is for Job no momentary outburst of passion. Long days and nights he has brooded over these bitter facts of experience, before he has spoken at all. Unweariedly, in presence of his friends' objections, he reiterates his charges. He has the right of the sufferer to speak, and he uses it. He reports the facts that he sees. Of the paradox involved in all this he can make nothing. What is clear to him, however, is that this paradox is a matter for reasoning, not for blind authority. God ought to meet him face to face, and have the matter out in plain words. Job fears not to face his judge, or to demand his answer from God. God knows that Job has done nothing to deserve this fury. The question at issue between maker and creature is therefore one that demands a direct statement and a clear decision. "Why, since You can do precisely as You choose, and since You know, as all-knower, the value of a righteous servant, do You choose, as enemy, to persecute the righteous with this fury and persistence of hate?" Here is the problem.

The human interest of the issue thus so clearly stated by Job lies, of course, in the universality of just such experiences of undeserved ill here upon earth. What Job saw of evil we can see ourselves today whenever we choose. Witness Armenia. Witness the tornadoes and the earthquakes. Less interesting to us is the thesis mentioned by Job's friends, in the antiquated form in which they state it, although, to be sure, a similar thesis, in altered forms, is prevalent among us still. And of dramatic significance only is the earnestness with which Job defends his own personal righteousness. So naïve a self-assurance as is his is not in accordance with our modern conscience, and it is seldom indeed that our day would see any man sincerely using this phraseology of Job regarding his own consciousness of rectitude. But what is today as fresh and real to us as it was to our poet is the fact that all about us, say in every child born with an unearned heredity of misery, or in every pang of the oppressed, or in every arbitrary coming of ill fortune, some form of innocence is beset with an evil that the sufferer has not deserved. Job wins dramatic sympathy as an extreme—but for the purpose all the more typical—case of this universal experience of unearned ill fortune. In every such case we therefore still have the interest that Job had in demanding the solution of this central problem of evil. Herein, I need not say, lies the permanent significance of the problem of Job—a problem that wholly outlasts any ancient Jewish controversy as to the question whether the divine justice always does or does not act as Job's friends, in their devotion to tradition, declare that it acts. Here, then, is the point where our poem touches a question, not merely of an older religion, but of philosophy, and of all time.

The general problem of evil has received, as is well known, a great deal of attention from the philosophers. Few of them, at least in European thought, have been as fearless in stating the issue as was the original author of Job. The solutions offered have, however, been very numerous. For our purposes they may be reduced to a few.

First, then, one may escape Job's paradox by declining altogether to view the world in teleological terms. Evils, such as death, disease, tempests, enemies, fires, are not, so one may declare, the works of God or of Satan, but are natural phenomena. Natural, too, are the phenomena of our desires, of our pains, sorrows, and failures. No divine purpose rules or overrules any of these things. That happens to us, at any time, which must happen, in view of our natural limitations and of our ignorance. The way to better things is to understand nature better than we now do. For this view—a view often maintained in our day—there is no problem of evil, in Job's sense, at all. Evil there indeed is, but the only rational problems are those of natural laws. I need not here further consider this method, not of solving but of abolishing the problem before us, since my intent is, in this paper, to suggest the possibility of some genuinely teleological answer to Job's question. I mention this first view only to recognize, historically, its existence.

In the second place, one may deal with our problem by attempting any one, or a number, of those familiar and popular compromises between the belief in a world of natural law and the belief in a teleological order, which are all, as compromises, reducible to the assertion that the presence of evil in the creation is a relatively insignificant, and an inevitable, incident of a plan that produces sentient creatures subject to law. Writers who expound such compromises have to point out that, since a burnt child dreads the fire, pain is, on the whole, useful as a warning. Evil is a transient discipline, whereby finite creatures learn their place in the system of things. Again, a sentient world cannot get on without some experience of suffering, since sentience means tenderness. Take away pain (so one still again often insists), take away pain and we should not learn our share of natural truth. Pain is the pedagogue to teach us natural science. The contagious diseases, for instance, are useful insofar as they lead us in the end to study bacteriology, and thus to get an insight into the life of certain beautiful creatures of God whose presence in the world we should otherwise blindly overlook! Moreover (to pass to still another variation of this sort of explanation), created beings obviously grow from less to more. First the lower, then the higher. Otherwise there could be no evolution. And were there no evolution, how much of edifying natural science we should miss! But if one is evolved, if one grows from less to more, there must be something to mark the stages of growth. Now evil is useful to mark the lower stages of evolution. If you are to be first an infant, then a man, or first a savage, then a civilized being, there must be evils attendant upon the earlier stages of your life—evils that make growth welcome and conscious. Thus, were there no colic and croup, were there no tumbles and crying spells in infancy, there would be no sufficient incentives to loving parents to hasten the growing robustness of their children, and no motives to impel the children to long to grow big! Just so, cannibalism is valuable as a mark of a lower grade of evolution. Had there been no cannibalism we should realize less joyously than we do what a respectable thing it is to have become civilized! In brief, evil is, as it were, the dirt of the natural order, whose value is that, when you wash it off, you thereby learn the charm of the bath of evolution.

The foregoing are mere hints of familiar methods of playing about the edges of our problem, as children play barefoot in the shallowest reaches of the foam of the sea. In our poem the speeches ascribed to Elihu contain the most hints of some such way of defining evil, as a merely transient incident of the discipline of the individual. With many writers explanations of this sort fill much space. They are even not without their proper place in popular discussion. But they have no interest for whoever has once come into the presence of Job's problem as it is in itself. A moment's thought reminds us of their superficiality. Pain is useful as a warning of danger. If we did not suffer, we should burn our hands off. Yes, but this explanation of one evil presupposes another, and a still unexplained and greater evil, namely, the existence of the danger of which we need to be thus warned. No doubt it is well that the past sufferings of the Armenians should teach the survivors, say the defenseless women and children, to have a wholesome fear in future of Turks. Does that explain, however, the need for the existence or for the murderous doings of the Turks? If I can only reach a given goal by passing over a given road, say of evolution, it may be well for me to consent to the toilsome journey. Does that explain why I was created so far from my goal? Discipline, toil, penalty, surgery—are all explicable as means to ends, if only it be presupposed that there exists, and that there is quite otherwise explicable, the necessity for the situations that involve such fearful expenses. One justifies the surgery, but not the disease; the toil, but not the existence of the need for the toil; the penalty, but not the situation that has made the penalty necessary, when one points out that evil is in so many cases medicinal or disciplinary or pro-phylactic—an incident of imperfect stages of evolution, or the price of a distant good attained through misery.

All such explanations, I insist, trade upon borrowed capital. But God, by hypothesis, is no borrower. He produces His own capital of ends and means. Every evil is explained on the foregoing plan only by presupposing at least an equal, and often a greater and a pre-existent evil, namely, the very state of things that renders the first evil the only physically possible way of reaching a given goal. But what Job wants his judge to explain is not that evil A is a physical means of warding off some other greater evil B, in this cruel world where the waters wear away even the stones, and where hopes of man are so much frailer than the stones; but why a God who can do whatever He wishes chooses situations where such a heaped-up mass of evil means become what we should call physical necessities to the ends now physically possible.

No real explanation of the presence of evil can succeed that declares evil to be a merely physical necessity for one who desires, in this present world, to reach a given goal. Job's business is not with physical accidents, but with the God who chose to make this present nature; and an answer to Job must show that evil is not a physical but a logical necessity—something whose non-existence would simply contradict the very essence, the very perfection of God's own nature and power. This talk of medicinal and disciplinary evil, perfectly fair when applied to our poor fate-bound human surgeons, judges, jailors, or teachers, becomes cruelly, even cynically trivial when applied to explain the ways of a God who is to choose not only the physical means to an end, but the very *Physis* itself in which path and goal are to exist together.

I confess, as a layman, that whenever, at a funeral, in the company of mourners who are immediately facing Job's own personal problem, and who are sometimes, to say the least, wide enough awake to desire not to be stayed with relative comforts, but to ask that terrible and uttermost question of God Himself, and to require the direct answer—that whenever, I say, in such company I have to listen to these halfway answers, to these superficial plashes in the wavelets at the water's edge of sorrow, while the black, unfathomed ocean of finite evil spreads out before our wide-opened eyes—well, at such times this trivial speech about useful burns and salutary medicines makes me, and I fancy others, simply and wearily heartsick. Some words are due to children at school, to peevish patients in the sickroom who need a little temporary quieting. But quite other speech is due to men and women when they are wakened to the higher reason of Job by the fierce anguish of our mortal life's ultimate facts. They deserve either our simple silence, or, if we are ready to speak, the speech of people who ourselves inquire as Job inquired.

A third method of dealing with our problem is in essence identical with the course which, in a very antiquated form, the friends of Job adopt. This method takes its best known expression in the doctrine that the presence of evil in the world is explained by the fact that the value of free will in moral agents logically involves, and so explains and justifies, the divine permission of the evil deeds of those finite beings who freely choose to sin, as well as the inevitable fruits of the sins. God creates agents with free will. He does so because the existence of such agents has of itself an infinite worth. Were there no free agents, the highest good could not be. But such agents, because they are free, can offend. The divine justice of necessity pursues such offenses with attendant evils. These evils, the result of sin, must, logically speaking, be permitted to exist, if God once creates the agents who have free will, and Himself remains, as He must logically do, a just God. How much ill thus results depends upon the choice of the free agents, not upon God, who wills to have only good chosen, but of necessity must leave His free creatures to their own devices, so far as concerns their power to sin.

This view has the advantage of undertaking to regard evil as a logically necessary part of a perfect moral order, and not as a mere incident of an imperfectly adjusted physical mechanism. So dignified a doctrine, by virtue of its long history and its high theological reputation, needs here no extended exposition. I assume it as familiar, and pass at once to its difficulties. It has its share of truth. There is, I doubt not, moral free will in the universe. But the presence of evil in the world simply cannot be explained by free will alone. This is easy to show. One who maintains this view asserts, in substance, "All real evils are the results of the acts of free and finite moral agents." These agents may be angels or men. If there is evil in the city, the Lord has *not* done it, except insofar as His justice has acted in readjusting wrongs already done. Such ill is due to the deeds of His creatures. But hereupon one asks at once, in presence of any ill, "Who did this?" Job's friends answer: "The sufferer himself; his deed wrought his own undoing. God punishes only the sinner. Everyone suffers for his own wrongdoing. Your ill is the result of your crime."

But Job, and all his defenders of innocence, must at once reply: "Empirically speaking, this is obviously, in our visible world, simply not true. The sufferer may suffer innocently. The ill is often undeserved. The fathers sin; the child, diseased from birth, degraded, or a born wretch, may pay the penalty. The Turk or the active rebel sins. Armenia's helpless women and babes cry in vain unto God for help."

Hereupon the reply comes, although not indeed from Job's friends: "Alas! it is so. Sin means suffering; but the innocent may suffer *for* the guilty. This, to be sure, is God's way. One cannot help it. It is so." But therewith the whole effort to explain evil as a logically necessary result of free will and of divine justice alone is simply abandoned. The unearned ills are not justly due to the free will that indeed partly caused them, but to God who declines to protect the innocent. God owes the Turk and the rebel their due. He also owes to His innocent creatures, the babes and the women, His shelter. He owes to the sinning father his penalty, but to the son, born in our visible world a lost soul from the womb, God owes the shelter of His almighty wing, and no penalty. Thus Job's cry is once more in place. The ways of God are not thus justified.

But the partisan of free will as the true explanation of ill may reiterate his view in a new form. He may insist that we see but a fragment. Perhaps the soul born here as if lost, or the wretch doomed to pangs now unearned, sinned of old, in some previous state of existence. Perhaps Karma is to blame. You expiate today the sins of your own former existences. Thus the Hindus varied the theme of our familiar doctrine. This is what Hindu friends might have said to Job. Well, admit even that, if you like; and what then follows? Admit that here or in former ages the free deed of every present sufferer earned as its penalty every ill, physical or moral, that appears as besetting just this sufferer today. Admit that, and what logically follows? It follows, so I must insist, that the moral world itself, which this free-will theory of the source of evil, thus abstractly stated, was to save, is destroyed in its very heart and center.

For consider. A suffers ill. B sees A suffering. Can B, the on-looker, help his suffering neighbor, A? Can he comfort him in any true way? No, a miserable comforter must B prove, like Job's friends, so long as B, believing in our present hypothesis, clings strictly to the logic of this abstract free-will explanation of the origin of evil. To A he says: "Well, you suffer for your own ill-doing. I therefore simply cannot relieve you. This is God's world of justice. If I tried to hinder God's justice from working in your case, I should at best only postpone your evil day. It would come, for God is just. You are hungry, thirsty, naked, sick, in prison. What can I do about it? All this is your own deed come back to you. God Himself, al-though justly punishing, is not the author of this evil. You are the sole originator of the ill." "Ah!" so A may cry out, "but can you not give me light, insight, instruction, sympathy? Can you not at least teach me to become good?" "No," B must reply, if he is a logical believer in the sole efficacy of the private free will of each finite agent as the one source, under the divine justice, of that agent's ill: "No, if you deserved light or any other comfort, God, being just, would enlighten you Himself, even if I absolutely re-fused. But if you do not deserve light, I should preach to you in vain, for God's justice would harden your heart against any such good fortune as I could offer you from without, even if I spoke with the tongues of men and of angels. Your free will is yours. No deed of mine could give you a good free will, for what I gave you from without would not be *your* free will at all. Nor can anyone but you cause your free will to be this or that. A great gulf is fixed between us. You and I, as sovereign free agents, live in God's holy world in sin-tight compartments and in evil-tight compartments too. I cannot hurt you, nor you me. You are damned for your own sins, while all I can do is to look out for my own salvation."

This, I say, is the logically inevitable result of asserting that every ill, physical or moral, that can happen to any agent is solely the result of that agent's own free will acting under the government of the divine justice. The only possible consequence would indeed be that we live, every soul of us, in separate—as it were, absolutely fireproof—free-will compartments, so that real cooperation as to good and ill is excluded. What more cynical denial of the reality of any sort of moral world could be imagined than is involved in this horrible thesis, which no sane partisan of the abstract and traditional free-will explanation of the source of evil will today maintain, precisely because no such partisan really knows or can know what his doctrine logically means, while still continuing to maintain it. Yet whenever one asserts with pious obscurity that "No harm can come to the righteous," one in fact implies, with logical necessity, just this cynical consequence.

There remains a fourth doctrine as to our problem. This doctrine is in essence the thesis of philosophical idealism, a thesis I myself feel bound to maintain, and, so far as space here permits, to explain. The theoretical basis of this view, the philosophical reasons for the notion of the divine nature which it implies, I cannot here explain. That is another argument. But I desire to indicate how the view in question deals with Job's problem.

This view first frankly admits that Job's problem is, upon Job's presuppositions, simply and absolutely insoluble. Grant Job's own presupposition that God is a being other than this world, that He is its external creator and ruler, and then all solutions fail. God is then either cruel or helpless, as regards all real finite ill of the sort that Job endures. Job, moreover, is right in demanding a reasonable answer to his question. The only possible answer is, however, one that undertakes to develop what I hold to be the immortal soul of the doctrine of the divine atonement. The answer to Job is: God is not in ultimate essence another being than yourself. He is the Absolute Being. You truly are one with God, part of His life. He is the very soul of your soul. And so, here is the first truth: When you suffer, *your sufferings are God's sufferings*—not His external work, not His external penalty, not the fruit of His neglect, but identically His own personal woe. In you God Himself suffers, precisely as you do, and has all your concern in overcoming this grief.

The true question then is: Why does God thus suffer? The sole possible, necessary, and sufficient answer is: Because without suffering, without ill, without woe, evil, tragedy, God's life could not be perfected. This grief is not a physical means to an external end. It is a logically necessary and eternal constituent of the divine life. It is logically necessary that the Captain of your salvation should be perfect through suffering. No outer nature compels Him. He chooses this because He chooses His own perfect selfhood. He is perfect. His world is the best possible world. Yet all its finite regions know not only of joy but of defeat and sorrow, for thus alone, in the completeness of His eternity, can God in His wholeness be triumphantly perfect.

This, I say, is my thesis. In the absolute oneness of God with the sufferer, in the concept of the suffering and therefore triumphant God, lies the logical solution of the problem of evil. The doctrine of philosophical idealism is, as regards its purely theoretical aspects, a fairly familiar metaphysical theory at the present time. One may, then, presuppose here as known the fact that, for reasons which I have not now to expound, the idealist maintains that there is in the universe but one perfectly real being, namely, the Absolute, that the Absolute is self-conscious, and that His world is essentially in its wholeness the fulfillment *in actu* of an all-perfect ideal. We ourselves exist as fragments of the absolute life, or better, as partial functions in the unity of the absolute and conscious process of the world. On the other hand, our existence and our individuality are not illusory, but are what they are in an organic unity with the whole life of the Absolute Being. This doctrine once presupposed, our present task is to inquire what case idealism can make for the thesis just indicated as its answer to Job's problem.

In endeavoring to grapple with the theoretical problem of the place of evil in a world that, on the whole, is to be conceived not only as good, but as perfect, there is happily one essentially decisive consideration concerning good and evil that falls directly within the scope of our own human experience, and which concerns matters at once familiar and momentous as well as too much neglected in philosophy. When we use such words as good, evil, perfect, we easily deceive ourselves by the merely abstract meanings we associate with each of the terms taken apart from the others. We forget the experiences from which the words have been abstracted. To these experiences we must return whenever we want really to comprehend the words. If we take the mere words, in their abstraction, it is easy to say, for instance, that if life has any evil in it at all, it must needs not be so perfect as life would be were there no evil in it whatever. Just so, speaking abstractly, it is easy to say that, in estimating life, one has to set the good over against the evil, and to compare their respective sums. It is easy to declare that, since we hate evil, wherever and just so far as we recognize it, our sole human interest in the world must be furthered by the removal of evil from the world. And thus viewing the case, one readily comes to say that if God views as not only good but perfect a world in which we find so much evil, the divine point of view must be very foreign to ours, so that Job's rebellious pessimism seems well in order, and Prometheus appears to defy the world ruler in a genuinely humane spirit. Shocked, however, by the apparent impiety of this result, some teachers, considering divine matters, still misled by the same one-sided use of words, have opposed one falsely abstract view by another, and have strangely asserted that the solution must be in proclaiming that since God's world, the real world, in order to be perfect, must be without evil, what we men call evil must be a mere illusion—a mirage of the human point of view—a dark vision which God, who sees all truth, sees not at all. To God, so this view asserts, the eternal world in its wholeness is not only perfect, but has merely the perfection of an utterly transparent crystal, unstained by any color of ill. Only mortal error imagines that there is any evil. There is no evil but only good in the real world, and that is why God finds the world perfect, whatever mortals dream.

Now neither of these abstract views is my view. I consider them both the result of a thoughtless trust in abstract words. I regard evil as a distinctly real fact, a fact just as real as the most helpless and hopeless sufferer finds it to be when he is in pain. Furthermore, I hold that God's point of view is not foreign to ours. I hold that God willingly, freely, and consciously suffers in us when we suffer, and that our grief is His. And despite all this I maintain that the world from God's point of view fulfills the divine ideal and is perfect. And I hold that when we abandon the one-sided abstract ideas which the words good, evil, and perfect suggest, and when we go back to the concrete experiences upon which these very words are founded, we can see, even within the limits of our own experience, facts that make these very paradoxes perfectly intelligible, and even commonplace.

As for that essentially pernicious view, nowadays somewhat current among a certain class of gentle but inconsequent people— the view that all evil is *merely* an illusion and that there is no such thing in God's world—I can say of it only in passing that it is often advanced as an idealistic view, but that, in my opinion, it is false idealism. Good idealism it is to regard all finite experience as an appearance, a hint, often a very poor hint, of deeper truth. Good idealism it is to admit that man can err about truth that lies beyond his finite range of experience. And very good idealism it is to assert that all truth, and so all finite experience, exists in and for the mind of God, and nowhere outside of or apart from God. But it is not good idealism to assert that any facts that fall within the range of finite experience are, even while they are experienced, mere illusions. God's truth is inclusive, not exclusive. What you experience God experiences. The difference lies only in this, that God sees in unity what you see in fragments. For the rest, if one said, "The source and seat of evil is only the error of mortal mind," one would but have changed the name of one's problem. If the evil were but the error, the error would still be the evil, and altering the name would not have diminished the horror of the evil of this finite world.

But I hasten from the false idealism to the true; from the abstractions to the enlightening insights of our life. As a fact, idealism does not say: The finite world is, as such, a mere illusion. A sound idealism says: Whatever we experience is a fragment, and, as far as it goes, a genuine fragment of the truth of the divine mind. With this principle before us, let us consider directly our own experiences of good and of evil, to see whether they are as abstractly opposed to each other as the mere words often suggest. We must begin with the elementary and even trivial facts. We shall soon come to something deeper.

By good, as we mortals experience it, we mean something that, when it comes or is expected, we actively welcome, try to attain or keep, and regard with content. By evil in general, as it is in our experience, we mean whatever we find in any sense repugnant and intolerable. I use the words repugnant and intolerable because I wish to indicate that words for evil frequently, like the words for good, directly refer to our actions as such. Commonly and rightly, when we speak of evil, we make reference to acts of resistance, of struggle, or shrinking, of flight, of removal of ourselves from a source of mischief—acts that not only follow upon the experience of evil, but that serve to define in a useful fashion what we mean by evil. The opposing acts of pursuit and of welcome define what we mean by good. By the evil which we experience we mean precisely whatever we regard as something to be gotten rid of, shrunken from, put out of sight, of hearing, or of memory, eschewed, expelled, assailed, or otherwise directly or indirectly resisted. By good we mean whatever we regard as something to be welcomed, pursued, won, grasped, held, persisted in, preserved. And we show all this in our acts in presence of any grade of good or evil, sensuous, aesthetic, ideal, moral. To shun, to flee, to resist, to destroy, these are our primary attitudes toward ill; the opposing acts are our primary attitudes toward the good; and whether you regard us as animals or as moralists, whether it is a sweet taste, a poem, a virtue, or God that we look to as good, and whether it is a burn or a temptation, an outward physical foe, or a stealthy, inward, ideal enemy that we regard as evil. In all our organs of voluntary movement, in all our deeds, in a turn of the eye, in a sigh, a groan, in a hostile gesture, in an act of silent contempt, we can show in endlessly varied ways the same general attitude of repugnance.

But man is a very complex creature. He has many organs. He performs many acts at once, and he experiences his performance of these acts in one highly complex life of consciousness. As the next feature of his life we all observe that he can at the same time shun one object and grasp at another. In this way he can have at once present to him a consciousness of good and a consciousness of ill. But so far in our account these sorts of experience appear merely as facts side by side. Man loves, and he *also* hates, loves this and hates that, assumes an attitude of repugnance toward one object while he welcomes another. So far the usual theory follows man's life, and calls it an experience of good and ill as mingled but ex-

clusively and abstractly opposed facts. For such a view the final
question as to the worth of a man's life is merely the question
whether there are more intense acts of satisfaction and of welcome
than of repugnance and disdain in his conscious life. [. . .]

Generalizing the lesson of experience we may then say: It is
logically impossible that a complete knower of truth should fail to
know, to experience, to have present to his insight, the fact of
actually existing evil. On the other hand, it is equally impossible
for one to know a higher good than comes from the subordination
of evil to good in a total experience. When one first loving, in an
elemental way, whatever you please, himself hinders, delays, thwarts
his elemental interest in the interest of some larger whole of experience, he not only knows more fact, but he possesses a higher
good than would or could be present to one who was aware neither
of the elemental impulse, nor of the thwarting of it in the tension
of a richer life. The knowing of the good, in the higher sense, depends upon contemplating the overcoming and subordination of
a less significant impulse, which survives even in order that it
should be subordinated. Now this law, this form of the knowledge
of the good, applies as well to the existence of moral as to that
of sensuous ill. If moral evil were simply destroyed and wiped
away from the external world, the knowledge of moral goodness
would also be destroyed. For the love of moral good is the thwarting of lower loves for the sake of the higher organization. What
is needed, then, for the definition of the divine knowledge of a
world that in its wholeness is perfect, is not a divine knowledge
that shall ignore, wipe out, and utterly make naught the existence
of any ill, whether physical or moral, but a divine knowledge to
which shall be present that love of the world as a whole which is
fulfilled in the endurance of physical ill, in the subordination of
moral ill, in the thwarting of impulses which survive even when
subordinated, in the acceptance of repugnances which are still
eternal, in the triumph over an enemy that endures even through
its eternal defeat, and in the discovery that the endless tension of
the finite world is included in the contemplative consciousness of
the repose and harmony of eternity. To view God's nature thus
is to view His nature as the whole idealistic theory views Him,

not as the Infinite One beyond the finite imperfections, but as the being whose unity determines the very constitution, the lack, the tension, and relative disharmony of the finite world.

The existence of evil, then, is not only consistent with the perfection of the universe, but is necessary for the very existence of that perfection. This is what we see when we no longer permit ourselves to be deceived by the abstract meanings of the words good and evil into thinking that these two opponents exist merely as mutually exclusive facts side by side in experience, but when we go back to the facts of life and perceive that all relatively higher good, in the trivial as in the more truly spiritual realm, is known only insofar as, from some higher reflective point of view, we accept as good the thwarting of an existent interest that is even thereby declared to be a relative ill, and love a tension of various impulses which even thereby involves, as the object of our love, the existence of what gives us aversion or grief.

Now if the love of God is more inclusive than the love of man, even as the divine world of experience is richer than the human world, we can simply set no human limit to the intensity of conflict, to the tragedies of existence, to the pangs of finitude, to the degree of moral ill, which in the end is included in the life that God not only loves but finds the fulfillment of the perfect ideal. If peace means satisfaction, acceptance of the whole of an experience as good, and if even we, in our weakness, can frequently find rest in the very presence of conflict and of tension, in the very endurance of ill in a good cause, in the hero's triumph over temptation, or in the mourner's tearless refusal to accept the lower comforts of forgetfulness, or to wish that the lost one's preciousness had been less painfully revealed by death—well, if even we know our little share of this harmony in the midst of the wrecks and disorders of life, what limit shall we set to the divine power to face this world of His own sorrows, and to find peace in the victory over all its ills?

But in this last expression I have pronounced the word that serves to link this theory as to the place of evil in a good world with the practical problem of every sufferer. Job's rebellion came from the thought that God, as a sovereign, is far off, and that, for His pleasure, His creature suffers. Our own theory comes to the mourner with the assurance: "Your suffering, just as it is in you, is God's suffering. No chasm divides you from God. He is not remote from you even in His eternity. He is here. His eternity means merely the completeness of His experience. But that completeness is inclusive. Your sorrow is one of the included facts." I do not say: "God sympathizes with you from without, would spare you if He could, pities you with helpless external pity merely as a father pities his children." I say: "God here sorrows, not *with* but *in* your sorrow. Your grief is identically His grief, and what you know as your loss, God knows as His loss, just in and through the very moment when you grieve."

But hereupon the sufferer perchance responds: "If this is God's loss, could He not have prevented it? To Him are present in unity all the worlds; and yet He must lack just this for which I grieve." I respond: "He suffers here that He may triumph. For the triumph of the wise is no easy thing. Their lives are not light, but sorrowful. Yet they rejoice in their sorrow, not, to be sure, because it is mere experience, but because, for them, it becomes part of a strenuous whole of life. They wander and find their home even in wandering. They long, and attain through their very love of longing. Peace they find in triumphant warfare. Contentment they have most of all in endurance. Sovereignty they win in endless service. The eternal world contains Gethsemane."

Yet the mourner may still insist: "If my sorrow is God's, His triumph is not mine. Mine is the woe. His is the peace." But my theory is a philosophy. It proposes to be coherent. I must persist: "It is your fault that you are thus sundered from God's triumph. His experience in its wholeness cannot now be yours, for you just as you—this individual—are now but a fragment, and see His truth as through a glass darkly. But if you see His truth at all, through even the dimmest light of a glimmering reason, remember, that truth is in fact your own truth, your own fulfillment, the whole from which your life cannot be divorced, the reality that you mean even when you most doubt, the desire of your heart even when you are most blind, the perfection that you unconsciously strove for even when you were an infant, the complete Self apart from whom you mean nothing, the very life that gives your life the only value it can have. In thought, if not in the fulfillment of thought, in aim if not in attainment of aim, in aspiration if not in the presence of the revealed fact, you can view God's triumph and peace as your triumph and peace. Your defeat will be no less real than it is, nor will you falsely call your evil a mere illusion. But you will see not only the grief but the truth, your truth, your rescue, your triumph."

Well, to what ill fortune does not just such reasoning apply? I insist: our conclusion is essentially universal. It discounts any evil that experience may contain. All the horrors of the natural order, all the concealments of the divine plan by our natural ignorance, find their general relation to the unity of the divine experience indicated in advance by this account of the problem of evil.

"Yes," one may continue, "ill fortune you have discovered, but how about moral evil? What if the sinner now triumphantly retorts: 'Aha! So my will is God's will. All then is well with me.'" I reply: What I have said disposes of moral ill precisely as definitely as of physical ill. What the evil will is to the good man, whose goodness depends upon its existence, but also upon the thwarting and the condemnation of its aim, just such is the sinner's will to the divine plan. God's will, we say to the sinner, is your will. Yes, but it is your will thwarted, scorned, overcome, defeated. In the eternal world you are seen, possessed, present, but your damnation is also seen including and thwarting you. Your apparent victory in this world stands simply for the vigor of your impulses. God wills you not to triumph. And that is the use of you in the world— the use of evil generally—to be hated but endured, to be triumphed over through the very fact of your presence, to be willed down even in the very life of which you are a part.

But to the serious moral agent we say: What you mean when you say that evil in this temporal world ought not to exist, and ought to be suppressed, is simply what God means by seeing that evil ought to be and is endlessly thwarted, endured, but subordinated. In the natural world you are the minister of God's triumph. Your deed is His. You can never clean the world of evil; but you can subordinate evil. The justification of the presence in the world of the morally evil becomes apparent to us mortals only insofar as this evil is overcome and condemned. It exists only that it may be cast down. Courage, then, for God works in you. In the order of time you embody in outer acts what is for Him the truth of His eternity.

HORACE M. KALLEN : JOB THE HUMANIST

The book of Job was originally a Greek tragedy in Hebrew, composed in the Euripidean tradition: such is the hypothesis of Horace M. Kallen (born 1882), American philosopher, Professor Emeritus of the New School for Social Research, New York. This hypothesis is not new (see Preface to Robert Lowth, "Of the Poem of Job"), but Kallen is its modern and most persistent advocate. In *The Book of Job as a Greek Tragedy* (New York, 1918), he presented an ingenious reconstruction of the biblical work. He believes that the original choral odes were later removed from their position in the tragedy and shifted into the dialogue to conceal the resemblance to a Greek play.

Kallen's book (reissued in 1959) includes an essay on "The Joban Philosophy of Life." Though the theme of Job is universal, Kallen posits the work within the context of Hebraic, prophetic thought, still vital in its author's time: A hoped-for future for Israel would redress the evil balance of the politically unfortunate present. Such ultimate readjustment presupposed the notion of change, of becoming, of futurity, and of a God "immanent in the movement of events," "dynamic continuity of nature, the creative history of the universe," "an all-generating and all-destroying Power," "a God that makes for righteousness."

Job realizes that "righteousness is already on the way to ritual; dogmas are hardening and religious practices are getting standardized . . . and the church motive is very nearly the sole controlling motive." Though on the surface the author of Job conforms to the official doctrine (which probably helped to preserve his work), he is in reality a dissenter. Like Euripides, he "knew the wisdom of conveying his heterodox doctrine by means of a seductive orthodox setting." In Job the Hebraic mind found its culmination: a "humanism terrible and unique"—a stance that happens to coincide with Kallen's own position in contemporary thought.

What follows is the last section of Kallen's essay.

With all its divergences from orthodoxy, Job is not a break with the Hebraic tradition. Rather is it a courageous continuation of that tradition, its most profound, its most vital and logical culmination. It is the summing up and generalization of the historic experience of the Jewish people. The God of Job is like the God of the prophets—the force of nature, manifesting itself with greatest clearness and definiteness in the movement of the universe rather than in its structure. The terms in which He is described throughout the drama are terms of action: the usual hypostasis of the pleasant emotions of men, of love, of goodness, of charity, is not made. The only human attribute declared of God is the attribute of justice, and that gets a peculiar significance through the fact that it is treated as an implication of His omnipotence. God is the dynamic of the universe, and the range of His power is co-extensive with it. His omnipotence is not deduced dialectically, it is observed empirically: Yahweh is the creator of heaven and earth, the *élan* of the whole panorama of nature, the source of both good and evil, the adjuster of destiny for men. In human terms He cannot be thought; being omnipotent, He is self-sufficient, absolute, consequently altogether incommensurable with human nature, the irreduceable surd of all experience, whose being and force can be acknowledged, but not reasoned with. There is no common measure, no ratio, between the infinite energy that is the life of the world and its creature, man, with all his interests and bias.

Both Job and his comforters are agreed on this: they vie with each other in the completeness of their pronouncements concerning it. But the consequences they draw from it are contradictory. Because there is no common measure, declare Eliphaz and his comrades, there can be for God no standards, no responsibility, no morality. These derive from God and are binding upon men. But since they derive from God, how can they be binding upon God? That any man should ask God "to enter into judgment with man" (Job 22:4) is, hence, presumption, blasphemy. Job, on the contrary, holds that God's responsibility to Himself alone is irresponsibility. And Yahweh concurs in this conception of His status: "Who then is he," He asks of Job, "who can stand before me? Who hath given unto me, that I should repay him? Whatsoever is under the whole heaven is mine" (41:2 f.). There can be no common denominator between God and man, and every attempt to establish one proves abortive.

Indeed, every demonstration of a particular moral direction in the universe can be met by an equally cogent demonstration of a will or *élan* in the opposite direction. At worst, God is unmoral—just with the justice of indifference. At best, He is inscrutable, opaque, a self-revelation unrevealing of anything at all. "Canst thou by searching find out God? Canst thou find out the Almighty unto perfection? It is as high as heaven; what canst thou do? Deeper than *sheol;* what canst thou know? The measure thereof is larger than the earth, and broader than the sea," Zophar declares to Job (11:7 ff.), reaffirming the universal compulsion, the inescapable grip of the principle underlying Job's earlier complaint (9:11 f.). The divine suddenness and divine elusiveness are one and the same (23:8 f.).

It is for this reason that the author of Job insists on our taking at its face value that revelation of Yahweh in nature and in society which is our experience; on our accepting as coordinate the loving-kindness and providence of the Lord with His cruelty and immorality. God's standards are not man's standards, nor God's ways man's ways: in the essential, the wicked also prosper, the righteous also go down to defeat. From any point of view that is human that you may choose, God has no preferences, nor can His will and interests be defined in terms of preference. He is the dynamical life of *all* nature, and He needs must be just to all. But this justice is nothing like the justice man conceives of and desires. Retribution it certainly is not. What is it then? Under the most favorable and deepest construction, it is the recognition that the life which is the source and foundation of all lives pertains to them all impartially, that it favors none of its creatures more than any other. Yahweh describes Himself as the wisdom that makes for the survival of the wild ass, the hawk, the eagle, the ostrich, of all living nature, and the wisdom that uproots mountains and annihilates angels. His justice is His wisdom, and this again is nothing else than power, force, the go and potency, generative and disintegrative, in things. It possesses nothing of the moral or the human; it is not foresight but performance, the originative and annihilative flowing of nature. His wisdom and might, His counsel and understanding are: to break up past rebuilding, to shut up past opening, to dry up the waters and send them out so that they overturn the earth.

According to the private bias of the human spirit, according to the preferences of man, considering the need of man alone, out of the very core of human nature, God is unjust and cannot and should not be justified. "God hath subverted me in my cause" (19:6), cries Job,

> I cry out of wrong, but I am not heard;
> I cry for help, but there is no justice. (19:7)

For the divine action beats on indifferently, or, if you prefer, with equal care for each and all of its creations. Its providence is in the fall of a sparrow, and microbe and man are alike its concern. Description and definition of it, please note, invariably proceeds by means of dynamic terms. It is a narrative of things doing, a history, not the analysis of a purpose nor the designation of a reason. God is Action, not Thought, and His reality is Change. Hebrew, significantly, possesses no word for *eternity:* the nearest approaches to it are "everlasting," "enduring," "world without end," literally, "world and beyond." God is Temporality, Becoming; and it is essentially as temporality, as the force that alters and creates, that He constitutes the ultimate environment of the human spirit. To it, morally indifferent, the spirit of man must adapt itself, must know it, propitiate it, control it. What he does can ultimately concern only his own realization of his inner worth and destiny, not God. All the protagonists of the tragedy—Job, Eliphaz and his comrades, Elihu—assert this fact. It is another common ground for their divergent conclusions.

What then, is man, and what is his status with regard to this all-enveloping and overwhelming changeful force in which he lives and moves and has his being? This force, clearly, did not come to be with him in view, nor had it especial regard for him in any of its creations. The world he lives in is not one that was made for him, but one in which he grew, and one in which he can maintain himself only by eternal vigilance: it is the *fear* of the Lord that is the beginning of wisdom. Man, says the poet, is born unto trouble, as the sparks fly upward (5:7). There is a warfare to him upon earth; he is born upon it, he dwells on it only by the mercy of the surrounding omnipotence, and then he dies. With death his hapless story ends. A more acceptable fate may be hoped for, but never achieved.

Merely to live as he lives, man needs the fear of the Lord—needs that wisdom which is to be gathered by the observation of nature, the study of history, the companionship of the wise. This is a wisdom that has nothing of the theoretical. Pure reason is its opposite. Its essence rather is practical intelligence, gumption, the knowledge of what to do and how to do it in the face of inharmonious situations and the march of time. It is foresight rather than insight; or better, it is the identification of insight with foresight. It is a thing empirical and unreasonable, rather than logical and rational. It assumes the reality of Change and Time, and its vision is a vision of adjustment rather than a vision of existence. As the refrain of the first chorus declares it:

> The fear of the Lord, that is Wisdom,
> And to depart from evil, understanding. (28:28)

And what does this painfully conditioned wisdom of man teach him concerning himself? It teaches him first of all its own weakness. Even as the righteousness which is the departure from evil, even as the vigilance which is the fear of the Lord, it fails to be a guarantee for prosperity: the viable and labile Cosmic Energy may be redirected by it; but also it may not. Suffering and death do not consider whether a man has been of the righteous or of the wicked. "They lie down alike in the dust, and the worm covereth them" (21:26). God, being indeed transcendental, transcends morality and manlike justice as well as everything else. For the justice that is His attribute, I cannot repeat too often, is just that justice of indifference, of cosmic impartiality whereby each creature of God's might makes its own destiny according to the implications of its own nature, without hindrance and without help. If, therefore, man seeks righteousness, he seeks it not because of any extrinsic advantage, but because, being what he is, righteousness is his proper virtue, the security and fulfillment of his inward excellence. If the righteous man falls, the divine will becomes in the fall the vindicator and avenger of the victim against its very self, for in the irrevocable and unalterable past there remains, irrevocably past, the tragic event. But a vindication of the dead does the dead no good. A future life might make the situation endurable; death is, however, complete extinction.

Consequently, the ultimate value of human existence is not existence merely; the ultimate value of human existence is the quality and distinction of existence of which consists a man's character, his nature as this or that kind of man. "Behold," declares Job, "I know that He will slay me; I have no hope. Nevertheless will I maintain my ways before Him" (13:15). "Till I die will I not put away mine integrity from me; my righteousness hold I fast, and will not let it go. My heart shall not reproach me so long as I live" (27:5 f.).

To cling to his integrity while he lives, to assert and to realize the excellences appropriate to his nature as a man, as this particular kind of man, knowing all the while that this is to be accomplished in a world that was not made for him, in which he shares his claim on the consideration of omnipotence with the infinitude of its creatures that alike manifest its powers—this is the destiny of man. He must take his chance in a world that doesn't care about him any more than about anything else. He must maintain his ways with courage rather than with faith, with self-respect rather than with humility—or better perhaps, with a faith that is courage, a humility that is self-respect. When ultimately confronted with the inward character of omnipotence, man realizes that, on its part, moral indifference alone can be genuine justice. Its providence, its indifference, its justice—they are all one. Otherwise, nothing else but the favored, the chosen creature could exist. Hence, when Yahweh reveals Himself to Job as the creative providence sustaining even the most impotent of living things and destroying even the strongest, Job realizes that not prosperity but excellence is the justification of human life, and the very indifference of Yahweh comforts him. "I know" he declares,

> that Thou canst do everything,
> And that no purpose of Thine can be restrained.
> By hearsay only had I heard of Thee,
> But now mine eye seeth Thee,
> Wherefore I recant my challenge, and am comforted
> Amid dust and ashes.   (42:2–6)

Such is the theory of life in which the ripest wisdom of the Hebraic tradition found expression. Its beginnings are strong in Jeremiah; its growth is a function of the progressive postponement of Yahweh's promised Golden Age, of the irony of a chosen people that suffers, of individual tragedies like Jeremiah's and Zerubbabel's. In it the soul of man comes to itself and is freed. It is a humanism terrible and unique. For, unlike the Greek humanism, it does not enfranchise the mind by interpreting the world in terms of its own substance, by declaring an ultimate happy destiny for man in a world immortally in harmony with his nature and needs; it is not an anthropomorphosis, not a pathetic fallacy. It is without illusion concerning the quality, extent, and possibilities of the life of man, without illusion concerning his relation to God. It accepts them, and makes of the human soul the citadel of man—even against omnipotence itself—wherein he cherishes his integrity, and, so cherishing, is victorious in the warfare of living even when life is lost.

This is why, on the confrontation of Hebraism with Hellenism, Hellenism conquered the Jewish mind itself: why the philosophic tradition has been dominated by Greek ideas, why religion has remained illusion rather than vision, why it is only with the coming of science that Hebraism begins to come into its own. For science yields power where it creates disillusion; it is a conquest of nature through knowledge. But the Hebraic mind had in Job attained disillusion without such compensating mastery of nature: its science was childishness. It had attained disillusion only with mastery of self, and such an excellence is too rare and difficult ever to become a common virtue of mankind.

PAUL WEISS : GOD, JOB, AND EVIL

Paul Weiss (born 1901), leading American speculative philosopher, has been associated with Yale University since 1945. He was a founding member of the Conference on Science, Philosophy and Religion, and founder of the *Review of Metaphysics*. His works indicate the range of his philosophic interests. Among them are *Nature and Man* (1947), *Man's Freedom* (1950), *Modes of Being* (1958), *The World of Art* (1961), *Art and Religion* (1963), *The Making of Men* (1967), and *Right and Wrong: A Philosophical Dialogue Between Father and Son* (1967); he also co-edited the *Collected Papers of Charles S. Peirce* (6 vols.; 1931–35). The essay on Job, here reprinted, appeared in *Commentary*, Vol. VI (1948).

Great literature is a universe framed in words. Offering a scheme of things more dramatic, more intelligible, more beautiful, more self-revealing than the universe in which we live, it at once inspires, restrains, and enriches the wise man, providing him with an endless source and a satisfying measure of spiritual growth.

The book of Job is surely one of the very great works of literature of the world. It touches the core of existence; it probes to the root of the problems of good and evil, the destiny of man, the meaning of friendship, the wisdom and goodness of God, and the justification of suffering.

We may call ourselves atheists. We may swear by the latest anthropological pronouncements that all values are relative except those that make anthropologists respectable. We may claim to have no use for anything other than the discoveries or rules of economics, history, politics, music, or physics. This will in no way prevent us from being radically informed and perhaps transformed by the book of Job. That book depends for its power on no prior commitment to any particular religion—or to religion at all.

The problem it deals with is unconfinable within any limited doctrine, philosophy, or creed. We must try to read it with the kind of sympathetic objectivity and resolute courage we normally reserve for our favorite modern writers—a Dostoevsky or a Freud, a Blake or a Kierkegaard—but then I think we will find in it much to despise as well as much to admire.

Though written in a magnificent style and sustaining brilliant insights, the book of Job is not a pleasant tale. It is not reasonable, and it violates our sense of what is right and wrong. Its value lies primarily in that it forces to the fore the mystery of human existence, where the righteous sometimes suffer and the evil apparently prosper mightily.

To get the most out of the book of Job, it is desirable, I think, to state the story in such a way as to stress traditionally neglected features. One will then be able to look in a fresh way at the perennial problem of evil, and perhaps even to make a little progress in grasping what existence means to man.

In outline the story is rather simple. A childishly conceived God, a childlike God in fact, boasts about Job to His angel Satan as a child might about a dog. Satan shrewdly observes that men well cushioned against the world of tragedy and disease, poverty and contempt, have no great temptation to abuse the source of their goods. God is provoked by this sensible remark. He sets Himself to prove that Job will stand firm though he lose all that is precious. God does not want to show that Job will stand firm in goodness, virtue, or decency. All that He wants to show is that if Job is cut off from the fat of existence he will not blaspheme in the face of God.

God, from a strictly legalistic point of view, is shown in the end to be right and Satan to be wrong. Job does not blaspheme in God's face. But of course no one could possibly do this, for that would be at one and the same time to see God and not to see Him, to know Him and not to know Him, to face Him and to turn away. But if it is simple blasphemy that is in point, there is no doubt but that God lost and Satan won, for Job blasphemed again and again, sincerely, roundly, and wholeheartedly.

What shocks us and should shock us is not Job's blasphemies, but God's. With a callousness, with a brutality, with a violence hard to equal in any literature, secular or divine, God, just to make a petulant point, proceeds to do almost everything the most villainous of beings could want. Not only does He kill, in one fell swoop, without excuse, explanation, or warrant, all of Job's cattle, but He follows this up by killing all Job's servants and then all his sons and daughters.

The inhumanity of the author (or of his God, if one prefers) has been almost matched by the insensitivity of those commentators who accept the prologue to the book of Job and do not feel a need to underscore an abhorrence of God's project and performance. Putting aside the question of whether Job's health and happiness are justifiably jeopardized because Satan is unconvinced by God's boasts, and ignoring the rights of cattle to love, there is the fact that the servants, if not the sons and daughters of Job, are human beings as vital, as precious, as worthy of life, dignity, and a defense against Satan as Job himself.

The author of the book of Job thought of Job as a pawn between God and Satan. But less than Job, infinitely less, was the value he set on Job's servants and children. He thought of them as rightfully used and even abused just to make Job uncomfortable, to try his faith, to confound Satan.

It is really amazing that Job should find, not the death of his servants or of his children, but that of his body cells, the most trying of experiences. Our modern torturers know better. They know that the core of a decent man can be more readily and vitally touched by killing his dependents than by making him sick or wracking him with pain.

Three friends come to comfort Job. He entertains them with a

long lament and a set of curses calculated to make the heart curl.
To this they reply with little human sympathy. They are friends
of an eternal law, not of a suffering spirit. Still, it is with considerable justice and good solid traditional wisdom that they observe
that Job is not as pure as he thinks he is. His sufferings, they insist,
are undoubtedly deserved.

In the epilogue, God reproves the three friends, apparently for
believing that human suffering comes from God and that it is be-
stowed on those who do wrong. If the reproof is just, we should
tremble for the souls of those who assure us that God is on the side
of what we have learned is the right. The refusal to affirm that good
men are the nurslings of God, to be fittingly rewarded before their
days are done, is today often called a lack of faith in religion. Actually, it is one of the characteristics of God as He appears in the
book of Job.

Job is not a pleasant person, rich or poor, in health or in sickness,
with children or without. His answer to his friends was that he was
at least as good as any—which he undoubtedly was, except for saying
so. He insists, a little too violently, that there is no wickedness in his
heart and that his conduct is above reproach. He suffers damnably
because of the searing pain to which he is subjected. But he suffers
also at least as much because he is overwhelmed with shame. He is
in anguish because he is looked on with contempt by the children
of those he despised. And even more than cure and peace, he wants
to argue with God and make God show due cause. But whatever
his faults, his sufferings were real. And his question, whether taken
to refer to him alone, to someone else, or to an indefinite number
of men, demands an answer: Why should a good man suffer?

After an interlude in which Elihu, a brash youngster, repeats
in principle what his elders said, God comes out of a whirlwind
and confronts them all. He answers that He is omnipotent and
therefore evidently possessed of a wisdom no man can rightly
measure or rightly judge, a proposition that will not withstand
logical scrutiny, and, so far as it does, cannot please those who think
of God as having the same ideas of goodness and justice as man.
The story ends with God reproving the friends (without making
clear the exact nature of their fault), and with an inadequate attempt by God to make amends to Job by making him wealthy and

respected once again, and by endowing him with a new set of children.

The book of Job does not explicitly answer the question it so unmistakably asks. Instead, it forces one to try to answer the question oneself and therefore to re-examine what one had previously believed about God and man, and the nature of good and evil.

There are at least ten different kinds of evil, though philosophers have been inclined to mention only three. Since there are no well-turned designations and definitions for most of them, we must make up a set as we go along. With some warrant in tradition, we can perhaps designate the different kinds of evil as *sin, bad intention, wickedness, guilt, vice, physical suffering, psychological suffering, social suffering, natural evil,* and *metaphysical evil.*

The most characteristically human evils are the first two, for they are privately inflicted. Of these, the more radical is the religious, what we normally speak of as *sin.* It can be defined in such a way as to be applicable both to those who, like the followers of Confucius and Marx, are without a God, and to those who, like Job, firmly believe in one. He sins who is disloyal to a primary value accepted on faith. Blasphemy is one form of sin and treason another, treason being in fact but practical blasphemy in the realm of the state. These and other forms of sin but begin a process of alienation from the land of consistent living and almost always end in a deserved spiritual and sometimes physical death.

All men take some supreme value to serve as the pivot and justification of the things they think and do. It is one which they have not rationally justified and can perhaps not rationally defend. On the contrary, it is usually what is needed in order to justify their use of reason and their activities. When they go counter to it, they go counter to themselves. He sins who denies his people, just as surely as does he who violates the fiats of his God.

The book of Job affirms—I think correctly—that it is not necessary for a man to sin (see 23:12; 13:15). Job was a righteous man, a man who lived up to the demands of his God, who feared God and shunned evil, who was *tam*, perfect, without blemish. This God affirms as well as Job. It never is denied.

Over against the theologians' belief that no mortal since the days of Adam can be without sin, is the testimony of the book of Job. It is not necessary that a man sin. But though we do not have to sin, all of us do. We are faithless again and again to the things we most cherish and which give our lives meaning and unity. The only thing "original" or unavoidable about sin is that each man sins in his own way.

Job is not a sinner. Since he suffers, suffering and the multiple evils of the world ought not to be attributed to man's failure to avoid sin. It is foolish to hope that a perfect world could be achieved if only men were true to God, the state, or science. He who claims that the solution of the problems left behind by the atomic bomb depends on man's willingness to subscribe to a single or triune God, to democracy or federalism, to physics or pragmatism, goes counter to the insights of the book of Job.

An apparent hair's breadth from sin and yet a world away is *bad intent,* ethical evil, the setting oneself to break an ethical command. Like sin, this is privately achieved. It is a matter of the inward parts. Unlike sin, it has a this-worldly reference always, and is concerned with the good as open to reason. The man of bad intent fails internally to live up to what reason commends.

He who wants to cheat the orphan and the widow, who steals, lies, kills, is one who violates what reason endorses as right. He who is not religious does not necessarily find these prospects more delightful than does he who is. A religious man may in fact at times be more unethical than an irreligious one, for a religion may demand of its adherents that, on behalf of it, they defy their reason and destroy the lives, property, and prospects of others.

The history of religion is in good part a story of the improvement of the morals of the gods. Throughout the ages we have edited supposed divine words to make them conform to what we know to be ethically correct. He who would avoid all ethical evil must not cling too close to the practices and faith of his fathers.

It is conceivable that a man might be without evil intent, though it is hard to believe that there ever was a man so insensitive that he never was tempted by the smell of novelty, a challenge to his daring, or the promptings of his conceit and flesh to think pleasantly of what his reason tells him is wrong.

Evil intent and suffering do not necessarily go together. There are those who intend to do good to others and those who intend to be good to themselves. Often it is the former who get the grit while the latter enjoy the grain. And Job affirms that there is no afterlife in which the balance will be righted (see 7:9).

The brutal fact of the matter is that God's good is not identical with what we take to be ethically good. This is evident occasionally to Job:

> Though I be righteous, mine own mouth shall condemn me;
> Though I be innocent, He shall prove me perverse.   (9:20)

But it is also affirmed by God. Despite Elihu's claim that

> The Almighty, whom we cannot find out, is excellent in power,
> Yet to judgment and plenteous justice He doeth no violence.
> $$(37:23)$$

God cries to Job out of the whirlwind:

> Wilt thou even make void my judgment?
> Wilt thou condemn Me, that thou mayest be justified?   (40:8)

If the book of Job be any guide, we must oppose those contemporary prophets who affirm that God's wisdom is ours, and that what we take to be good, God will eventually endorse.

Every man has evil intentions, if only for passing moments. Fortunately for our society and civilization, most of us do not allow such intentions to pass the threshold of the mind and be expressed in practice. Privately and occasionally unethical in intent, we publicly and regularly do much that is good. Though we may not escape the first and second forms of evil, most of us avoid the third, *wickedness*, the evil of carrying out evil intentions.

Job, who was a little too sure that he was righteous and well intentioned, was quite right in insisting that he was not wicked (see 29:14). Those who are wicked are the enemies of mankind. Yet they seem to prosper (21:7–13). Why should this be so?

Philosophers such as Maimonides (twelfth century) and Gersonides (thirteenth–fourteenth centuries) thought the answer was to be found in the theory that God's providential care did not extend to individuals. They held that men prospered or suffered as the outcome of natural laws, and regardless of whether or not they conformed to a religious or ethical demand. But their theory does not cover the issue. Putting aside the fact that the story of Job had God and Satan actually interfering with the lives and fortunes of individual men, there is the fact that the participants have no doubt but that God could apportion health, wealth, children, and reputation in any way He wished. To the question, why is it that God did not reward the good and punish the bad, the answer given in the book of Job is that God has His own business, that He does not use our standards, that He has His own reasons, that His idea of the good is beyond the reach of man's knowledge.

The philosophers and the Bible are not, however, altogether opposed. It is possible to hold that God does not interfere with the detailed workings of the world and that He has His own standards of what ought to be and what ought to be done. The philosophers, I think, are right in affirming that God does not—in fact, cannot—interfere with the ways of the world. But the author of the book of Job is right in thinking that God does not allow man's standard of true virtue, right action, and real justice to dictate to Him what He is to do. With scathing scorn God asks Job:

> Knowest thou the ordinances of the heavens?
> Canst thou establish the dominion thereof in the earth?   (38:33)
> Doth the hawk soar by thy wisdom?   (39:26)

He who is wicked does not necessarily incur the wrath of God. Nor does he necessarily suffer. If a man ought to avoid wickedness, the reason cannot be that he would thereby escape either the anger of God or natural ills. We do not know what God will be angry about and whether, if He were, He could or would do anything to those who aroused Him.

A man ought to avoid wickedness because otherwise he stands in his own light. It is of his nature to need his fellows and to be obligated to preserve and enhance the good that is theirs. He who is wicked opposes himself, since he does what the very completeness of his nature requires that he should not do. He may gain the whole world, but since he thereby loses himself, it cannot be himself whom he profits.

It is not true that the wicked prosper. They may be at their ease, thcy may have pleasure, property, admiration, honor, security. They may be unconscious of any wrong. Everyone may account them happy. Yet it would be wrong to say that they really prosper, since they defeat themselves, forcing themselves as they do further and further away from the status of a complete man.

The wicked never really prosper. But do not the good suffer? And if they do, can the suffering be justified?

The answer to this question requires, I think, some grasp of the fourth form of evil, *guilt.*

A man ought to intend to do the good and ought to avoid injuring others. But he ought also not neglect the plight of any. Every single being deserves to be helped, cherished, loved. Yet he who concentrates on one here must slight others there. Each has only finite energy, finite funds, finite interest; none can be everywhere. Each thus fails to fulfill an obligation to realize the good completely. Not necessarily wicked, each is necessarily guilty, humanly evil—one who fails to do all that ought to be done.

Eliphaz correctly charges Job with a neglect of hosts of needy (22:7). He spoils the charge by supposing that Job deliberately neglected the needy. To be sure, so long as he had a shekel and another did not, Job was chargeable as selfish, as having a narrow vision, as being unwilling to extend himself. But since his actions were not rooted in a deliberate malicious intent, he could not be rightly said to be wicked. He was, however, guilty.

Even if Job gave up all that he owned, he would still be guilty. He would be guilty of failing to fulfill an infinite obligation to do good to every being everywhere. Just as no man can claim that his poverty frees him from a duty to repay a loan, so no one can claim to be without guilt because unable to fulfill this infinite obligation. Job, even if he had given up all his possessions, which he was far from doing, would still have been infinitely guilty of neglecting the needs of most of mankind.

A guilty man deserves to be punished. Were there a God and were He just, did He measure punishment according to human standards of right and wrong, everyone would be subject to infinite punishment. Anything less than this would be an undeserved bounty, warranting paeans of thanks to any God that there might be. It is some such view as this, I think, that is characteristic of

much of Jewish thought. Job, in his belief that he deserved to
prosper, goes counter to the dark, somber, and reasonable temper
of most Jews to the effect that men deserve nought but punishment. Every reward for the Jew is an unwarranted blessing, a sign
of the infinite mercy of a just God.

Job deserved punishment. He was in fact a guilty man who was
made to suffer less than he ought. Zophar rightly says to him:

> Know therefore that God exacteth of thee less than thine
> iniquity deserveth.   (11:6)

But what Zophar did not say or see is that Job is no more guilty
than anyone else, that his suffering was no evidence of his being
more wicked, of his having unethical thoughts, or of his being irreligious. And what none of them sees or says is that the point could
be made without referring to God at all. Despite our guilt, we
have the good fortune to live in a universe where only some of
us suffer and then only part of the time.

A fifth form of evil is *vice*, the habit of doing what injures
others. This, though it looms large in the writings of ethicists and
is of great interest to educators and lawmakers, is not dealt with
in the book of Job. We must therefore regretfully pass it by, but
not before we remark that it is produced by men and not by God,
that it is independent of intent, and that it need not entail suffering.

The sixth, seventh, and eighth forms of evil can be dealt with
together as different modes of suffering. Men suffer in their bodies,
physically; in their minds, *psychologically*; and as both together,
socially. Job suffered in all three ways (7:5; 30:17; 7:13 ff.; 19:9,
13, 17 f.).

Torn in his body, by his mind, and from his fellow man, Job
has no place to rest. In him evil has found a lodging; there it
festers and grows. His sufferings are real, painfully real, or everything we could possibly know is nought but an allusion.

Those philosophers who assure us that such sufferings are like
ugly spots in paintings, which disappear when seen as part of the
beautiful whole they make possible, overlook a slight point: it is
a living man who suffers.

The suffering may seem like nothing from the perspective of the
world. But it is all the world to him who suffers. It is real, it is

vital, it is ultimate; it must be reckoned with. As the story of Job makes abundantly clear, it has nothing necessarily to do with other forms of evil. It is to be conquered, not by improving our morals, but by improving our bodies, our minds, and our societies.

Good men will undoubtedly help us advance in medicine, psychology, and politics more than those who are bad. But it will not be because they are religiously or ethically good that they will make progress in these fields, but because they are good as doctors, psychologists, and sociologists.

It is not necessary that men should suffer. Some remain healthy throughout their days, others are perpetually at peace with themselves, and still others are perfectly at home with their fellows. It is hard to see why any one man might not enjoy all three types of good. In any case, it is one of the tasks of all to make this true of each.

Beyond these evils, usually neglected in this anthropocentric age, is a ninth, a *natural* evil, an evil embodied in the wild, destructive forces of nature. Cataclysms of all kinds, earthquakes, tidal waves, and hurricanes, "the *leviathan* and the *behemoth*," are forces of destruction which

> esteemeth iron as straw
> and brass as rotten wood.   (41:19)

They ought not to be. They do not arise, however, because there is something bad in man. The wind does not blow violently, the earth does not rock, because men sin or kill. To suppose that nature is geared to the goodness and badness of men is to suppose either a mysterious harmony between ethics and physics, or that spirits can really move mountains.

It is God, according to the book of Job, who is responsible for the forces of nature.

> Out of whose womb came the ice?
> And the hoar-frost of heaven, who hath gendered it?   (38:29)

It is God

> Who hath cleft a channel for the waterflood
> Or a way for the lightning of the thunder,
> To cause it to rain on a land where no man is.   (38:25 f.)

But then, either God is responsible for natural evils, or He has His own mysterious reasons for allowing what He does, or the universe and its evils are independent of Him. The first of these alternatives is untenable. If God is responsible for the occurrence of evils, it must be because He is not good and therefore not God. We must take one or both of the remaining alternatives, unpalatable though they are to the traditionally minded. The former says that God is not necessarily on the side of what men term the right, while the latter says that God does not interfere with the workings of the universe. As we saw earlier in discussing wickedness, these two are compatible: men and God may not only have different standards of goodness but may be quite independent in nature.

God has His own standards of goodness and does not disturb the natural order of things. If "providence" be understood to refer to an irresistible divine force supporting what men take to be good, there is then no providence. But God could offer material which the universe might utilize in its own way, and God could preserve whatever goods the universe throws up on the shores of time. If He did, He would exhibit a providential concern for the universe and its inhabitants, but one that does not conflict with the brutal fact that there are both human and natural evils.

No one of the foregoing nine forms of evil is necessary. It is conceivable that none of them might be. To be sure, wherever there are men, there is the evil of guilt; but men need not exist. To be sure, if we have a universe of interplaying things, there will be destructive natural forces, but the universe might conceivably reach a stage of equilibrium. Each atom might vibrate in place and interfere with nothing beyond. What could not be avoided by the things in any universe whatsoever is the tenth kind of evil, *metaphysical* evil, the evil of being one among many, of possessing only a fragment of reality, of lacking the reality and thus the power and good possessed by all the others.

Any universe whatsoever, created or uncreated, is one in which each part is less than perfect precisely because it is other than the rest, and is deprived therefore of the reality the rest contain. God might have made, could He make anything at all, a better universe than this, for He could have eliminated or muted some of the forms of evil that now prevail. But He could not have made this universe in detail or as a whole completely free of all defect. No matter how good and concerned God might be, and no matter how few of the other nine types of evil happen to exist, there is always metaphysical evil to mark the fact that the universe is not God and God not the universe.

Much of the foregoing can be summarized in four questions and answers:

Why do bad men prosper? They do not.

Why does God not make bad men suffer more than they do? He does not interfere with the workings of the universe on the whole or in detail.

Why do good men suffer? Suffering and goodness have quite dissimilar causes.

Is God on the side of the right? God has His own standards. But to be religious is to have a faith that His standards will eventually be ours.

GILBERT MURRAY :
BEYOND GOOD AND EVIL

Gilbert Murray (1866–1957), England's best known classical scholar, is known for his *History of Ancient Greek Literature* (1897), *Rise of the Greek Epic* (1907), *Five Stages of Greek Religion* (1925), and his critical editions of Euripides (3 vols.; 1901, 1904, 1910) and Aeschylus (1937). His concern with peace and international understanding is articulated in his *Faith, War, and Policy* (1918) and *Liberality and Civilization* (1938). He was an ardent supporter of the League of Nations and a member of the Committee for Intellectual Co-operation, representing "the deeper spirit of the League." His reflection on Job, though not profound, is interesting; the short piece here reprinted is taken from *Aeschylus: The Creator of Tragedy* (Oxford, 1940).

I think there can be no doubt that the moral sense of civilized man, or of anything that claims the flattering title of *homo sapiens* in whatever stage of development, is at times shocked and bewildered by the behavior of the external world. He is its slave, and it cares nothing for him: its values are not his values; and the more he thinks of the world as alive and acting by conscious, quasi-human will, the more profoundly is he shocked. The fires, floods, and famines, the great inevitable miseries of nature, are not things any good man would think of causing or permitting even against his worst enemies, if he had control over them. The rebellion of certain religions against the ruler of the world, so far as the ordinary run of events can serve as evidence of His character and intentions, is a rebellion of the moral sense not exactly against facts, but against the claim that facts because they are facts must be good. It is to a large extent the protest of the "rebel passion," pity, and has led to much fine, imaginative work. In itself, the rebellion is not a solution of any difficulty; but it often leads to interesting attempts at solving the main problem.

One of the most impressive, no doubt, is the book of Job. The course of thought in Job, though often sublime, is not on the whole lucid, a fact that has led critics to conclude that it is a good deal interpolated. But the main lines can be made out. It is a "theodicy," an attempt to "justify the ways of God to man." Its dramatic form, as well as its philosophical substance, is without parallel in our remains of Hebrew literature. And we may remember that some biblical scholars have thought it was actually inspired by the *Prometheus* of Aeschylus, which the author may have read, or heard about, in Egypt.

The book begins with a mythological setting in which the story is represented as the result of a sort of bet upon the part of Satan that, though Job while prosperous is perfectly pious, he can be made to "curse God" if he is sufficiently tormented and afflicted. The Almighty enters into the spirit of this atrocious proposal, and every kind of torment is showered upon the innocent man. It is like torturing your faithful dog to see if you can make him bite you. So much for the mythological prologue.

Then comes the real substance of the book. It is a discussion of the just or unjust government of the world. Through most of the book the divine justice is taken for granted, which seems to imply the conclusion that, since Job is made miserable by Jehovah, he must be wicked. He must deserve all that he gets. This is the view of the comforters, but Job never admits it. Like the faithful dog who will never turn against his master, he says, "Though He slay me, yet will I trust in Him" (13:15),[1] but he steadfastly refuses to confess to sins that he has not committed or to a general wickedness of which he is not conscious. He cannot see the justice or the reason of his afflictions; he states his innocence and craves a reply. He would like to see the case against him in black and white: "Oh that one would hear me! Behold, my desire is that the Almighty should answer me and that mine adversary had written a book" (31:35).

Elihu the Buzite is thoroughly shocked by this attitude of Job. His belly becomes like wine that has no vent; it is ready to burst with indignation, like new bottles. He undertakes to make an answer. God must be righteous and cannot do wrong. Therefore Job is committing a grave sin in protesting his innocence, and thus attempting to judge the justice of God (see 40:8). He goes on to argue that God owes Job nothing: Job's goodness cannot benefit Him nor Job's wickedness hurt Him. It is exactly the view rejected by Plutarch[2] but reasserted by certain medieval theologians, that animals have no cause to complain if man tortures them, because he has no duties toward them. On moral grounds this is a pretty miserable answer, yet it is essentially the same as the answer made by Jehovah Himself. "Who is this that darkeneth knowledge? . . . Where wast thou when I laid the foundations of the earth? Declare, if thou hast understanding. Who hath laid the measures thereof? . . . Whereupon are the foundations fashioned? Or who laid the corner-stone thereof, when the morning stars sang together, and all the sons of God shouted for joy?" (38:2–7). Later on, after long insistence on the puny and ephemeral nature of Job, the Almighty comes to the central argument: "Wilt thou disannul my judgment? Wilt thou condemn me, that thou mayest be righteous? Hast thou an arm like God, or canst thou thunder with a voice like Him?" (40:8 f.).

If Plato or Aristotle had been present at this discussion, I think they would have felt as explosive as Elihu the Buzite, but on different grounds. They would have pointed out that Jehovah was not answering the real question at all. No one had doubted God's power, it was His justice they had questioned; and His only answer has been to reassert His power again and again in a storm of magnificent rhetoric, and demand how a worm like Job dares to ask any question at all. God does not show, or even say, that He is righteous by human standards of righteousness; what he does assert is that He is, in Nietzsche's phrase, *Jenseits von Gut und Böse* (Beyond Good and Evil), and that the puny standards by which man judges right and wrong simply do not apply to the power that rules the universe. If God's rule conflicts with human morality, that is because human morality is such a limited thing, not valid beyond particular regions of time and space. It is impertinence in man to expect God to be "righteous." This can be defended as a real and profound answer. But it is one that would have utterly shocked Plato or Aristotle. The democratic Greek instinctively cared more for law and justice, *nomos* and *dikaiosune*. The Oriental, accustomed to the rule of a despot or patriarch, cared most for obedience to the supreme power.

ARTHUR S. PEAKE : JOB'S VICTORY

Arthur S. Peake (1865–1929), Protestant theologian, was a professor of Biblical Exegesis at the University of Manchester. He is also the author of *A Critical Introduction to the New Testament* (1909), *Commentary on Jeremiah* (1910–12), *The Revelation of John* (1919), and *The Servant of Yahweh and Other Lectures* (1931). His study on Job (from which the section below is quoted) is a chapter in an overall discussion of the problem of suffering, from the biblical prophets to the apocalyptic writings and early Christianity: *The Problem of Suffering in the Old Testament* (London, 1904).

It is in his debate with God that the interest of Job's speeches is most intense. He charges God, sometimes in language of tremendous realism, with inflicting his intolerable pains. His are the poisoned arrows that have consumed his strength. It is God who assails him like a giant, and dashes him in pieces, God who cruelly persecutes him, breaks him with a tempest and dissolves him in the storm. It is God's terrors that dismay him, His presence that troubles him, the horrible dreams He sends that affright him. So, with the Almighty for his enemy, he is driven to bay, and turns on God with the plain speech of the desperate:

> Therefore I will not refrain my mouth;
> I will speak in the anguish of my spirit;
> I will complain in the bitterness of my soul. (7:11)

> My soul is weary of my life;
> I will give free course to my complaint;
> I will speak in the bitterness of my soul. (10:1)
> Hold your peace, let me alone, that I may speak,
> And let come on me what will. (13:13)

The friends have made eloquent speeches about the might and majesty of God, His inscrutable wisdom and the mystery of His ways. But Job is well aware of it all, nay he himself does not lag behind the friends in his descriptions of it. But this only makes matters worse. There can be no immorality like that of omnipotence and omniscience uncontrolled by goodness. Such Job feels to be the Immorality who governs the universe.

> Perfect and wicked He destroys.
> If the scourge slay suddenly
> At the trial of the innocent He mocks.
> The earth is given into the hand of the wicked,
> The faces of its judges He covereth;
> If not, then who is it?   (9:22 ff.)

Of the prosperity of the wicked Job cites abundance of proofs. Sometimes he speaks as if God were simply indifferent to moral distinctions, slaying good and bad without discrimination. At other times he speaks as if God directly favored the wicked. The difference is largely one of mood and expression; the thought he means to utter is that the government of the world is radically immoral. No destiny controls God's actions, He is free with a sovereign freedom in the colossal wrongs He permits Himself to do. His actions are arbitrary, and it is just the incalculable waywardness of His dealings with man that strikes such terror into the heart.

Not observation, but his own calamity, revealed to Job the profound injustice of God. Maddened by his pain, goaded by the cruel judgment of his friends, the hostility of God, at first so perplexing to him, comes at last to seem only too characteristic. His own misery sharpens his insight into the misery of the world. Yet he is preoccupied far more with the issues between himself and God than with God's relations to mankind. From the first he had been predestined in God's secret counsel to his cruel fate. His long and prosperous career had all been part of God's sinister design. With fiendish malignity He had lulled His servant into security and a sense of His loving care, that He might dash him into a misery, made unspeakably more wretched by its contrast with his happiness, and by the stripping of the mask of love from God's hate. And now his Adversary is determined to establish his guilt. He knows that Job is innocent, yet He is the Almighty, who can easily put him in the wrong. What chance has a frail ignorant man against a deity who can entrap him so easily by his subtle ques-

tions into self-condemnation, or who by the sheer terror of His
majesty can strike him dumb or force him into confession of sin?
He skulks behind the veil; will neither listen nor reply. If He
respects so far the decencies of justice that He justifies His action
by real sins of Job, He can do it only by raking up the long dead
past, and dragging to light the sins of his youth, when passion
was unchecked by mature experience and judgment. But He has
no magnanimity. He spies on man's minutest actions, will not for
a moment release him from His maddening watchfulness. How
petty must be His character, since He follows frail man with persecution so untiring.

> What is man that Thou magnifiest him,
> And settest Thy heart upon him;
> And visitest him every morning,
> And every moment dost test him?   (7:17 f.)

Even granted that he had sinned, his sin cannot hurt the Almighty. Is a puny man so formidable that God dare not relax His
vigilance? If Job were the tossing tumultuous sea, conquered by
God in primeval times, but still chafing against the restraints He
imposed upon it, and flinging upward its heaven-assaulting waves,
then he might be a menace to God. How fitly matched with that
mighty conquest of the chaos monster is the miracle that has sub-
dued a weak, mortal man!

In all the surging turmoil of Job's soul one thing stands fast, the
certainty of his own integrity. He affirms it again and again: he is
a just, a blameless man; there is no violence in his hands, and his
prayer is pure. He is sure that God knows that he is not wicked,
and though He has determined to slay him, he will maintain his
ways before Him. His righteousness he holds fast, and will not let
it go. This consciousness finds its noblest expression in Job's great
defense of his past life, which perhaps touches the loftiest point
of Old Testament ethics (chapters 29–31). Sure of himself and
the justice of his cause, he brings his self-vindication to its close,
with a challenge to Yahweh that He should answer him, and the
proud declaration that as prince he would draw near to God,
bearing the indictment his adversary had written (31:35 ff.).

Yet the poet has wonderfully shown us the clashing currents
in Job's breast by the strange incoherence of his language about

God. He is torn between the bitter present and the happy memory, between the God who is torturing him and the God of whose goodness he had drunk so deeply in the past. And side by side with all his incisive complaints of God's cruelty, and scorn of His malignant pettiness, side by side even with the firm assertion of His immorality, stand other utterances that recognize His righteousness. He bases the confidence he expresses in one of his less gloomy moments on the conviction that a godless man shall not come before Him. He warns the friends that God will not suffer Himself to be flattered by lies. It is therefore natural that appeal should alternate with invective. The appeal is in some cases, indeed, rather remonstrance.

Why had God suffered him to be born? Why does He contend with him, why hide His face? What are the sins God has to bring against him? Is it good for Him to despise His own work, or, when He has lavished so much care on fashioning His servant, wantonly to destroy him? But the tone of remonstrance is softened into the tone of pathetic appeal. Would that he knew where he might find Him, that he might lay bare his case or utter his supplication. From the injustice of man he turns to God, in the moving words: "My friends scorn me, but my eye pours out tears unto God" (16:20). If he could only come face to face with God, He would not contend with him in the greatness of His power, but would give heed to his plea. He appeals to God to relax His incessant watchfulness, and give him a respite from his pain. Would that He might hide him in *sheol*, keep him in secret till His wrath were past. Here the poet advances to one of his deepest thoughts. Not only does Job appeal from man to God, but he appeals from God to God. There seems to be an irrational element in his thought. Job asks God to save him from God's wrath, to place him out of its reach, till it has spent itself. He appeals to God against God, as if God had a higher and a lower self. Behind the wrathful he catches a glimpse of the gracious God. There is no umpire between them, but would not God Himself give security to God for Job? So he wins, if he cannot hold fast, the conviction that his witness is in heaven, and He that vouches for him is on high. This reaches its climax in the famous passage, 19:25 ff., in which Job expresses his conviction that his vindicator lives, and that his innocence will at last be established. And though he does not look forward to a vindication in his lifetime, yet he believes that he will be permitted to know that his character is cleared. Not that he anticipates a happy immortality, or escape from *sheol*'s dismal gloom. He prizes his honor and fair fame above his happiness, and with the vision of God as his avenger he will be content.

The schism in God, which seems so strange, is a reflection of the schism in Job's experience. His mind swings to and fro between the memory of blessed fellowship and the pang of his present curse. When his pain is hard to bear, or he is stung by the calm injustice of his friends, he can think of God only as his unrelenting foe. But as the thought of his former life in God's favor fills his soul, he turns back with yearning and tenderness to those happy days when God watched over him in love, and he walked through the darkness in His light, when he called upon Him and He answered him. Still his own heart goes out to God, how gladly he would renew the old communion. And though the anger of God now hotly pursues him, he feels that it will not last. It is only a temporary aberration that has seized Him, not, as Job elsewhere affirms, a long cherished and subtly framed design to which He is giving effect. If He would only hide him in *sheol*, forget him till His anger had burned out, and then remember him, how gladly he would wait the full time in that dreary home, so that he might at last renew the happy intercourse, forgetting God's wayward mood.

But this hope he sadly sets aside. There can be few things more pathetic in all literature than his appeal to God to be gracious to him before it is too late. Soon he must die, and when God's inexplicable wrath has spent itself, He will think remorsefully of His servant whose loyal love He has so cruelly spurned. And He will think on him in love, and long for the familiar intercourse. But His vain regrets will come too late, Job will have passed beyond recall:

> For now shall I lie down in the dust,
> And Thou wilt seek me diligently, but I shall not be. (7:21)

Again and again Job had challenged God to appear and defend His action. He had implored Him to fulfill two conditions, to suspend the persecution from which he is suffering and not to overwhelm him with the dread of His presence:

> Only do not two things unto me,
> Then will I not hide myself from Thee:
> Withdraw Thy hand far from me;
> And let not Thy terror make me afraid.
> Then call Thou, and I will answer;
> Or let me speak, and answer Thou me.   (13:20 ff.)

But God fulfills neither of Job's conditions. When He appears, He does not take His rod from the sufferer, and He speaks out of the whirlwind. Moreover, not only does He leave Job on the rack and appall him with the storm, but He deigns to give no reply to Job's questions, no defense of His own conduct. Rather He speaks roughly to the sufferer, pressing him with questions, which convict him of his ignorance. The reader is at first distracted between his wonder at the poet's genius and his disappointment and even resentment at the character of Yahweh's reply. Surely, he thinks, God will now make clear the mystery, but no word is said to explain to Job why he suffers. There is no comfort offered him, but what seems like a brutal mockery.

Yet if we look more closely we shall see that the speeches of Yahweh are not mere irrelevant irony. Job has taken on himself to criticize the government of the universe. But has he ever realized what the universe is, or how complex the problem of its control? So God brings before him its wonderful phenomena in language of surpassing beauty. The mighty work of its creation, the curbing of the rebellious sea, the land of the dead, the home of light and of darkness, the ordered march of the constellations, the treasuries of snow and hail, which God has stored to overwhelm His enemies; the frost that binds the streams, or the rain that quenches the desert's thirst—all pass before Job's mind and all are too vast, too obscure, for him to comprehend. Then God sketches a series of swift pictures of His animal creation, of whose secrets Job is profoundly ignorant. Thus He brings home to him the limitation of his outlook, thus Job comes to learn the wide range of God's interests.

And as we reflect more deeply we see a relevance in the divine speeches that at first we are apt to miss. Job's language had not stopped short of blasphemy, and though he pleaded that his friends must not take too seriously the words of a desperate man, yet he deserved a sharp lesson to cure his presumption. True, he had freely confessed God's might and wisdom, he had beforehand said that God would not contend with him in the greatness of His power. But he needed to have the detail bitten into his imagination, that the vague generality might become vivid and concrete. For much of the mischief with Job lay in his self-absorption. He dwells on God's immoral control of the lot of man, but even more specially on God's immoral treatment of himself. God bids the self-centered sufferer look away at the wide universe, then he will come to a juster estimate of man's place. But even if he looks at the sentient life of the world, he will realize that man is only one among many of the objects of God's concern. All those glorious pictures of the animal creation that God flashes before his eyes are meant to show him that man's importance may easily be overrated. Especially is this the case with those unsubdued denizens of the wilderness, who live their life wholly independent of man. There, too, God sends the fertilizing shower, causing it "to rain on a land where no man is" (38:26).

When Job confesses that he has sinned in speaking of things too wonderful for him, and with self-abhorrence repents in dust and ashes, the question arises whether we are to see in this a verification of his dread that the terror of God's majesty and His insoluble questions would force him into self-condemnation. It would be to miss the deepest teaching the poet has to give us, were we to think so. By confronting him with nature, God has taken him out of himself, and, convinced him of his relative insignificance. Yet even that is not the chief thing. It is no accident that the poet refrains from putting in God's mouth any explanation of Job's sufferings. To men oppressed by the mystery of their own or the world's pain, the explanation of an individual case is of little worth, unless it admits of wider application. And for Job himself the explanation is unneeded. He has received a new experience:

> I had heard of Thee by the hearing of the ear;
> But now mine eye seeth Thee,
> Wherefore I abhor myself, and repent
> In dust and ashes. (42:5 f.)

It is the vision of God that has released him from his problem. His suffering is as mysterious as ever, but, plain or mysterious, why should it vex him any longer? He has seen God, and has entered into rest. The only answer we can get to the problem of pain is, the poet would tell us, this answer. The soul's certainty is the soul's secret. The spirit has escaped its difficulties by soaring above them. If we know God, no other knowledge matters. For ourselves, we have won our way to unspeakable peace. As we dwell in the secret place of the Most High and abide under the shadow of the Almighty, we see the universe from a new point of view. We can give no answer to its questions, no solution of its baffling riddles. But since we know God we can trust Him to the uttermost; we know, incredible though it may seem, that the world's misery does not contradict the love of God. It was therefore with deliberate intent that the poet put on God's lips no hint of the reason of Job's suffering. To trust God when we understand Him would be but a sorry triumph for religion. To trust God, when we have every reason for distrusting Him, save our inward certainty of Him, is the supreme victory of religion. This is the victory that Job achieves. But he can achieve it only as God takes the initiative and gives him the revelation of Himself.

Yet God, by the very action He took at the Satan's instigation, placed not only Job but Himself on His trial. If the Satan is to be convinced that Job's piety is disinterested, it must be through the tests that he imposes. For God to accept the challenge meant that He accepted a grave responsibility. Job has to be the involuntary subject of this experiment; he must suffer that God's confidence may be justified. To some at any rate this will not seem a complete vindication of God's action; it, too, must go with other partially solved mysteries.

The difficulty would probably be less to a Semite than to ourselves. Yet the author felt it, and for that reason added or retained the epilogue. It is not that Job needed his restoration in order to regain his confidence in God. Had he been doomed to end his days in pain, he could walk through the valley in the memory of the vision of God. But then the reader would have been very unfavorably impressed by God's treatment of him. Now he feels that God has made amends to His loyal servant for the pain He has made him endure. To estimate the epilogue aright, we must not forget that the author had to keep the treatment of his subject within the limits of the earthly life, and could not work with the conception of a happy immortality. And we must remember that the compensation given to Job is to clear God's character, not in any way to reaffirm the old theory that the righteous must be fortunate.

EMIL G. KRAELING :
A THEODICY—AND MORE

The book of Job as a theodicy and what "is more than a theodicy" is analyzed by the Old Testament scholar Emil G. Kraeling (born 1892), with an appropriate reference to Kant's treatise on the subject (see Introduction, chapter VII). Professor Kraeling is the author of *Aram and Israel* (1918), *The Brooklyn Museum Aramaic Papyri* (1953), and *The Old Testament since the Reformation* (1955). The exposition here reproduced is from *The Book of the Ways of God* (London, 1938).

The book does not raise the issue [of the lack of correspondence between sin and punishment] to leave it standing as an unanswerable indictment: it defends God against the attacks that our reason reads out of the situation. To appreciate this defense, and to see it in its proper perspective, it may be well to recall to mind what possible line a theodicy of the kind that Kant declared permissible may take. The defender of God's righteousness, so the philosopher says, must prove either that what seems contrary to purpose in the world is not really so, or that, even if it should be so, it has to be regarded as an inevitable consequence of the nature of things, or that it at least is not caused by the supreme creator of all things, but merely by the beings of this world to whom something may be imputed (i.e., either men, or possibly also higher beings, whether good or evil spirits). Are any or all of these the three possible approaches utilized in the book of Job?

Now, the first line, that of showing that what seems contrary to purpose is not really so, is taken by the three friends, when they describe Job's sufferings as punitive, and the lack of correspondence between sin and punishment in the world in general as only a temporary maladjustment, which is invariably corrected by "late" retribution. So far as Job's case is concerned, their explanation is inaccurate, and the hero rightly rejects it. But Job is a saint, who has not his like on earth; an argument that is inapplicable in his case is not necessarily inapplicable in other cases. This explanation of the sufferings of men ordinarily carries more weight than can be granted it in this particular connection. It has a powerful ally in the conscience of the sinner, who will admit what the saint denied, and will confess with the crucified malefactor, "We receive the due reward of our deeds" (Luke 23:41). It has occupied an important place in theodicy discussions, and hence it is well that it was included in the general picture of the book, even though it proves insufficient here. The same thing applies, though in lesser degree, to the line taken by Elihu and the related 5:17 f., that suffering has a pedagogical purpose. This point is not repudiated by the hero, but it is not nearly as satisfactory an explanation of his case as Elihu thinks. Surely the gain to Job's morality or spirituality is disproportionate to the enormous machinery of destruction that has been loosed against him! But we must not forget that the pedagogical theory may cover many other cases, and likewise has an ally in the religious consciousness of the believer. A third explanation of the meaningfulness of suffering is implied in the introductory narrative, and thus remains in the background of the reader's mind throughout, viz., that suffering gives a man the opportunity to prove his virtue. This theory, put forward also in Greece by the Stoics, has, indeed, a very great significance, as a reader of Emerson's *Essay on Character* will appreciate. Still, if it had been put forward in the form of a hypothesis, rather than, as at present, in the form of incontrovertible narrative, it might not have carried any more weight with Job than do the other explanations of his plight.

It will thus appear that the book of Job does not leave much out of consideration that can be said in favor of the purposefulness of suffering. In the greatest of Christian theodicies—one that sprang from a fusion of the Stoic and Neoplatonic with the Apostolic tradition, Augustine's *City of God*—we find only two arguments marshaled that we have not considered: namely, that suffering is a punishment for original sin, and that it serves to prevent man from being too satisfied on this earth and to awaken in him a longing for immortality. And the latter point can, with a little stretch of the imagination, even be regarded as latent in 19:25–27.

The case chosen for the theodicy debate is an extreme one, but by virtue of that very fact it vividly illustrates the insufficiency of the teleological explanations of suffering in some cases, and the impossibility of persuading serious doubters of the justice of God by this approach. It is a great thing that the book of Job shows us the hero embattled with those who promulgate explanations of this kind and utterly unconvinced by them. True, they go beyond the bounds of the permissible in their cocksure deductions, as though they had an absolute knowledge of the ways of God. But even if they were more moderate, and advanced only tentative suggestions, the result would still be the same. A sufferer like Job would have to refuse to see any earthly purpose in what befell him. Only a metaphysical explanation that is not subject to disproof by experience can show a sufficient degree of resistance to withstand criticism in a situation like that.

But the book of Job also illustrates the third of the possible approaches mentioned by Kant—that of attributing evil to beings other than God. This explanation is advanced in the bold introductory narrative 1–2:10 as an actual fact. It is, however, a fact not known to any of the contenders of the dialogue, who conduct themselves as though such celestial complications were entirely beyond their horizon. The story, of course, suggests this justification of God only for the particular case of Job. It is by no means clear that the inexplicable trials of other men proceed from the same source. Still less is it said that the ultimate origin of evil as such is to be explained in similar fashion. Nevertheless, one is tempted to extend its meaning.

The theory is skillfully applied. At the very outset it relieves God of the onus of having originated the plan of bringing misfortune upon Job, and yet preserves the theistic position that God controls all things by making His permission essential before Satan can act. If it makes the All-wise seem less good when He allows His faithful worshipper to be treated with such gross injustice, this is offset by the ultimate purpose of glorifying both God and His servant Job. God's supreme wisdom is demonstrated by Job's rectitude and God's goodness through what He does to compensate Job. [. . .]

But the Satan who is made responsible for all the trouble is not an evil spirit. He is a zealot for righteousness who shares the hypothesis of Genesis 6:5 that all the thoughts of the heart of man are evil, and who is unwilling to believe that there is such a thing as a righteous man. He here wants to inflict misfortune on Job for the purpose of eliciting the sinfulness that he believes to be latent in this favorite of the Lord. This is a demonstration of cruelty on his part, and yet, to a greater degree, a proof of his inferior knowledge, which was unable to search the heart and the reins. In short, the story is many-sided. It indicates that God, out of consideration for celestial beings, sometimes permits things to happen that are contrary to His love, in order that some desirable end may be attained. In this case it was a great end—to prove beyond a doubt that there is such a thing as an unselfish love of God among men.

What shall we say of the value of this approach? It verges closely upon the "dualistic" theodicy which was developed in its most consistent form in Zoroastrianism, and which Pierre Bayle,[1] the opponent of Leibniz, regarded as the only reasonable explanation of the existence of evil. But dualism endangers either the unity or the moral nature of the idea of God. Our book, in the glorious freedom of unbroken mythological thinking, which is able to enliven characters and situations as no mere abstract formula can, steers skillfully between this Scylla and Charybdis. It is a fine thing, however, that the theory is not dealt with by any of the speakers in the great debate, or even alluded to by God Himself, but stands in splendid isolation as a poetic glimpse of a reality hidden from mortal eyes. It thus has a humbling effect on the human mind, which is left by God to move upon a lower plane, totally unconscious of the vast range of possibilities that exist behind the curtain of terrestrial existence.

Perhaps the second approach referred to by Kant—that of showing that, if there be anything contrary to purpose in the world, it is inherent in the nature of things—offers more promise. Does our book make use of it? This question can be raised only with regard to the great section 38–42:6, for here alone one ascends to so vast a perspective as the arrangements of the world as such. Have we in this case a biblical prototype of the doctrine of the harmony of the cosmos which engaged many minds from Plotinus down to the eighteenth-century thinkers and poets? In those latter days the great Leibniz set forth how it is in the nature of things to be limited, and how evil is nothing else but limitation of capacity with resultant deficiency. The eternal verities themselves imposed this situation on the creator of this best of all possible worlds. Shaftesbury,[2] more aesthetic and less speculative, emphasized the harmonious beauty of the world, counting misfortune and pain as but the momentary disharmonies of music that are at once dissolved into harmony, and Pope[3] sang in the *First Epistle to Lord Bolingbroke*:

> All nature is but art unknown to thee,
> All chance direction that thou canst not see,
> All discord harmony, not understood,
> All partial evil, universal good,
> And spite of pride, in erring reason's spite
> One truth is clear, whatever is is right.

But the force of this type of argument depends on a fairly satisfactory state of affairs in the world or in individual human life. Hence we find that the optimism of the eighteenth century was sadly shaken by the great earthquake of Lisbon on November 1, 1755, in which sixty thousand human beings perished. Goethe recalls the tremendous effect of this event, which occurred during his boyhood, when he writes,

> Perhaps the demon of terror did not at any time so quickly and powerfully spread his tremors over the earth. The boy who repeatedly became aware of this was not a little disturbed. God the creator of heaven and earth, whom Luther's explanation of the first article of the creed presented as so wise and merciful, had by no means shown Himself fatherly in consigning the righteous to destruction along with the wicked. In vain the young mind sought to stabilize itself over against these impressions, which was the more impossible since the wise men and scribes could not agree as to how a phenomenon of this kind was to be regarded.

In France Voltaire, too, who had been an adherent of Leibniz, abandoned his optimism, and began to cast scorn upon this view of life. By the same token, one cannot imagine Job in his dire predicament, or the reader who puts himself in his place, as being impressed by a philosophical argument to the effect that the world in its totality is good, or that evil is only an unavoidable by-product of creation. He might answer this whole line of argument with Lotze,[4]

> One may say that evil appears only in the minor sphere, but disappears when one ponders the great totality; but what does this comfort, the force of which depends on the arrangement of a given period of history, avail, and what becomes of it when we reverse it and say: in the greater sphere there is indeed harmony, but when one looks more closely into things, the world is full of misery? Whoever justifies evil as a means of divine pedagogy does not think of all the sufferings of the animal world, or of the incomprehensible decay of so much intellectual life in history, and thereby limits God's omnipotence; for every pedagogy employs evil only if there is no other way out. Whoever concedes this limitation, not subtly but openly, and believing with Leibniz that in every dilemma between God's omnipotence and goodness he must choose the latter, and so explains evil out of the limitations that the immemorial necessity of the everlasting truths imposed on the creative freedom of God, also fails to satisfy us. For it is the least demonstrable of all assertions that the validity of the everlasting truths is responsible for the evil in the world; to any impartial observation of nature, evil is dependent rather on certain arrangements of reality, alongside of which, on the basis of the same eternal verities, other arrangements are conceivable. If one holds fast to a distinction between necessary laws and the creative freedom of God (with which we do not agree), then doubtless evil must belong to that which did not have to be, but was created through freedom.

But if a theodicy of the second type is at all attempted in 38–42:6, then it is a less ambitious one than that of the philosophers of the age of rationalism. [. . .] The section seems, indeed, to reflect the claim that there is a teleology visible in the great totality. The same implication still remains if one stresses the thought that we here have a tripartite argument to prove the foolhardiness of criticizing God—first the proof of the inability of Job to understand or duplicate the mysterious arrangements of nature (chapters 38–39), then the proof of the impossibility of his assuming or improving on the government of the world (40:8–14), and finally the proof of his incompetence to cope with the most formidable crea-

tures (40:15–41:26). For all this presupposes that the world
government is very wonderful, both when it produces that which
is teleological in relation to man and that which is not. And in
railing at human inability to understand or to duplicate these
things, the section sets forth an indirect praise of God's wisdom
that can hardly be excelled.

God has not attempted to frighten or browbeat Job into submission, but has addressed Himself to his reason in extended
poetic argument. If He speaks powerfully, or even with biting
sarcasm, it is because His infinite superiority to man has been
disregarded. This trend of thought itself, even in the mouth of a
man, would carry considerable weight; how much more when it
is put into the mouth of Him who alone knows the secrets of
heaven and earth. And Job does not give in grudgingly, but is
freely persuaded.

> Now I know that Thou canst do all things,
> And that no plan of Thine can be restrained.   (42:2)

God, so the poet would have us realize, has infinite power, but He
also has a purpose which His power serves. The existence of such
a purpose must not be questioned, because we cannot discern it
at every point. We see so much of it in the great arrangements
of the world that we must believe in its existence where our understanding fails us.

This manner of combating the arguments that reason adduces
against the divine world government is more effective than that
followed by Pope or Shaftesbury, because it invokes the thought
that, according to Max Weber,[5] constitutes the only consistent
theodicy the Western world has to offer, the doctrine of the *deus
absconditus,* the inscrutable God. This is not just an *ad hoc* creation of theologians: it is inevitably rooted in the nature of true,
unspoiled religion that the deity should remain clothed in mystery
and passing all understanding. Otto[6] has set this forth with particular force, and has shown how the atmosphere of chapters 38 f.
reflects the recognition of the mysterious element in God in rare
purity. Dissatisfied as reason may be with the fact that the defender of God's righteousness quits the rational battleground at this
point, it must resign itself to the situation, and realize that if, as

Kant says, it is arrogant to defend God, it is still more arrogant to assail Him.

It thus appears that our book of Job is the classic treatment of the theodicy problem, in poetic form, covering the latter almost in its full range so far as a philosophy that accepts theism may go. This is the reason for its timeless value and perennial interest for the nobler spirits of the human race. Nowhere have the case against God and the case for God been put so powerfully as in the pages of this ancient work of the Eastern sages.

But the book is more than a theodicy: it offers yet another solution of the greatest of all problems—that of its dissolution. This will appear when 42:5–6 are taken into the picture. The man who has repentantly put aside his criticism of God is shown at peace with Him in the attitude of faith. In thus exhibiting faith as the ultimate necessity, the book illustrates a situation that prevails for any philosophy when it comes to the end of all our thoughts in the matter of theodicy. Pierre Bayle drew this conclusion from his denial of the pre-established harmony, as did Laurentius Valla[7] in his discourse on the freedom of the will. And Lotze likewise concludes his previously quoted criticism of all rational theodicies by saying:

> Hence let us change slightly the rule laid down by Leibniz, and say where an absolute contradiction exists between God's goodness and His omnipotence, we will decide that our finite wisdom is at an end and that we cannot comprehend the solution *in which we believe.*

Thus the philosophers take refuge in faith, just as a venerable theologian does when he writes, "Can the world process be understood—hypothetically—as grounded in and ruled by love? Nay, not understood but believed!"

It is this same ultimate realization that we find reflected in this final section of Job. For if the rebellious hero here becomes a joyous confessor, and recognizes the divine omnipotence and voluntaristic purposefulness of God, this is not entirely due to the effect of the arguments of chapters 38 f. on his reason, but is partly the result of his experience of the divine reality.

> I had heard of Thee by the hearing of the ear,
> But now mine eye hath seen Thee. (42:5)

Such an experience deters from one-sided emphasis on the intellectual, and gives importance also to the realms of feeling and of the will. In that glorious encounter of the divine reality, which is made a seeing with the senses, in the ancient parable, Job becomes completely convinced of the divine justice. All the doubts and questions that had troubled him are dispelled before that appearance as the shadows that are no more when the day-star is risen. He no longer needs a rational theodicy. He is ready to believe without understanding, knowing that no understanding is possible. There is not the faintest touch of sadness in the acceptance of the latter limitation. His tortured mind gladly comes to rest when the bounds that are set for it, as for the primeval ocean, are pointed out by the creator: "Thus far shalt thou go, and no further" (38:11).

And now we must glance back once more to observe how the way to such an insight was already prepared by the titanic struggle of Job in chapters 3–19, prior to his sudden and unaccountable fall into worldly skepticism. There we behold him breaking through the thought of the divine omnipotence, which he sets forth as terrifying and subversive to piety (9:2 f.), to a realization of God's incomprehensible love. Clinging to this love of God, he faces death and the hostile world in such a way that, instead of his case being a stumbling block to religion as such, it becomes a veritable living proof of its indestructible power. Here at the end of the book the fruits of this great battle are garnered in. We find the hero freed from the only stain that marred him, and, oblivious of his earthly assailants, communing with the creator.

Thus the book of Job enters into that exalted sphere where the religious experience looms so large that nothing else matters. It touches hands here with great and noble words of Israel's sweet singers. The poet of Psalm 73, too, confesses that he was once driven almost to the point of despair as he contemplated how misfortune had come upon him in spite of his piety, while the evildoers, who doubt God's omniscience or His concern about earthly affairs, prospered. He overcame his doubts by heeding the final fate of the ungodly. Though still in his unfortunate condition, he emphasizes the fact that "the Lord is his portion" (as do Pss. 16:5; 119:57; 142:62; Lam. 3:24), but he does it in a form indicating an allegiance to God that can brook no interference from any physical hindrance.

Whom have I in heaven (but Thee)?
And having Thee I delight not (in anything that is) upon earth,
Though my flesh and my heart fail,
But God is the rock of my heart and my portion forever.

(Ps. 73:25 f.)

To this man of exceeding piety the joy of fellowship with God outweighs all adversities, just as the Psalmist asserts, "Thy loving-kindness is better than life" (Ps. 63:4).

What follows in the book—Job's triumph over his adversaries and their enforced recognition of his sainthood, as well as the final picture of his restored prosperity—only serves, by its subtle humor, to throw into bold relief the element of the beatific that sometimes attends the experience of God. It is as though we had suddenly emerged through a door of a cathedral, and stand without in the sharp sunlight, where men move about in all their worldly manners and pursuits. We find ourselves longing for the interior of the building, with its twilight and odor of incense—above all, for that marvelous choir. For here we felt the very walls breathing the divine reality, as religious men have experienced it at all times. Terror and bliss, exaltation and humiliation, have come to them as they stood in its presence, asking nought else but this, and knowing that there is nothing in the world that unveils in like measure the nethermost depths and the towering heights of life, so that he who is the recipient of this mercy has tasted the full range of what it can offer, and has lived tremendously. The benison of this experience illumines the whole edifice of the book of Job, and casts a radiance upon him who enters unshod into this, its holy of holies.

W. O. E. OESTERLEY AND T. H. ROBINSON :
THE THREE STAGES OF THE BOOK

W. O. E. Oesterley, Professor of Hebrew and Old Testament Exegesis, King's College, London, and Theodore H. Robinson, Professor of Semitic Languages, University College, Cardiff, collaborated in the writing of *A History of Israel* (2 vols.; Oxford, 1932), *Hebrew Religion: Its Origin and*

Development (New York, 1930), and *An Introduction to the Books of the Old Testament* (London, 1934). The latter work, from which the selection that follows is taken, is an analysis of the development of the biblical writings, their origin and history, and an account of the various formulations of biblical thought. Speaking of the book of Job, our authors maintain that suffering becomes a problem only "when it conflicts with the religious theory of a single ruler of the whole universe, who is at once omnipotent, wise, and good," a doctrine that does not appear in the ancient world outside Israel. The question "is an inevitable corollary of that ethical monotheism in which Judaism stood alone." However, is there an answer to the question?

We cannot leave the book without noting the difficulty that commentators have found in satisfying themselves in regard to the answer the book gives to the problem stated therein—the inequality of suffering and its apparent injustice. We should, however, remark that there are two problems. One is the purely personal one, and concerns God's attitude to Job himself. Is He the friend or the enemy of His faithful servant? This receives a certain answer in the great passage 19:25 ff., where Job is at least assured that God must and will vindicate him. The other problem is more general, and the book as it stands contains no less than three different attempts to solve it.

In the first place we have the explanation offered by the popular tale. Here the suffering of the hero is due not to any fault of his own, but to the jealous cynicism of the Satan. "Doth Job fear God for nought?" (1:9) is a valid question, not only for ancient Israel, but for every other age in human history—we think, inevitably, of Glaucon's description of the perfectly righteous man.[1] Like Plato, the storyteller could find no answer except in the humiliation and hopeless agony of the faultless man, and his suffering becomes a test, the only valid test, of *disinterested* righteousness.

Such a solution may help the sufferer, but it does not touch the heart of the problem. Is God justified in torturing a perfectly good and innocent person, merely to prove that he *is* good and innocent? It is a justification of God, a theodicy, that is needed, and the demand for a further explanation is the motive inspiring the poet to whom we owe the greater part of the book. In the poem, the friends insist that suffering can be explained only as punishment due to, and proportioned to, sin, but one of the obvious aims of the book is to challenge this theory. The striking fact in the poet's

discussion is that the divine pronouncement at the end contains
no hint at an answer. God simply presents Himself as He is, and
Job is cowed, and "abhors himself in dust and ashes" (42:6). This
is no solution of the problem, and the poet cannot have intended
it to be understood as one. In other words, it looks as though he
had deliberately told his readers that there was no solution—at
least none that the human mind could appreciate.

What, then, does Job's final attitude imply? We must remember
that we are dealing with an Eastern, especially with a Jewish,
mind, and we must not expect that our own feelings and instincts
will meet with full satisfaction in what appeals to an ancient Jew,
great poet and deep thinker though he be. With this in mind let
us look once more at the *dénouement*. Job has appealed to God to
appear, and is prepared "as a prince to enter His presence" (31:37),
bearing a convincing statement of his case with him. In answer
to this challenge God does appear, and presents Himself in all
His creative majesty. At once Job forgets his case, and ceases to be
urged by his problems. In the presence of God these things vanish
away, and only God is left.

True, the experience is one that instills into him the deepest
awe and self-contempt, but these are just the aspects of the matter
that would be inevitable to the ancient Oriental. Translated into
modern terms, however, we may surely say that the supreme lesson
of the close of this book is that when once a man has really stood
face to face with God, he has no more doubts. The question may
have no logical answer, the problem may find no formal solution,
but that does not matter; the sufferer has seen God, and that is
enough. In that vision, and in the knowledge it brings, he can rest
in patience and spiritual contentment. In him is fulfilled that
which was spoken by the prophet, "he shall look away out of the
agony of his soul, and shall be satisfied by his knowledge" (Isa.
53:11).

The third attempt at a solution belongs to a point of view best
represented by the Elihu speeches, though it may, possibly, be
detected elsewhere. Here we have the position of a reader of the
popular story and of the poem, who felt that there was one very
serious fault in Job's character, which needed correction. Throughout the debate he has insisted on his substantial righteousness.
He may have done what was wrong in the sight of God, but such

sins were insignificant and unconscious. While many will feel that this determined self-justification was the natural, almost inevitable, reaction of the sufferer to the theology of the three friends, it can also be interpreted as evidence of a self-righteous Pharisaism, and in that light it was viewed by the author of the Elihu speeches.

This gives him a clue: there is a double purpose in Job's calamities. In the first place they bring to light a deep-seated and subtle weakness. Prosperity would never have shown that Job was so fatally "righteous in his own eyes" (32:1); in the crucible of adversity this spiritual dross has risen to the surface. But, further, Job's sufferings have offered a remedy for the disease. The poem ended with the hero lying contrite and penitent at the feet of God. He "abhors himself in dust and ashes" (42:6). His self-righteousness has gone, and it was the purging fires of pain that had rid him of this subtle impurity of soul.

Our first perusal of the book may have left us with the feeling that the essential theme is handled in a confusing and uncertain fashion. It is only when we recognize the fact that Job is the result of a growth in which three main stages can be distinguished, and that each stage presents its own view of the problem, that the various lines of thought are clear, and the book takes its proper place in the story of man's developing knowledge of God.

HAYIM GREENBERG : IN DUST AND ASHES

The Russian-born Hayim Greenberg (1889–1953) came to the United States in 1924. Both in prerevolutionary Russia and in America he was one of the leaders in the Hebrew culture movement and in Labor Zionism. He edited *Der Yiddischer Kemfer* (1924–53) and *The Jewish Frontier* (1934–53). A brilliant speaker, he lectured in Yiddish, Hebrew, and English throughout the United States. His essays were collected in *The Inner Eye* (two volumes, 1953–64), from which the article here reprinted is taken. It was written in 1940.

What is God doing now? Where is He, if He exists anywhere at all? Is He perhaps directing this devilish spectacle, this most terrible bloodbath which our planet has ever witnessed, from behind the scenes? Is it His hand that guides the millions of Cains who spare neither mothers nor daughters and rain their bombs on babes in their cribs as well as on grey heads? Or is He neutral? Has He perhaps isolated Himself somewhere in the vastness of space and does not care what is going on in this remote little provincial corner of the universe that is called the earth? Or does He suffer together with us? Does He shed tears over every drop of innocent blood, yet is Himself too weak and helpless, chained by dumb necessity or subject to the chaos of accident?

What is God doing now? Where is He, if He exists anywhere at all? In colonial Puritan Massachusetts one could only ask such questions at the risk of one's life. Today such words, or a close paraphrase of them, serve as the title of an article in a theological journal (*The Christian Century*).

But let not the reader be frightened. The Reverend [Henry H.] Crane, a Methodist preacher from Detroit who wrote the article in *The Christian Century*, only toyed momentarily with a nihilist phrase. He is not a heretic, God forbid, or a blasphemer. On the contrary, he regards himself as a confirmed believer, and when he looks at the present-day world, at the torment and suffering of hundreds of millions of God's creatures, his faith is not affected, and doubt does not enter his heart for a moment. Do not expect the cynical curse of a man deeply shaken to fall from his pious lips. He knows who is our Father in heaven, and he is sure that this Father will deal with His creatures paternally. If he seems to ask heretical questions, it is only for the purpose of providing pious answers. His own faith remains steadfast as a rock. And anyone who suspects that the world is abandoned and orphaned is only a fool and an enemy of Christianity. The Methodist Reverend from Michigan understands the deep mystery of creation and of everything that happens—he knows that eternal secret for the sake of which Eliphaz once left his native Yemen to go to the land of Uz, there to pour the salt of his comfort on the wounds of his friend Job.

The secret is really a very simple one, and only those do not know it who *refuse* to know it. Two times two is four. When it rains the grass grows and sheep wax fat. Hail destroys the crops. If one doesn't wash one's face, pimples appear on it. And whenever you see suffering, look for sins, those pimples on the face of the world. Eliphaz of Yemen is the physicist of theology, its natural scientist and also its lawyer. Reward and punishment are laws of nature set up by God, ever since Genesis and lasting till . . . well, till the last. And when Job sits in dust and ashes, his entire body covered with sores, bereaved of sons and daughters, without a roof over his head, his wife unable to bear his suffering and advising him to curse God and die (2:9) and thus be freed of his pain, then Eliphaz of Yemen examines Job from his ash-covered head down to his dust-covered toes and "consoles" him with the famous verse: "Where is the innocent man who is lost, and where are the just who have been destroyed?" (4:7).

Job suffers, ergo he has sinned; and if he denies his sins, he commits the still greater sin of blasphemy, of slandering God that He punishes an innocent man, or of doubting the correctness of God's bookkeeping.

An old and discredited teaching? There seems to exist no such thing. Idols do not die so lightly, and absurd pieties have a way of coming back to life. Today we hear from Detroit the same "wisdom" with which a Semitic sheikh consoled his friend thousands of years ago. Neither is the Reverend Crane the only Eliphaz in the religious thinking of today, among Christians, among Moslems, and also among Jews. Scratch the average pietist—wherever people practice piety—and you will uncover a pre-Job man who conceives the Lord of the Universe in terms of a just king of flesh and blood.

The Eliphaz from Detroit is not the only one who tries to persuade us that Hitler is God's rod, by means of which He whips all of us for our sins. Only the other day I heard the same explanation from a prominent Jewish leader in pre-Hitler Germany. Both the Methodist Reverend and the one-time leader are pious, each in his own way. Both have read the prophets, and both consider it reasonable that just as the God of Vengeance once punished Israel by means of the hosts of Assyria, so He now punishes the entire world for its sins by means of Nazi tanks and planes. Both pietists fail to realize how their God has become a barbarian. In prehistoric times, God punished sinful mankind without the aid of people. The punishment came directly from heaven. Such was the Deluge, and such too was the destruction of Sodom and Gomorrah. But it would seem that the forces of nature at the command of their creator are not sufficient, and in historic times the Lord of the Universe has resorted to hired gangsters, Assyria or Babylonia, Mongols or Romans; and in our own day it is Hitler. With fiery justice God punishes the sinful at the hands of those who are a thousand-fold more sinful, and intentionally converts a great people to first-class wickedness so that they should settle His scores with second-class sinners. Seeing that God's law of love was not sufficiently well practiced in Poland and in Scandinavia, in France and in Belgium, He transformed scores of millions of Germans into sadistic murderers and sent them to cure the other nations of their lack of love. Were a mortal king to do anything of the sort, we would regard him as an insane tyrant. But when the Lord of the Universe does this, it is necessary to put on an expression of piety and to recite a benediction. Yes, "Blessed be the true judge. . . ."

It is the old need to justify the ways of God. He is just and His judgment is just, and I, John Doe, will demonstrate how and why He is just. Sometimes a Bedouin sheikh takes it upon himself to do the justifying, sometimes a prophet, and sometimes a western European philosopher like Leibniz, or a University Counsellor like [Friedrich] Paulsen. For two generations on end Paulsen taught his theodicy, which had all the charm of the one-time Catholic explanation of the existence of poverty on earth: poverty exists so that the rich should have an opportunity to give charity and thus assure themselves of the hereafter. Everything fits, that is, and everywhere we behold God's wisdom and justice and love. Had not God created the little worms so that the birds should be fed and sing the glory of the sunrise? Stupid little worms. They had not studied in medieval Catholic schools, and cannot understand their rôle in the universe. Yet the sense of it is so simple. Evil is the shadow, or the background, of good (any painter will readily explain the eternal laws of contrast on his canvases), and, as Paulsen once assured us, the judges and prosecutors in ancient Athens were the proper framework for Socrates—without their evil and idiotic death sentence the moral courage and the wisdom of Socrates would not have emerged so boldly.

And another German sophist (David Friedrich Strauss), equally determined to justify the ways of God from the standpoint of a more secular piety, even developed a purely logical (though not experimentally demonstrated) proof that the world was in perfect order and that whatever happened in it was equally in order. He reasoned as follows: "If the world were something which had better not have been created, this implies that such a thought about the world, which is part of the world, had also better not have been thought. But if the idea that the world is evil is an evil idea, it is proof that the world is not evil." Not in vain did Nietzsche use to argue that such demonstrated optimism was enough to drive any sensitive person to suicide. Nietzsche, I sometimes think, would have thought more highly of the blasphemous "philosophy" of the tailor of Jewish lore who regarded the Lord of the Universe as a poor craftsman. When the rabbi reproached the tailor for taking six weeks to make a pair of trousers for him, while it took God no more than six days to create the entire world, the tailor was not impressed. "Yes, Rabbi," he said, "but just see what a world created in a hurry looks like. On the other hand, regard these trousers which I have made for you. It's a pleasure to look at them. So how can you compare them with a cheap job such as God made?"

The rabbi in the folk anecdote was no doubt deeply shocked by the tailor's remarks. One more strict than he would have had the tailor excommunicated; one more sensitive would have mourned. All rationalist justifiers of the ways of God, from Eliphaz of Yemen to the Reverend Crane of Detroit, would no doubt have been ready to tear him apart for his vulgarity. And yet there is more sincerity and honesty in the spiteful humor of the dissatisfied tailor than in all the justification-of-God theories. Consequently, the tailor is also more profoundly religious.

In 1755—on All Saints' Day, of all days—Lisbon was destroyed by an earthquake. About thirty thousand persons perished that day, many of them while praying in churches. Jean Jacques Rousseau interpreted the catastrophe in Lisbon as God's punishment for man's sins. For, verily, why do people crowd in the slums of big cities when nature wished them to live in her maternal bosom? (This from Rousseau, a Swiss, who knew very well how many Swiss perished annually "in the bosom of nature" as a result of snow slides and other natural calamities.) It did not even occur to him that if earthquakes are a punishment for crowding in big cities, then it would have been only just on the part of the Almighty to destroy Paris and London, which were bigger cities than

Lisbon. The priests of Paris followed a similar interpretation, and thundered from their pulpits that the earthquake was Heaven's punishment on the people of Lisbon for their sins. This was a generation before the French Revolution, and the Parisian *paters* knew that no one would dare ask them why the Portuguese of Lisbon were more sinful than the French of Paris or the Spaniards of Madrid. But we should be grateful both to Rousseau and to the Catholic priests of Paris, for with their mental calisthenics on the subject of nature's and God's justice, they aroused Voltaire's sarcasm (*Candide*). Voltaire's hero, Professor Pangloss (a professor of the exact science of "metaphysicotheologicocosmonicology"), could also demonstrate that everything in the world is purposefully ordained to serve justice and welfare: Don't you realize that the nose was created to provide a platform for glasses; and had we no feet, we would not be able to put on stockings; nature contains rocks to provide building material for palaces; pigs were created to provide us with smoked pork. But Voltaire was no atheist; he merely disdained the piety of nonsense and self-delusion. He rejected rational theodicy. If we are to rely on our limited human reason, he would no doubt have shared Bertrand Russell's blasphemous statement that "in a world so full of contradictions I cannot find God; I can more easily assume that it was created by a mischievous Mephistopheles in an exceptionally devilish mood." Russell is a self-proclaimed atheist, while Voltaire was such an independent spirit that he had the courage to be heretical about heresy itself. He was a Deist, but he never undertook to analyze rationally the ways of the Almighty, and even less so to explain them to others.

It would be unnatural, and also the greatest disappointment of our time, were the events the world is now experiencing not to give rise to the need for religious self-searching. But in this search we must not be guided by Eliphaz of Yemen. Earthquakes and floods, wars and pogroms can and should give rise to moods of repentance and a sense of general sinfulness. But these have nothing to do with the concept of a cosmic police magistrate who doles out reward and punishment for good deeds and for transgressions. No one ever demonstrated the existence of such a God in the past, nor can it be done today. Were the rule of reward and punishment to be operative, Berlin and Munich, Rome and Naples would have to be first on the list for destruction (and even in these cities it would perhaps first be necessary to send angels to mark the doors of those to be spared, as was done in Egypt when the first-born died). And (I hope the universal God will not punish me for my chauvinist remark) on the basis of reward and punishment, Jews today should suffer less, rather than more, than all other peoples. For though I do not regard the Jews as perfect saints, I am fully convinced that they sinned less than others. Religious thought must, once and for all, renounce rationalist interpretation and justification of the ways of God. There exists no science of God, and no way of studying His ways. And whoever seeks a sign of God's justice and goodness in the events of the world, an empirical and demonstrable confirmation that He exists and that He is the bearer of the highest good, will never find it; and if one claims that he has found such confirmation, this is conscious or unconscious falsehood. If one is to be honest with oneself, one must either deny the existence of God or come to the conclusion reached by the hero of the Latin drama *Thyestes*: "I have always maintained and I will continue to maintain that the gods exist in heaven but that they take no interest in the doings of mankind. Were they to take an interest, then the good would flourish and the evil would suffer." This is the only possible conclusion if one is to retain a rationalist conception of the world. Religious man, on the other hand, must learn from Job to believe without understanding, to trust without explanations.

Whence then comes wisdom? And where is the place of understanding? Seeing it is hidden from the eyes of all living, and kept close from the fowls of the air.
God understands the way thereof, and He knows the place thereof.

(28:20, 21, 23)

Job was comforted when he sat in dust and ashes. Who comforted him? Not his friends with their theological scholarship, not even God Himself. God's voice from the storm explained nothing to Job—it merely expanded the area of his not knowing and not understanding; it opened before him unlimited horizons of the inconceivable and impenetrable, and deepened the mystery of existence. Job was consoled by the realization that his suffering was a drop in the endless mystery of being and living.

Whoever seeks proofs will never find them. Whoever cannot join the Psalmist in declaring, "Even though I go through the valley of the shadow of death, I will fear no evil, for Thou art with me" (Ps. 23:4), has not reached the height of the courage of resignation which is faith. Rationally, Ivan Karamazoff will always be right: "There is no justification for the tear of even a single suffering child." Believing man must cease to look for confirmations which he can grasp with his reason and touch with his hands. Those who test God and wait for a sign from Him still believe in a monotheist idol, which they will reject sooner or later. The more profoundly religious man always considered such testing as the viper of disbelief, dark Satan trying to seduce him. In the New Testament we read how Satan tempted Jesus. If you are the son of God, he said to him, then command these stones to become transformed into loaves of bread. . . . If you are the son of God, then leap from this peak, for is it not said in the Scriptures that He will command His angels to guard you in all your ways . . . they will carry you in their arms lest your foot stumble on a rock. . . . But the son of God is sure of his sonhood and needs no proof of God's fatherhood. He answers contemptuously: Go away, Seducer (Matt. 4:3–10). One who lacks dumb faith in God even when he hangs on a Roman cross without being conscious of any sin, one who cannot praise God even as he sits in dust and ashes and has no explanation for his suffering, nor any *sign* from above—such a person is, in the final analysis, not a believer.

The true believer practices the most heroic defiance in the world. His logic may be most strange and paradoxical, as in the case of Job, who declared, "Even though He slay me will I believe in Him" (13:15). Those who regard such an attitude as absurd cannot be proved wrong, but people who reason thus have nothing to do with religion.

V

The Ways of God Are a Mystery

RUDOLF OTTO :

THE ELEMENT OF THE MYSTERIOUS

Rudolf Otto (1869–1937), German Protestant theologian and historian of religion, first probed into the rational aspect of religious concepts (*Naturalistische und religiöse Weltansicht* [1904]; English translation: *Naturalism and Religion* [London, 1907]) before he attempted to analyze the non-rational, supra-rational elements in faith. The presentation of this analysis, *Das Heilige* (1917; English version: *The Idea of the Holy* [Oxford, 1923]), has since become a classic. Otto proposes that all language tends to stress the conceptual, rational attributes of God, who Himself is not, nor indeed can be, comprehended in them. Otto employs the terms holy, or sacred, or numinous (from the Latin *numen*) to designate "this unnamed Something" that lives at the real core of religion. The religious experience transcends the ethical, moral, sphere, and focuses on the awful, mysterious, the *tremendum*, the majestic, the wholly other. Such experience of the deity pervades religions, from the primitive to the highly developed and sophisticated. A choice example of what Otto has in mind is Job 38–41. The excerpt that follows is taken from *The Idea of the Holy*, chapter VIII ("The Numinous in the Old Testament").

In the thirty-eighth chapter of Job we have the element of the mysterious displayed in rare purity and completeness, and this chapter may well rank among the most remarkable in the history of religion. Job has been reasoning with his friends against Elohim

[God], and—as far as concerns them—he has been obviously in the right. They are compelled to be dumb before him. And then Elohim Himself appears to conduct His own defense in person. And He conducts it to such effect that Job avows himself to be overpowered —truly and rightly overpowered—not merely silenced by superior strength. Then he confesses: "Therefore I abhor myself and repent in dust and ashes" (42:6). That is an admission of inward convincement and conviction, not of impotent collapse and submission to merely superior power. Nor is there here at all the frame of mind to which St. Paul now and then gives utterance; e.g., "Shall the thing formed say to Him that formed it, Why hast Thou made me thus? Hath not the potter power over the clay, of the same lump to make one vessel unto honor, and another unto dishonor?" (Rom. 9:20). To interpret the passage in Job thus would be a misunderstanding of it. This chapter does not proclaim, as Paul does, the renunciation of, the realization of the impossibility of, a "theodicy"; rather, it aims at putting forward a real theodicy of its own, and a better one than that of Job's friends—a theodicy able to convince even a Job, and not only to convince him, but utterly to still every inward doubt that assailed his soul. For latent in the weird experience that Job underwent in the revelation of Elohim is at once an inward relaxing of his soul's anguish and an appeasement, an appeasement that would alone and in itself perfectly suffice as the solution of the problem of the book of Job, even without Job's rehabilitation in chapter 42, which is merely a later addition to the real narrative. But what is this strange "moment" of experience that operates at once as a vindication of God to Job and a reconciliation of Job to God?

In the words put into the mouth of Elohim, nearly every note is sounded that the situation may prepare one to expect a priori: the summons to Job, and the demonstration of God's overwhelming power, His sublimity and greatness, and His surpassing wisdom. This last would yield forthwith a plausible and rational solution of the whole problem, if only the argument were here completed with some such sentences as: "My ways are higher than your ways; in my deeds and my actions I have ends that you understand not"; viz., the testing or purification of the godly man, or ends that concern the whole universe as such, into which the single man must fit himself with all his sufferings.

If you start from rational ideas and concepts, you absolutely thirst for such a conclusion to the discourse. But nothing of the kind follows; nor does the chapter intend at all to suggest such teleological reflections or solutions. In the last resort it relies on something quite different from anything that can be exhaustively rendered in rational concepts, namely, on the sheer absolute wondrousness that transcends thought, on the *mysterium*, presented in its pure, non-rational form. All the glorious examples from nature speak very plainly in this sense. The eagle, that "dwelleth and abideth on the rock, upon the crag of the rock, and the strong place," whose "eyes behold afar off" her prey, and whose "young ones also suck up blood, and where the slain are, there is she" (39:26–30)—this eagle is in truth no evidence for the teleological wisdom that "prepares all cunningly and well," but is rather the creature of strangeness and marvel, in whom the wondrousness of its creator becomes apparent. And the same is true of the ostrich with its inexplicable instincts. The ostrich is indeed, as here depicted, and "rationally" considered, a crucial difficulty rather than an evidence of wisdom, and it affords singularly little help if we are seeking purpose in nature: "For she leaveth her eggs in the earth, and warmeth them in the dust, and forgetteth that the foot may crush them or that the wild beast may break them. She is hardened against her young ones, as though they were not hers; her labor is in vain without fear; because God hath deprived her of wisdom, neither hath He imparted to her understanding" (39:14–17).

It is the same with the wild ass (39:5) and the wild ox (39:9). These are beasts whose complete "dysteleology" or negation of purposiveness is truly magnificently depicted; but, nevertheless, with their mysterious instincts and the riddle of their generation, this very negation of purpose becomes a thing of baffling significance, as in the case of the wild goat (39:1) and the hind. The "wisdom" of the inward parts (38:36), and the "knowledge" of dayspring, winds, and clouds, with the mysterious ways in which they come and go, arise and vanish, shift and veer and re-form; and the wonderful Pleiades aloft in heaven, with Orion and "Arcturus and his sons"—these serve but to emphasize the same lesson. It is conjectured that the descriptions of the hippopotamus (*behemoth*) and crocodile (*leviathan*) (in 40:15 ff.) are a later interpolation. This may well be the fact; but, if so, it must be admitted that the interpolator has felt the point of the entire section extraordinarily well. He only brings to its grossest expression the thought intended by all the other examples of animals; they gave portents only, he gives us "monsters"—but "the monstrous" is just the "mysterious" in a gross form. Assuredly these beasts would be the most unfortunate examples that one could hit upon if searching for evidences of the purposefulness of the divine "wisdom." But they, no less than all the previous examples and the whole context, tenor, and sense of the entire passage, do express in masterly fashion the downright stupendousness, the wellnigh demonic and wholly incomprehensible character of the eternal creative power; how, incalculable and "wholly other," it mocks at all conceiving but can yet stir the mind to its depths, fascinate and overbrim the heart. What is meant is the mysterium not as mysterious simply, but at the same time also as "fascinating" and "august"; and here, too, these latter meanings live, not in any explicit concepts, but in the tone, the enthusiasm, in the very rhythm of the entire exposition. And here is indeed the point of the whole passage, comprising alike the theodicy and the appeasement and calming of Job's soul. The mysterium, simply as such, would merely (as discussed above) be a part of the "absolute inconceivability" of the *numen*, and that, though it might strike Job utterly dumb, could not convince him inwardly. That of which we are conscious is rather an intrinsic value in the incomprehensible—a value inexpressible, positive, and "fascinating." This is incommensurable with thoughts of rational human teleology and is not assimilated to them: it remains in all its mystery. But it is as it becomes felt in consciousness that Elohim is justified and at the same time Job's soul brought to peace.

G. K. CHESTERTON :

MAN IS MOST COMFORTED BY PARADOXES

Gilbert Keith Chesterton (1874–1936) is known for his poems, his many novels, literary and social criticism, and essays in the cause of Roman Catholicism (to which he converted in 1922). Keenly and with a sharp wit he fought smugness, egotism, and the self-sufficiency of his time, and both

optimism and pessimism. It has been said of him that he was "essentially a
poet who has gotten loose in the realm of theology." The book of Job was
one of the young Chesterton's favorite readings, and its impact remained
strong throughout his life. The essay on Job that follows (slightly abridged)
is an introduction to *The Book of Job* (London, 1916).

The book of Job is among the other Old Testament books both
a philosophical riddle and a historical riddle. It is the philosophical
riddle that concerns us in such an introduction as this; so we may
dismiss first the few words of general explanation or warning which
should be said about the historical aspect. Controversy has long
raged about which parts of this epic belong to its original scheme
and which are interpolations of considerably later date. The doctors disagree, as it is the business of doctors to do; but upon the
whole the trend of investigation has always been in the direction
of maintaining that the parts interpolated, if any, were the prose
prologue and epilogue, and possibly the speech of the young man
who comes in with an apology at the end. I do not profess to be
competent to decide such questions.

But whatever decision the reader may come to concerning
them, there is a general truth to be remembered in this connection.
When you deal with any ancient artistic creation, do not suppose
that it is anything against it that it grew gradually. The book of
Job may have grown gradually just as Westminster Abbey grew
gradually. But the people who made the old folk poetry, like the
people who made Westminster Abbey, did not attach that importance to the actual date and the actual author, that importance
which is entirely the creation of the almost insane individualism of
modern times. We may put aside the case of Job, as one complicated with religious difficulties, and take any other, say the case of
the *Iliad*. Many people have maintained the characteristic formula
of modern skepticism, that Homer was not written by Homer, but
by another person of the same name. Just in the same way many
have maintained that Moses was not Moses but another person
called Moses. But the thing really to be remembered in the matter
of the *Iliad* is that if other people did interpolate the passages,
the thing did not create the same sense of shock as would be created by such proceedings in these individualistic times. The creation
of the tribal epic was to some extent regarded as a tribal work, like

the building of the tribal temple. Believe then, if you will, that the prologue of Job and the epilogue and the speech of Elihu are things inserted after the original work was composed. But do not suppose that such insertions have that obvious and spurious character which would belong to any insertions in a modern, individualistic book. [. . .]

Without going into questions of unity as understood by the scholars, we may say of the scholarly riddle that the book has unity in the sense that all great traditional creations have unity; in the sense that Canterbury Cathedral has unity. And the same is broadly true of what I have called the philosophical riddle. There is a real sense in which the book of Job stands apart from most of the books included in the canon of the Old Testament. But here again those are wrong who insist on the entire absence of unity. Those are wrong who maintain that the Old Testament is a mere loose library; that it has no consistency or aim. Whether the result was achieved by some supernal spiritual truth, or by a steady national tradition, or merely by an ingenious selection in aftertimes, the books of the Old Testament have a quite perceptible unity. [. . .]

The central idea of the great part of the Old Testament may be called the idea of the loneliness of God. God is not the only chief character of the Old Testament; God is properly the only character in the Old Testament. Compared with His clearness of purpose, all the other wills are heavy and automatic, like those of animals; compared with His actuality, all the sons of flesh are shadows. Again and again the note is struck, "With whom hath He taken counsel?" (Isa. 40:14). "I have trodden the winepress alone, and of the peoples there was no man with me" (Isa. 63:3). All the patriarchs and prophets are merely His tools or weapons; for the Lord is a man of war. He uses Joshua like an axe or Moses like a measuring rod. For Him, Samson is only a sword and Isaiah a trumpet. The saints of Christianity are supposed to be like God, to be, as it were, little statuettes of Him. The Old Testament hero is no more supposed to be of the same nature as God than a saw or a hammer is supposed to be of the same shape as the carpenter. This is the main key and characteristic of the Hebrew scriptures as a whole. There are, indeed, in those scriptures innumerable instances of the sort of rugged humor, keen emotion, and powerful individuality which is never wanting in great primitive prose and poetry.

Nevertheless the main characteristic remains: the sense not merely that God is stronger than man, not merely that God is more secret than man, but that He means more, that He knows better what He is doing, that compared with Him we have something of the vagueness, the unreason, and the vagrancy of the beasts that perish. "It is He that sitteth above the earth, and the inhabitants thereof are as grasshoppers" (Isa. 40:22). We might almost put it thus. The book is so intent upon asserting the personality of God that it almost asserts the impersonality of man. Unless this gigantic cosmic brain has conceived a thing, that thing is insecure and void; man has not enough tenacity to ensure its continuance. "Except the Lord build the house, they labor in vain that build it. Except the Lord keep the city, the watchman waketh but in vain" (Ps. 127:1).

Everywhere else, then, the Old Testament positively rejoices in the obliteration of man in comparison with the divine purpose. The book of Job stands definitely alone because the book of Job definitely asks, "But what is the purpose of God? Is it worth the sacrifice even of our miserable humanity? Of course, it is easy enough to wipe out our own paltry wills for the sake of a will that is grander and kinder. But is it grander and kinder? Let God use His tools; let God break His tools. But what is He doing, and what are they being broken for?" It is because of this question that we have to attack as a philosophical riddle the riddle of the book of Job.

The present importance of the book of Job cannot be expressed adequately even by saying that it is the most interesting of ancient books. We may almost say of the book of Job that it is the most interesting of modern books. In truth, of course, neither of the two phrases covers the matter, because fundamental human religion and fundamental human irreligion are both at once old and new; philosophy is either eternal or it is not philosophy. The modern habit of saying "This is my opinion, but I may be wrong" is entirely irrational. If I say that it may be wrong, I say that is not my opinion. The modern habit of saying "Every man has a different philosophy; this is my philosophy and it suits me"—the habit of saying this is mere weak-mindedness. A cosmic philosophy is not constructed to fit a man; a cosmic philosophy is constructed to fit a cosmos. A man can no more possess a private religion than he can possess a private sun and moon.

The first of the intellectual beauties of the book of Job is that it is all concerned with this desire to know the actuality; the desire to know what is, and not merely what seems. If moderns were writing the book, we should probably find that Job and his comforters got on quite well together by the simple operation of referring their differences to what is called the temperament, saying that the comforters were by nature "optimists" and Job by nature a "pessimist." And they would be quite comfortable, as people can often be, for some time at least, by agreeing to say what is obviously untrue. For if the word "pessimist" means anything at all, then emphatically Job is not a pessimist. His case alone is sufficient to refute the modern absurdity of referring everything to physical temperament. Job does not in any sense look at life in a gloomy way. If wishing to be happy and being quite ready to be happy constitute an optimist, Job is an optimist. He is a perplexed optimist; he is an exasperated optimist; he is an outraged and insulted optimist. He wishes the universe to justify itself, not because he wishes it to be caught out, but because he really wishes it to be justified. He demands an explanation from God, but he does not do it at all in the spirit in which [John] Hampden might demand an explanation from Charles I. He does it in the spirit in which a wife might demand an explanation from her husband whom she really respected. He remonstrates with his Maker because he is proud of his Maker. He even speaks of the Almighty as his enemy, but he never doubts, at the back of his mind, that his enemy has some kind of a case which he does not understand. In a fine and famous blasphemy he says, "Oh, that mine adversary had written a book!" (31:35). It never really occurs to him that it could possibly be a bad book. He is anxious to be convinced, that is, he thinks that God could convince him. In short, we may say again that if the word optimist means anything (which I doubt), Job is an optimist. He shakes the pillars of the world and strikes insanely at the heavens; he lashes the stars, but it is not to silence them; it is to make them speak.

In the same way we may speak of the official optimists, the comforters of Job. Again, if the word pessimist means anything (which I doubt), the comforters of Job may be called pessimists rather than optimists. All that they really believe is not that God is good but that God is so strong that it is much more judicious to call Him good. It would be the exaggeration of censure to call them evolutionists; but they have something of the vital error of the evolutionary optimist. They will keep on saying that everything in the universe fits into everything else: as if there were anything comforting about a number of nasty things all fitting into each other. We shall see later how God in the great climax of the poem turns this particular argument altogether upside down.

When, at the end of the poem, God enters (somewhat abruptly), is struck the sudden and splendid note which makes the thing as great as it is. All the human beings through the story, and Job especially, have been asking questions of God. A more trivial poet would have made God enter in some sense or other in order to answer the questions. By a touch truly to be called inspired, when God enters, it is to ask a number more questions on His own account. In this drama of skepticism God Himself takes up the rôle of skeptic. He does what all the great voices defending religion have always done. He does, for instance, what Socrates did. He turns rationalism against itself. He seems to say that if it comes to asking questions, He can ask some questions which will fling down and flatten out all conceivable human questioners. The poet by an exquisite intuition has made God ironically accept a kind of controversial equality with His accusers. He is willing to regard it as if it were a fair intellectual duel: "Gird up now thy loins like a man; for I will demand of thee, and answer thou me" (38:3). The everlasting adopts an enormous and sardonic humility. He is quite willing to be prosecuted. He only asks for the right which every prosecuted person possesses; He asks to be allowed to cross-examine the witness for the prosecution. And He carries yet further the correctness of the legal parallel. For the first question, essentially speaking, which He asks of Job is the question that any criminal accused by Job would be most entitled to ask. He asks Job who he is. And Job, being a man of candid intellect, takes a little time to consider, and comes to the conclusion that he does not know.

This is the first great fact to notice about the speech of God, which is the culmination of the inquiry. It represents all human skeptics routed by a higher skepticism. It is this method, used sometimes by supreme and sometimes by mediocre minds, that has ever since been the logical weapon of the true mystic. Socrates, as I have said, used it when he showed that if you only allowed him enough sophistry he could destroy all the sophists. Jesus Christ used it when he reminded the Sadducees, who could not imagine the nature of marriage in heaven, that if it came to that they had not really imagined the nature of marriage at all. In the break up of Christian theology in the eighteenth century, [Joseph] Butler used it, when he pointed out that rationalistic arguments could be used as much against vague religion as against doctrinal religion, as much against rationalist ethics as against Christian ethics. It is the root and reason of the fact that men who have religious faith have also philosophic doubt. These are the small streams of the delta; the book of Job is the first great cataract that creates the river. In dealing with the arrogant asserter of doubt, it is not the right method to tell him to stop doubting. It is rather the right method to tell him to go on doubting, to doubt a little more, to doubt every day newer and wilder things in the universe, until at last, by some strange enlightenment, he may begin to doubt himself.

This, I say, is the first fact touching the speech; the fine inspiration by which God comes in at the end, not to answer riddles, but to propound them. The other great fact which, taken together with this one, makes the whole work religious instead of merely philosophical is that other great surprise which makes Job suddenly satisfied with the mere presentation of something impenetrable. Verbally speaking the enigmas of Jehovah seem darker and more desolate than the enigmas of Job; yet Job was comfortless before the speech of Jehovah and is comforted after it. He has been told nothing, but he feels the terrible and tingling atmosphere of something which is too good to be told. The refusal of God to explain His design is itself a burning hint of His design. The riddles of God are more satisfying than the solutions of man.

Thirdly, of course, it is one of the splendid strokes that God rebukes alike the man who accused and the men who defended Him; that He knocks down pessimists and optimists with the same hammer. And it is in connection with the mechanical and supercilious comforters of Job that there occurs the still deeper and finer inversion of which I have spoken. The mechanical optimist endeavors to justify the universe avowedly upon the ground that it is a rational and consecutive pattern. He points out that the fine thing about the world is that it can all be explained. That is the one point, if I may put it so, on which God, in return, is explicit to the point of violence. God says, in effect, that if there is one fine thing

about the world, as far as men are concerned, it is that it cannot be
explained. He insists on the inexplicableness of everything; "Hath
the rain a father? . . . Out of whose womb came the ice?" (38:28 f.).
He goes farther, and insists on the positive and palpable unreason of
things; "Hast thou sent the rain upon the desert where no man is,
and upon the wilderness wherein there is no man?" (38:26). God
will make man see things, if it is only against the black background
of nonentity. God will make Job see a startling universe if He can
only do it by making Job see an idiotic universe. To startle man,
God becomes for an instant a blasphemer; one might almost say
that God becomes for an instant an atheist. He unrolls before Job
a long panorama of created things, the horse, the eagle, the raven,
the wild ass, the peacock, the ostrich, the crocodile. He so describes
each of them that it sounds like a monster walking in the sun. The
whole is a sort of psalm or rhapsody of the sense of wonder. The
maker of all things is astonished at the things He has Himself
made.

This we may call the third point. Job puts forward a note of
interrogation; God answers with a note of exclamation. Instead of
proving to Job that it is an explicable world, He insists that it is
a much stranger world than Job ever thought it was. Lastly, the
poet has achieved in this speech, with that unconscious artistic
accuracy found in so many of the simpler epics, another and much
more delicate thing. Without once relaxing the rigid impenetrability
of Jehovah in His deliberate declaration, he has contrived to let fall
here and there in the metaphors, in the parenthetical imagery, sudden and splendid suggestions that the secret of God is a bright
and not a sad one—semi-accidental suggestions, like light seen for
an instant through the cracks of a closed door.

It would be difficult to praise too highly, in a purely poetical
sense, the instinctive exactitude and ease with which these more
optimistic insinuations are let fall in other connections, as if the
Almighty Himself were scarcely aware that He was letting them
out. For instance, there is that famous passage where Jehovah, with
devastating sarcasm, asks Job where he was when the foundations
of the world were laid, and then (as if merely fixing a date) mentions the time when the sons of God shouted for joy (38:4-7). One
cannot help feeling, even upon this meager information, that they
must have had something to shout about. Or again, when God is

speaking of snow and hail in the mere catalogue of the physical cosmos, He speaks of them as a treasury that He has laid up against the day of battle—a hint of some huge Armageddon in which evil shall be at last overthrown.

Nothing could be better, artistically speaking, than this optimism breaking through agnosticism like fiery gold round the edges of a black cloud. Those who look superficially at the barbaric origin of the epic may think it fanciful to read so much artistic significance into its casual similes or accidental phrases. But no one who is well acquainted with great examples of semi-barbaric poetry, as in *The Song of Roland* or the old ballads, will fall into this mistake. No one who knows what primitive poetry is can fail to realize that while its conscious form is simple some of its finer effects are subtle. The *Iliad* contrives to express the idea that Hector and Sarpedon have a certain tone or tint of sad and chivalrous resignation, not bitter enough to be called pessimism and not jovial enough to be called optimism; Homer could never have said this in elaborate words. But somehow he contrives to say it in simple words. *The Song of Roland* contrives to express the idea that Christianity imposes upon its heroes a paradox: a paradox of great humility in the matter of their sins combined with great ferocity in the matter of their ideas. Of course *The Song of Roland* could not say this; but it conveys this. In the same way, the book of Job must be credited with many subtle effects which were in the author's soul without being, perhaps, in the author's mind. And of these by far the most important remains even yet to be stated.

I do not know, and I doubt whether even scholars know, if the book of Job had a great effect or had any effect upon the after development of Jewish thought. But if it did have any effect it may have saved them from an enormous collapse and decay. Here in this book the question is really asked whether God invariably punishes vice with terrestrial punishment and rewards virtue with terrestrial prosperity. If the Jews had answered that question wrongly they might have lost all their after influence in human history. They might have sunk even down to the level of modern well-educated society. For when once people have begun to believe that prosperity is the reward of virtue, their next calamity is obvious. If prosperity is regarded as the reward of virtue it will be regarded as the symptom of virtue. Men will leave off the heavy task of making good men successful. They will adopt the easier task of making out successful men good. This, which has happened throughout modern commerce and journalism, is the ultimate Nemesis of the wicked optimism of the comforters of Job. If the Jews could be saved from it, the book of Job saved them.

The book of Job is chiefly remarkable, as I have insisted throughout, for the fact that it does not end in a way that is conventionally satisfactory. Job is not told that his misfortunes were due to his sins or a part of any plan for his improvement. But in the prologue we see Job tormented not because he was the worst of men, but because he was the best. It is the lesson of the whole work that man is most comforted by paradoxes. Here is the very darkest and strangest of the paradoxes; and it is by all human testimony the most reassuring. I need not suggest what a high and strange history awaited this paradox of the best man in the worst fortune. I need not say that in the freest and most philosophical sense there is one Old Testament figure who is truly a type; or say what is prefigured in the wounds of Job.

WALTER KAUFMANN : AN UNCANNY WORLD

In his *Critique of Religion and Philosophy* (1958), the philosopher Walter Kaufmann (born 1921) noted that "a great deal of the book could have been presented in the form of a commentary on the book of Job" (section 79). Indeed, his is one of the boldest and most incisive and sensitive reflections on the Joban problem. His analysis stresses Job's protest against divine injustice and his denial of God's goodness—issues carefully avoided by theological moralists. In his *The Faith of a Heretic* (New York, 1961), Kaufmann devotes sections 41 and 42 to Job. The three pseudo-solutions mentioned in the first paragraph refer to: (1) Satan, whom "some of the lesser minds invoked to solve the problem of suffering"; (2) immortality of the soul or an eventual resurrection of the dead; (3) the assertion—in flat defiance of experience— that "everybody gets precisely what he deserves."

The one book of the Old Testament that is given over to an extended consideration of the problem of suffering, the book of

Job, rejects the first of these pseudo-solutions out of hand, refuses
to take up the second, and repudiates the third emphatically.

The frame story, unlike the core of the book, is in prose. Here
Satan appears, and the few words put into his mouth show a master's touch. As Heymann Steinthal, one of the founders of *Völker-
psychologie,* remarked in the first essay of *Zu Bibel und Religions-
philosophie* (1890): probably nowhere in world literature before
Goethe's Mephistopheles, who was deliberately modeled in the
image of the prologue to Job, can we find words that are equally
"Mephistophelic." After Satan has remarked that he has been
walking up and down on the earth, the Lord asks him whether
he has noticed "my servant Job, that there is none like him in the
earth, a blameless and upright man who fears God and turns away
from evil. Then Satan answered the Lord: Does Job fear God for
nothing? Have You not put a hedge around him and his house and
all that he has, on every side? You have blessed the work of his
hands, and his possessions have increased in the land. But put
forth Your hand now and touch all that he has, and he will curse
You to Your face. And the Lord said to Satan: Behold, all that he
has is in your power; only on him do not put forth your hand"
(1:8–12).

Job loses everything but does not curse God. The Lord asks
Satan what he thinks of Job now, and Satan replies: "Skin for skin.
All that a man has he will give for his life. But put forth Your
hand now and touch his bone and his flesh, and he will curse You
to Your face. And the Lord said to Satan: Behold, he is in your
power, only spare his life" (2:4 ff.). Now Job is afflicted "with
loathsome sores from the sole of his foot to the crown of his head"
(2:7); he sits down in ashes, and three friends come to comfort
him. At first they cannot recognize him, then they sit on the ground
with him seven days and nights, "and no one spoke a word, for
they saw that his suffering was very great. After this Job opened
his mouth and cursed the day of his birth" (2:13–3:1)—in magnificent poetry.

From this point, at the beginning of the third chapter, through
the first half of the last chapter (42), great poetic speeches alternate. First, Job's alternate with those of his three friends, several
times over; then a fourth friend joins in—a later interpolation, according to some scholars—and then God Himself delivers His

reply to Job, speaking out of the whirlwind. In the last half of the last chapter, the prose narrative is resumed.

Throughout, it does not occur to anybody even to try to solve the problem of suffering by pointing to Satan. God's omnipotence is never questioned, and all concerned apparently realize that no reference to Satan can explain Job's suffering without in effect denying either God's justice or His omnipotence. Job's friends refuse to question either of these. All four of them take the same stand: it being certain that God is both almighty and just, the only conclusion possible is that Job deserves his suffering. Since he is suffering, he must have sinned.

Job refuses to accept their reasoning. He never questions either God's existence or His omnipotence; but God's justice, mercy, and goodness he not only questions but denies outright. This is a highly unusual approach to the problem: almost all Christian theologians and philosophers who have dealt with the problem of suffering have clung to God's moral perfection while in effect, though hardly ever admittedly, they have denied His omnipotence.

In the Old Testament there is no exact equivalent of "omnipotence," though *shaddai* is generally translated as Almighty. It is a numinous term which stresses mysterious and unbounded power, not a cerebral concept. The play on words in Isaiah 13:6 and Joel 1:15 shows that in biblical times the word was associated with *shod*, devastation. Nowhere else in the Bible does *shaddai* appear so constantly as the name of God as in the book of Job. But the claim that God's omnipotence is not questioned in the book does not rest merely on the use of a word. Rather, the point is that it does not occur to anybody that God might simply be unable to prevent Job's suffering.

Job's denial of God's goodness takes many forms. In chapter 3, in powerful verse, he curses the day when he was born; then the first friend replies, and Job's response surpasses even his previous speech, reaching a climax in chapter 7: "I will not restrain my mouth; I will speak in the anguish of my spirit; I will complain in the bitterness of my soul. . . . When I say, 'My bed will comfort me, my couch will ease my complaint,' then Thou dost scare me with dreams and terrify me with visions, so that I would choose strangling and death rather than my bones. I loathe my life; I would not live for ever. . . . If I sin, what do I do to Thee, watcher of men? Why hast Thou made me Thy mark? . . . Why dost Thou not pardon my transgression and take away my iniquity?" (7:11–21). Job does not say that he has done evil, but insists that, even if he had, this would not justify God's treatment of him. If a child has done wrong, a loving father has no excuse for tormenting him cruelly without respite. Centuries in advance, Job replies to generations of philosophers and theologians.

The second friend speaks, and Job in his reply says: "I am blameless; I regard not myself; I loathe my life. It is all one; therefore I say, He destroys both the blameless and the wicked. When disaster brings sudden death, He mocks at the calamity of the innocent. The earth is given into the hand of the wicked; He covers the faces of its judges—if it is not He, who then is it?" (9:21–24). Job, like the early prophets, has no patience with the utopian religion that divorces God from reality and uses the name of God as a synonym for moral perfection. He echoes Amos' "Does evil befall a city, and the Lord has not done it?" (Amos 3:6). The innocent suffer and the wicked flourish, and Job insists that God is responsible: "If it is not He, who then is it?"

To be sure, occasionally one may detect something of poetic justice in history, but Job asks (21:17): "How often is it?" And two verses later: "You say, 'God stores up their iniquity for their sons.' . . . What do they care for their houses after them?"

Later, Job gives an account of his righteousness: "I was eyes to the blind, and feet to the lame" (29:15); and two chapters later he offers a famous "negative confession" in which he lists the things he did not do. And in both cases we may well marvel at the exalted standards that find expression here. To take offense at Job's conviction of his own righteousness and to suppose that for that he after all deserved his afflictions is surely to miss the point of the book and to side with his friends: Job is not presented to us as a historic figure but as a character who is, as we are assured at the outset in the words of the Lord, "blameless"; and the Lord adds that "there is none like him on the earth" (1:8). Nor does the Lord, when He finally speaks from the whirlwind, accuse Job of any sin. The point is clearly that, even if there were a human being who had never done any wrong at all and who was "eyes to the blind and feet to the lame," there would not be any reason at all to suppose that he would be less likely than others to come down with some dreadful disease or to suffer unspeakable torments.

Indeed, that is the point of the Lord's great speech. Far from insisting that there is some hidden justice in the world after all, or from claiming that everything is really rational if only we look at it intelligently, God goes out of His way to point out how utterly weird ever so many things are. He says in effect: the problem of suffering is no isolated problem; it fits a pattern, the world is not so rational as Job's comforters suppose; it is uncanny. God does not claim to be good, and Job in his final reply does not change his mind on this point: he reaffirms that God can do all things. And then the Lord says in the prose conclusion that Job's friends have aroused His anger, "for you have not spoken of me what is right, as my servant Job has; . . . and my servant Job shall pray for you, for I will accept his prayer not to deal with you according to your folly; for you have not spoken of me what is right as my servant Job has" (42:7 f.).

The last words of the book seem offensive at first. "The Lord restored the fortunes of Job when he had prayed for his friends; and the Lord gave Job twice as much as he had before" (42:10). Also, Job again had seven sons and three daughters, even as he had had seven sons and three daughters at the beginning, before all ten had been killed early in the book. But, after all, the book does not say or imply that this vindicates God's mercy or justice, or that Job felt that his second set of ten children was fair compensation for the first. There is no need to charge this strange conclusion either to an insensitive editor who had missed the point of all that went before or to an old folk tale. Probably it did come from a folk tale, but the author knew what he was doing in retaining this conclusion. It underlines the weirdness of the ways of the world, which is nothing less than grotesque.

Nietzsche remarked in *The Dawn* how Christian scholars and preachers had spread "the art of reading badly." The usual treatment of the book of Job furnishes a fine example of that. Again and again one reads and hears that in the end Job is given twice as many children as he had in the beginning, and his forthright denial of the justice of God, which the Lord Himself accepts as "right" in the end, is simply ignored. Worst of all, it is accepted as a commonplace that the ethic of the Old Testament is an ethic of prudence and rewards, as if the point were that it pays to be good. Clearly, it is the whole point of the book of Job that this is not so, but Protestant scholars and preachers have often claimed that Job's friends represent the ethic of the Old Testament. This is rather like claiming that the sinners in Dante's *Inferno* represent the Christian virtues. If it should be countered that large numbers of Jews in Old Testament times were probably like the friends of Job rather than like Job himself or the author of the book, it is equally probable that most Christians in the age of faith resembled the sinners in Dante's hell rather than the poet or the saints in his heaven.

Still, it might be objected that the authors of most of the other books of the Old Testament are closer to Job's friends than to the author of the book of Job. But this is simply not so. This common claim involves a thorough misunderstanding of the ethic of the Old Testament. Not even the moralistic historians who considered it essential to grade the behavior of the kings of Israel and Judah inferred, like the friends of Job, that success proved virtue; failure, sin. Omri, one of the most powerful kings, who would certainly have been glorified in the annals of any other nation, and who died in splendor and peace, was said to have done "more evil than all who were before him" (I Kings 16); but of Josiah, who suffered a disastrous defeat at Megiddo and was slain in battle, it was said that "he did what was right in the eyes of the Lord, and walked in all the way of David" (II Kings 22).

To be sure, we encounter perennial appeals to the consequences of moral and immoral conduct, but in the overwhelming majority of cases it is the nation that stands to profit or to suffer, not the individual. The dominant ethic of the Old Testament does not invite comparison with the ethic of the Roman Church but rather with the ethic of ancient republican Rome: the individual is expected to subordinate his own pleasure and profit to the interests of the commonwealth; it is presupposed that ethical conduct involves such unselfishness. Even as the ancient Roman did his stint and risked his life when called upon, and then, if he survived, returned to the anonymity of private life without even expecting fame, the ancient Hebrew, too, is called upon to do what will benefit the people as a whole, if only in the long run, and to refrain from doing what will hurt the people, even if only after his death.

In this respect, too, Jesus does *not* stand in the prophetic tradition: in the Gospels this ancient appeal to selflessness is no longer encountered; it is presupposed that every soul is concerned with how *he* may enter the kingdom of heaven, and prudence has come to mean enlightened selfishness.

This is not the way the New Testament is usually read; and such an important matter cannot be settled in passing.

Between the age of the prophets and the time of Jesus, the whole climate of thought had changed about as much as it had in Rome between the time of the first Brutus and the age of Caesar Augustus. Concern with oneself and the other world was common indeed, though by no means universal—and Jesus and the evangelists were not as independent of their age as Moses and some of the prophets had been of theirs. The author of the book of Job had been more independent, too.

The author of Job had been at one with the prophetic ethic in his radical opposition to the vulgar ethic of his day, and of all times, and in his radical opposition to syncretism. In an age in which the ancient sense of solidarity was crumbling and the individual experienced his sufferings in that utter solitude which is now once again the mark of modernity, the author of Job refused all the comforts that go with the assurance that God is perfectly merciful and just—the promises that being moral pays either in this life or the next—and, with a radicalism that has parallels in Amos and the other prophets of his type, but scarcely in the Gospels, claimed that God was neither just nor the embodiment of mercy or perfection.

Those who believe in God because their experience of life and the facts of nature prove His existence must have led sheltered lives and closed their hearts to the voice of their brothers' blood. "Behold the tears of the oppressed, and they had no one to comfort them! On the side of the oppressors there was power, and there was no one to comfort them. And I thought the dead who are already dead more fortunate than the living who are still alive; but better than both is he who has not yet been, and has not seen the evil deeds done under the sun" (Eccles. 4:1 ff.). Whether Ecclesiastes, who "saw all the oppressions that are practiced under the sun" (Eccles. 4:1), retained any faith in God is a moot point, but Jeremiah and Job and the psalmists who speak in a similar vein did. Pagan piety rose to similar heights of despair and created tragedies.

The deepest difference between religions is not that between polytheism and monotheism. To which camp would one assign Sophocles? Even the difference between theism and atheism is not nearly so profound as that between those who feel and those who do not feel their brothers' torments. The Buddha, like the prophets and the Greek tragedians, did, though he did not believe in any deity. There is no inkling of such piety in the callous religiousness of those who note the regularities of nature, find some proof in that of the existence of a God or gods, and practice magic, rites, or pray to ensure rain, success, or speedy passage into heaven.

Natural theology is a form of heathenism, represented in the Bible by the friends of Job. The only theism worthy of our respect believes in God not because of the way the world is made but in spite of that. The only theism that is no less profound than the Buddha's atheism is that represented in the Bible by Job and Jeremiah.

Their piety is a cry in the night, born of suffering so intense that they cannot contain it and must shriek, speak, accuse, and argue with God—not about Him—for there is no other human being who would understand, and the prose of dialogue could not be faithful to the poetry of anguish. In time, theologians come to wrench some useful phrases out of Latin versions of a Hebrew outcry, blind with tears, and try to win some argument about a point of dogma. Scribes, who preceded them, carved phrases out of context, too, and used them in their arguments about the law. But for all that, Jewish piety has been a ceaseless cry in the night, rarely unaware of "all the oppressions that are practiced under the sun," a faith in spite of, not a heathenish, complacent faith because.

The profound detachment of Job's words at the end of the first chapter is certainly possible for an infidel: not being wedded to the things of this world, being able to let them go—and yet not repudiating them in the first place like the great Christian ascetics and the Buddha and his followers. In the form of an anthropomorphic faith, these words express one of the most admirable attitudes possible for man: to be able to give up what life takes away, without being unable to enjoy what life gives us in the first place; to remember that we came naked from the womb and shall return naked; to accept what life gives us as if it were God's own gift, full of wonders beyond price; and to be able to part with everything. To try to fashion something from suffering, to relish our triumphs, and to endure defeats without resentment: all that is compatible with the faith of a heretic.

H. WHEELER ROBINSON : LIFE—A MYSTERY

In his *The Religious Ideas of the Old Testament* (New York, 1913), H. Wheeler Robinson (1872–1945), British biblical scholar, distinguishes five biblical attitudes to the problem of the suffering of the innocent: (1) Wait! (2) There may be life beyond death for the righteous. (3) Life is a dark mystery. (4) Life is a bright mystery of a divine purpose higher than our grasp. (5) The suffering of the innocent may avail for the guilty. The book of Job documents the fourth attitude; its discussion follows that of Ecclesiastes, whose world "presents an inexplicable mystery of non-moral happenings, a mystery without hope of solution by man."

[. . .] But it was also possible for other men, of a different temperament and outlook, to see in life a mystery, not of darkness, but of light. This is essentially the answer reached in the most important discussion of the problem of suffering the Old Testament contains—the poem of Job. The personal fortunes of Job are intended to exemplify that fact of experience which constitutes one side of the problem before us—the possibility of the concurrence of practical innocence with terrible suffering. The explanation of this suffering as retributive, offered by the three friends, is dismissed as quite inadequate; the extension of this view, that the suffering is disciplinary, offered by Eliphaz, and in particular by the additional speeches of Elihu, is also rejected by Job. The position reached by Job himself, after the tentative longing for the restoration of his life after imminent death, is that of a direct challenge of the providence of God—a challenge that is at the same time an appeal to the heart of God, to reveal His true self in the vindication of Job. The speeches of the Almighty, describing the wonders of the universe, seem at first sight away from the point of the challenge. Yet they must have been intended by the author of the poem to suggest that the ways of God are *necessarily* a mystery to the human mind, a mystery before which the only right attitude is trustful humility. This Job himself acknowledges in the final chapter of the poem (42:1–6). But the contribution of the book as a whole to the problem of suffering certainly goes beyond this. The prose prologue and epilogue may possibly have been incorporated by the author from an independent and older source, but they are an integral part of the work as he left it. Now, in the epilogue, besides the naïve restoration to Job of twice as much as he had before, Yahweh repeatedly speaks of "my servant Job," and declares him right in what he has said. If we ask what was the service that the suffering Job had rendered, we are thrown back to the opening scenes of the book, the heavenly court in which Yahweh entrusts the cause of disinterested religion to the unconscious fidelity of Job. The very point of the book is the mystery of this service; the suffering must be borne under the pressure of an ever recurrent and finally unanswered "Why?" Neither at the beginning nor at the end is Job admitted to the secret of that heavenly court, which would be an adequate explanation of his suffering. But the author of the book asks us to believe that there is innocent suffering that must be explained on these lines—suffering that is the necessary condition for the manifestation of the deepest piety. The service could not be rendered without the trial; its issues lie beyond the horizon of the man who is tried. Personal religion has intrinsic worth for God, whose treatment of men belongs to a higher level than that of a merely juristic scheme of moral government.

JAMES B. CONANT :
JOB: THE TWOFOLD ANSWER

James Bryant Conant (born 1893) combines the faculties of scientist, educator, and administrator. He was a Professor of Chemistry at Harvard University before becoming its President (1933–53); served his country as High Commissioner for Germany (1953–55); was concerned with the educational process (*Education in a Divided World,* 1948, and *Education and Liberty,* 1953); and wrote textbooks on organic chemistry and on the function of science (*On Understanding Science,* 1947, and *Science and Common Sense,* 1947). His *Modern Science and Modern Man* (New York, 1952), is based on the Bumpton Lectures at Columbia University, 1952; the lectures analyze the significance of recent developments in the physical sciences. A reflection on Job, here reprinted, appears in the chapter "Science and Spiritual Values."

The problem of evil as set forth in the book of Job is not the problem of evil conduct on the part of humans but the problem of why good men suffer grievous calamities. The problem is recurring; what one of us has not felt its bruising impact within the year? Of the answers given by Job's comforters, none suggested that some evils of the flesh could be overcome by human action. Yet this in essence seems to me the eighteenth century's rationalistic answer to Job's laments. It was an answer that ever since has been echoed by ardent supporters of the work of scientists. Forty years ago it was widely accepted by what are now called "liberal" Christians; in the last twenty years, doubts as to its validity have been expressed by certain Protestant leaders as well as Catholics. The liberal tradition, it is constantly asserted today, has been forced "by the wry advance of world events to adjust its large principles to the hard reality of things as they are." Of the world events, Hitler, Stalin, and the explosion of the atomic bomb are usually cited as examples.

If I read the book of Job correctly, its lesson is a denial of the assumption that the universe is explicable in human terms; it is a corrective to the presumption of human beings in applying their standards of value to the cosmos. The Lord rebukes Job's three comforters for their attempt to persuade the sufferer that he must have sinned by arguing that otherwise he would not have been afflicted. The universe is not constructed along the lines of an automatic machine distributing rewards and punishments—at least not in this world of mortals. As to a future life, the book of Job reflects the Judaic as contrasted to the Christian position; the New Testament answer to the problem of evil is largely absent in the Old Testament. And as to the exact meaning of that answer, Christians have been debating for nearly two thousand years.

Salvation by good works as opposed to salvation by faith, I shall not discuss. Rather, I wish to stay within the setting of the book of Job. The writer presents two answers, it seems to me, to the question of why men and women of the purest character may suffer the most hideous afflictions. The first is essentially that the universe is inexplicable. With almost a stoic resignation, Job accepts this fact and ceases to lament. This is the philosophic answer; the other is the spiritual one. It may be expressed in Job's own words. After the Lord had answered him out of the whirlwind, Job said, "I have heard of Thee by the hearing of the ear; but now mine eye seeth Thee. Wherefore I abhor myself, and repent in dust and ashes."

Taken literally, this passage means something very specific in theological terms to an orthodox Jew or fundamentalist Christian. Taken symbolically, it has deep spiritual meaning for those who interpret broadly the Judaic-Christian literature. I shall so regard it. Indeed, to those who ask, "What do you mean by the term 'spiritual values'?" I would reply by reference to this episode in the book of Job.

To explain further what I have in mind, let me give one example of an evaluation that seems to me significant. People have undergone a spiritual enrichment as a consequence of their sufferings, I would say, if they have become less rebellious in their attitude toward the universe, less frightened of the future, more sympathetic toward other people; on the other hand, those who have become more embittered, more apprehensive, more hostile have suffered a spiritual deterioration. Such changes are only partially indicated by the verbal formulations of the individual in question; the state of a person's spirit is indicated far more by actions than by formal statements of a philosophy of life. Judgments of the type I have just mentioned seem to me to have meaning and to be concerned with a value we may well call spiritual.

The twofold answer of the book of Job stands in sharp contradiction to the belligerent optimism of a typical nineteenth-century materialist. For such a person there was only one explanation of Job's afflictions—ignorance. Disease could be conquered if scientists kept at work and people were sensible enough to follow their advice; so, many an intelligent person maintained as early as the 1800's. And as a bit of prophecy, I submit, fewer statements by optimists have ever been more right. This needs to be emphasized in these days when prophets of gloom are so readily listened to on all sides. We have been triumphantly successful in our efforts to right the scales of apparent injustice in this vale of tears, at least as regards the ills of the flesh; and it was this type of affliction—Satan's touching "his bone and his flesh"—that finally moved Job to question God's justice.

But it is one thing to make great progress in curing or preventing disease and another to say that *all* the afflictions of man can be overcome by human intelligence. Yet this almost became the creed of those who, throughout the nineteenth century and well into this, proclaimed the coming salvation of man on this earth by the good works known as science! This outlook on the world has become embodied—one might almost say enshrined—in the set of doctrines known as dialectical materialism. One version of these doctrines is the official philosophy of the Kremlin and all those who obey its injunctions and slavishly follow its moods. Another version is, I believe, the accepted philosophy of the Communists of Yugoslavia; in less belligerent and doctrinaire form, the Russian version is accepted by some non-Communist Marxists in English-speaking countries. But in all its forms, it breathes that spirit of the mid-nineteenth century which was carrying forward the rationalistic optimism of the eighteenth.

To the doctrinaire dialectical materialist, the book of Job is worse than nonsense—it is an opiate of the people. His answer to the problem of all evil, to calamities of all sorts, is essentially as follows: Through science all evils may be overcome. By "science" he means science based on the doctrine of dialectical materialism, the laws that govern not only inanimate nature but the development of society as well. Of these laws, the recognition of the triad—thesis, antithesis, synthesis—as illustrated by the equation, heat plus ice equals water, is usually given prominence in popular expositions.

I do not propose to discuss the grim political consequences of accepting the Soviet interpretation of dialectical materialism. Philosophically the whole doctrine seems to me utter nonsense. It presents in the most dogmatic and extravagant form the optimism of those scientists who are interested in translating their discoveries into practical effects. It is a creed suited in a crude way to the scientist turned inventor, for it glorifies his rôle; more than that, it denies that the scientist ever was anything more than an inventor or ever could be. Indeed, this point of view has been widely publicized by some non-Marxists who to my mind have unwittingly swallowed a bit of the Communist bait!

I have purposely placed before you a false dichotomy—the book of Job taken literally or dialectical materialism. I have already suggested, I hope, my own predilection; I would not repudiate the nineteenth-century optimism about the continued improvement, with the aid of science, of all the practical arts (including the art of human relations). I would not, however, subscribe to any "in principle" argument about what science can accomplish. I would be certain that for the next century, under the best conditions, the areas of uncertainty and empiricism would remain enormous. As to the book of Job, I would subscribe to the answer that the universe is essentially inexplicable, and I would interpret Job's vision symbolically, using this as one entrance to the whole area of inquiry that can be designated as the universe of spiritual values.

VI

Job as a Lesson in Faith

G. W. F. HEGEL : CONFIDENCE

G. W. F. Hegel's (1770–1831) *Lectures on the Philosophy of Religion* were published in the original German in 1832; the text was based on students' lecture notes taken at the University of Berlin. A second, corrected, version, which made use of some of Hegel's own papers, was issued in 1840. Though this edition, too, bears the signs of informality and casualness, the *Lectures* are an important introduction to Hegel's philosophy of religion. The note on Job appears in the chapter "The Religion of Sublimity," within the division "The Religion of Spiritual Individuality." Hegel refers to the "conscious subject" that knows that God is "this unity which brings about a state of well-being proportionate to the well-doing, and that this connection exists." "It is this kind of harmony of which Man is conscious in this sphere of thought." Hegel then continues with the passage here reprinted.

The English translation of *Lectures,* in three volumes, is based on the second edition of the original.

The consciousness that these are thus joined together constitutes that faith, that confidence, which is a fundamental and praiseworthy trait of the Jewish people. The Old Testament Scriptures, the Psalms especially, are full of this confidence.

This, too, is the line of thought that is represented in the book of Job, the only book whose connection with the standpoint of the Jewish people is not sufficiently recognized. Job extols his innocence, finds his destiny unjust; he is discontented, i.e., there is in him a contradiction—the consciousness of the righteousness which is absolute, and the want of correspondence between his condition and this righteousness. It is recognized as being an end of God's that He makes things go well with the good man.

What the argument points to is that this discontent, this despondency, ought to be brought under the control of pure and absolute confidence. Job asks, "What doth God give me as a reward from on high? Should it not be the unrighteous man who is rejected thus?" His friends answer in the same sense, only they put it in the reverse way, "Because thou art unhappy, therefore we conclude that thou art not righteous." God does this in order that He may protect man from the sin of pride.

God Himself at last speaks: "Who is this that talks thus without understanding? Where wast thou when I laid the foundations of the earth?" (38:2, 4). Then comes a very beautiful and magnificent description of God's power, and Job says, "I know it; he is a man without knowledge who thinks he may hide his counsel" (42:2 f.). This subjection is what is finally reached; on the one hand, there is the demand that it should go well with the righteous, and, on the other, even the feeling of discontent when this is not the case has to be given up. It is this resignation, this acknowledgment of God's power, that restores to Job his property and the happiness he had before. It is on this acknowledgment of God's power that there follows the re-establishment of his happiness. Still, at the same time, this good fortune is not regarded as something that can be demanded by finite man as a right, independent of the power of God.

This confidence in God, this unity, and the consciousness of this harmony of the power, and at the same time of the wisdom and righteousness of God, are based on the thought that God is determined within Himself as end, and has an end.

SÖREN KIERKEGAARD : THE LORD GAVE, AND THE LORD HATH TAKEN AWAY

The enigmatic, lonely Danish thinker, Sören Kierkegaard (1813–55), disregarded in his own generation, has become a central spokesman for existential philosophy in ours. He rejected Hegel's preoccupation with the universal, in which all subjective differences are overcome; rejected also philosophic and religious thought based on abstract, speculative reason and aiming at disinterested, objective truth. His concern was the existent individual —the concrete, singular, particular person—in his daring (because objectively undefinable) relationship with God. In contradistinction to the God of ethics, whose command pertains to universal human obligations, Kierkegaard posits the God of faith, who speaks to individual man and who imposes upon him a particular, at times even paradoxical, duty. The command to sacrifice his son was addressed to Abraham alone and perceived by him alone (*Fear and Trembling*). The man of faith stands as a solitary creature before his creator. He "knows" nothing. Or, rather, with Socrates, he knows only that there is "truth" as "the ultimate ground of all things," but he has no knowledge of what that truth is. The only thing Socrates "could say about it was that he knew nothing of it." This not knowing is the root of faith. Man "possesses God not in virtue of any objective consideration, but in virtue of the boundless passion of inwardness." In search for inwardness, for subjective truth, man must disentangle himself from the world and "become again one self before God." In a short work, *Repetition* (published in 1843, the same year in which he issued his *Fear and Trembling*), he has his hero (i.e., himself) undergo such transformation. He presents Job as a man who lost his possessions and his bodily weal, but regained his self, was granted "repetition" of his original estate, because, paradoxically, "he lost his case before God."

Kierkegaard published another analysis of Job in one of the four *Edifying Discourses* (1843) (reprinted below); here the presentation is based on the verse, "The Lord gave, and the Lord hath taken away . . ." (1:21)—words that Kierkegaard heard his pious father pronounce at the death of three of his children.

The three parts of the verse "The Lord gave," etc., seem, in Kierkegaard's exegesis, to allude to the three themes in chapters 38–42:6: the Lord's demonstration of the created universe as the act of this "giving," Job's exclusion from this grand picture as the act of God's "taking away" of what Job claimed as his, and Job's final submission as evidence that the "giving" is greater than the "taking away," that even in this taking away God is manifest, so that nothing but "praise" is in order. That in the end Job emerges as a greater man than he was is the view of the author of the book of Job; Kierkegaard injects this element into his Job of the initial chapters of the book.

> Then Job arose, and rent his mantle, and shaved his head, and
> fell upon the ground, and worshipped, and said: Naked came
> I out of my mother's womb, and naked shall I return thither;
> the Lord gave, and the Lord hath taken away; blessed be the
> name of the Lord.   (1:20–21)

Not only do we call that man a teacher of men who through
some particularly happy talent discovered, or by unremitting toil
and continued perseverance brought to light, one or another truth;
left what he had acquired as a principle of knowledge, which the
following generations strove to understand, and through this understanding to appropriate to themselves. Perhaps, in an even stricter
sense, we also call that one a teacher of men who had no doctrine
to pass on to others, but who merely left himself as a pattern to
succeeding generations, his life as a principle of guidance to every
man, his name as an assurance to the many, his own deeds as an
encouragement to the striving. Such a teacher and guide of men
was Job, whose significance is due by no means to what he said
but to what he did. He has indeed left a saying which because of
its brevity and its beauty has become a proverb, preserved from generation to generation, and no one has been presumptuous enough
to add anything to it or to take anything away from it. But the
expression itself is not the guidance, and Job's significance lies not
in the fact that he said it, but in the fact that he acted in accordance with it. The expression itself is truly beautiful and worthy of
consideration, but if another had used it, or if Job had been different, or if he had uttered it under different circumstances, then
the word itself would have become something different—significant,
if, as uttered, it would otherwise have been so, but not significant
from the fact that he acted in asserting it, so that the expression
itself was the action. If Job had devoted his whole life to empha-
sizing this word, if he had regarded it as the sum and fulfillment
of what a man ought to let life teach him, if he had constantly only
taught it, but had never himself practiced it, had never himself
acted in accordance with what he taught, then Job would have been
a different kind of man, his significance different. Then would Job's
name have been forgotten, or it would have been unimportant
whether anyone remembered it or not, the principal thing being
the content of the word, the richness of the thought it embodied.

If the race had accepted the saying, then it would have been this that one generation transmitted to the next; while now, on the contrary, it is Job himself who guides the generations. When one generation has served its time, fulfilled its duty, fought its battle, then Job has guided it; when the new generation, with its innumerable ranks and every individual among them in his place, stands ready to begin the journey, then Job is again present, takes his place, which is the outpost of humanity. If the generation sees only happy days and prosperous times, then Job faithfully goes with them; and if, nevertheless, an individual in his thought experiences the terrible, is apprehensive because of his conception of what life may conceal of horror and distress, of the fact that no one knows when the hour of despair may strike for him, then his troubled thought resorts to Job, dwells upon him, is reassured by him. For Job keeps faithfully by his side and comforts him, not as if he had thus suffered once for all what he would never again have to endure, but he comforts him as one who witnesses that the terror is endured, the horror experienced, the battle of despair waged, to the honor of God, to his own salvation, to the profit and happiness of others. In joyful days, in fortunate times, Job walks by the side of the race and guarantees it its happiness, combats the apprehensive dream that some horror may suddenly befall a man and have power to destroy his soul as its certain prey.

Only the thoughtless man could wish that Job should not accompany him, that his venerable name should not remind him of what he seeks to forget—that terror and anxiety exist in life. Only the selfish man could wish that Job had not existed, so that the idea of his suffering might not disturb with its austere earnestness his own unsubstantial joy, and frighten him out of his intoxicated security in obduracy and perdition. In stormy times, when the foundation of existence is shaken, when the moment trembles in fearful expectation of what may happen, when every explanation is silent at the sight of the wild uproar, when a man's heart groans in despair, and "in bitterness of soul" he cries to heaven, then Job still walks at the side of the race and guarantees that there is a victory, guarantees that even if the individual loses in the strife, there is still a God, who, as with every human temptation, even if a man fails to endure it, will still make its outcome such that we may be able to bear it; yea, more glorious than any human expectation. Only the defiant could wish that Job had not existed, so that he might absolutely free his soul from the last vestiges of love which still remained in the plaintive shriek of despair; so that he might complain, aye, even curse life; so that there might be no consonance of faith and confidence and humility in his speech; so that in his defiance he might stifle the shriek so that it might not even seem as if there were anyone whom it defied. Only the effeminate could wish that Job had not existed, so that he might relinquish every thought, the sooner the better; might renounce every emotion in the most abhorrent impotence and completely efface himself in the most wretched and miserable oblivion.

The expression that, when it is mentioned, at once reminds us of Job, immediately becomes vividly present in everyone's thought, is a plain and simple one; it conceals no secret wisdom that must be unearthed from the depths. If a child learns this word, if it is entrusted to him as an endowment, he does not understand for what purpose he will use it; when he understands the word, he understands essentially the same thing by it as does the wisest. Still, the child does not understand it, or rather he does not understand Job; for what he does not comprehend is all the distress and wretchedness with which Job was tested. About that the child can have only a dark premonition; and yet, happy the child who understood the word and got an impression of what he did not comprehend, that it was the most terrible thing imaginable; who possessed, before sorrow and adversity made its thought cunning, the convincing and childishly vivid conviction that it was in truth the most terrible. When the youth turns his attention to this word, then he understands it, and understands it essentially the same as do the child and the wisest. Still he perhaps does not understand it, or rather, he does not understand Job, does not understand why all the distress and wretchedness should come in which Job was tried; and yet happy the youth who understood the word and humbly bowed before what he did not understand, before his own distress made his thought wayward, as if he had discovered what no one had known before. When the adult reflects on this word, then he understands essentially the same by it as did the child and the wisest. He understands, too, the wretchedness and distress in which Job was tried; and yet, perhaps he does not understand Job, for he cannot understand how Job was able to say it; and yet, happy the man who understood the word, and steadfastly admired what he did not understand, before his own distress and wretchedness made him also distrustful of Job. When the man who has been tried, who fought the good fight through remembering this saying, mentions it, then he understands it, and understands it essentially the same as the child and as the wisest understood it; he understands Job's misery, he understands how Job could say it. He understands the word, he interprets it, even though he never speaks about it, more gloriously than the one who spent a whole lifetime in explaining this one word.

Only the one who has been tried, who tested the word through himself being tested, only he interprets the word correctly; and only such a disciple, only such an interpreter, does Job desire. Only such a one learns from Job what there is to learn, the most beautiful and blessed truth, compared with which all other art and all other wisdom is very unessential. Therefore we rightly call Job a teacher of mankind, not of certain individual men, for he offers himself to every man as his pattern, beckons to everyone by his glorious example, summons everyone in his beautiful words. While the more simple-minded man, the one less gifted, or the one less favored by time and circumstances, if not enviously yet in troubled despondency, may sometimes have wished for the talent and the opportunity to be able to understand and absorb himself in those things that scholars from time to time have discovered, may also have felt a desire in his soul to be able to teach others, and not always be the one to receive instruction, Job does not tempt him in this way. How, too, could human wisdom help here? Would it perhaps seek to make that more intelligible which the simplest and the child easily understood, and understood as well as the wisest! How would the art of eloquence and fluency help here? Would it be able to produce in the speaker or in some other man what the simplest is able to do as well as the wisest—action! Would not human wisdom rather tend to make everything more difficult? Would not eloquence, which, despite its pretentiousness, is nevertheless unable to express the differences that always dwell in the heart of man, rather benumb the power of action and allow it to slumber in extensive reflection! But even if this is true, and even if, as a result of this, the speaker endeavors to avoid intruding disturbingly between the striving individual and the beautiful pattern which is equally near to every man, so that he may not increase sorrow by increasing wisdom; even if he takes care not to ensnare himself in the splendid words of human persuasiveness, which are very unfruitful, still it by no means follows that the reflection and the development might not have their own significance. If the one reflecting had not hitherto known this word, then it would always be an advantage to him that he had learned to know it; if he had known it, but had had no occasion to test it, then it would always be an advantage to him that he had learned to understand what he perhaps might sometime have to use. If he had tested it, but it had deceived him, if he even believed that it was the word that had deceived him, then it would be advantageous to him that he had previously reflected upon it, before he fled from it in the unrest of the strife and the haste of battle! Perhaps the reflection would sometime become significant to him; it might perhaps happen that the reflection would become vividly present in his soul just when he needed it in order to penetrate the confused thoughts of his restless heart; it might perhaps happen that what the reflection had understood only in part would sometime gather itself regenerated in the moment of decision; that what reflection had sowed in corruption would spring up in the day of need in the incorruptible life of action.

So let us endeavor to understand Job better in his beautiful words: "The Lord gave, the Lord hath taken away; blessed be the name of the Lord!"

In the land toward the east there lived a man whose name was Job. He was blessed with lands, innumerable herds, and rich pastures; "his words had lifted up the fallen, and had strengthened the feeble knees" (4:4); his tent was blessed as if it rested in the lap of heaven, and in this tent he lived with his seven sons and three daughters; and "the secret of the Lord" abode there with him (29:4). And Job was an old man; his joy in life was his pleasure in his children, over whom he watched that no evil might come upon them. There he sat one day alone by his fireside, while his children were gathered at a festival at the oldest brother's house. There he offered burnt offerings for each one individually, there he also disposed his heart to joy in the thought of his children. As he sat there in the quiet confidence of happiness, there came a messenger, and before he could speak there came another, and while this one was still speaking, there came a third, but the fourth messenger brought news concerning his sons and daughters, that the house had been overthrown and had buried them all. "Then Job stood up and rent his mantle, and shaved his head, and fell down upon the ground, and worshipped" (1:20). His sorrow did not express itself in many words, or rather he did not utter a single one; only his appearance bore witness that his heart was broken. Could you wish it otherwise! Is not that one who prides himself on not being able to sorrow in the day of sorrow put to shame by not being able to rejoice in the day of gladness? Is not the sight of such imperturbability unpleasant and distressing, almost revolting, while it is affecting to see an honorable old man, who but now sat in the gladness of the Lord, sitting with his fatherly countenance downcast, his mantle rent and his head shaven! Since he had thus surrendered himself to sorrow, not in despair but stirred by human emotion, he was swift to judge between God and himself, and the words of his judgment are these: "Naked I came forth from my mother's womb, and naked shall I return thither" (1:21). With these words the struggle was decided, and every claim that would demand something from the Lord, which He did not wish to give, or would desire to retain something, as if it had not been a gift, was brought to silence in his soul. Then follows the confession from the man whom not sorrow alone but worship as well had prostrated on the ground: "The Lord gave, and the Lord hath taken away. Blessed be the name of the Lord!"

The Lord gave, the Lord took. What first arrests the attention is that Job said, "The Lord gave." Is not this word irrelevant to the occasion; does it not contain something different from what lay in the event itself? If a man in a single moment is deprived of everything dear to him, and deprived of the most precious of all, the loss will perhaps at first so overwhelm him that he will not even trust himself to express it, even if in his heart he is conscious before God that he has lost everything. Or he will not permit the loss to rest with its crushing weight upon his soul, but he will put it away from him, and in his heart's agitation he will say, "The Lord took." And thus to humble oneself before the Lord in silence and humility is indeed worthy of praise and emulation, and in the struggle such a man saves his soul though he loses all his gladness.

But Job! At the moment when the Lord took everything, he did not say first "The Lord took," but he said first "The Lord gave." The word is short, but in its brevity it perfectly expresses what it wishes to indicate, that Job's soul is not crushed down in silent submission to sorrow, but that his heart first expanded in gratitude; that the loss of everything first made him thankful to the Lord that He had given him all the blessings that He now took from him. It did not happen with him, as Joseph predicted, that the abundance of the seven fruitful years would be entirely forgotten in the seven lean years. The nature of his gratitude was not the same as in that long vanished time when he accepted every good and perfect gift from the hand of God with thanksgiving; but still his gratitude was sincere, as was his conception about the goodness of God which now became living in his soul. Now he is reminded of everything the Lord had given, some individual thing perhaps with even greater thankfulness than when he had received it. It was not become less beautiful to him because it was taken away, nor more beautiful, but still beautiful as before, beautiful because the Lord gave it, and what now might seem more beautiful to him is not the gift but the goodness of God. He is reminded again of his abundant prosperity, his eyes rest once more upon the rich pastures and follow the numerous herds; he remembers what joy there was in having seven sons and three daughters, who now needed no offering except that of thankfulness for having had them. He is reminded of those who perhaps still remembered him with gratitude, the many he had instructed, "whose weak hands he had strengthened, whose feeble knees he had upheld" (4:4). He is reminded of the glorious days when he was powerful and esteemed by the people, "when the young men hid themselves out of reverence for him, and the old men arose and remained standing" (29:8). He remembers with thankfulness that his step had not turned away from the way of righteousness, that he had rescued the poor who complained, and the fatherless who had no helper; and therefore, even in this moment, the "blessing of the forsaken" (29:13) was upon him as before.

The Lord gave. It is a short word, but to Job it signified so very much; for Job's memory was not so short, nor was his thankfulness so forgetful. While thankfulness rested in his soul with its quiet sadness, he bade a gentle and friendly farewell to everything at once, and in this farewell everything disappeared like a beautiful memory; moreover, it seemed as if it were not the Lord who took it, but Job who gave it back to Him. When therefore Job had said, "The Lord gave," then was his mind well prepared to please God also with the next word, "The Lord took."

Perhaps there might be someone who on the day of sorrow was also reminded that he had seen happy days, and his soul would become even more impatient. "Had he never known happiness, then the pain would not have overcome him, for what is pain, after all, other than an idea that he does not have who knows nothing else, but now happiness had so educated and developed him as to make him conscious of the pain." Thus his happiness became pernicious to him; it was never lost but only lacking, and it tempted him more in the lack than ever before. What had been the delight of his eyes, he desired to see again, and his ingratitude punished him by conjuring it up as more beautiful than it had formerly been. What his soul had rejoiced in, it now thirsted for again, and his ingratitude punished him by painting it as more desirable than it had previously been. What he had once been capable of doing, that he now wished to be able to do again, and his ingratitude punished him with visions that had never had reality. Thus he condemned his soul to living famished in the never satisfied craving of want.

Or there awakened a consuming passion in his soul, because he had not even enjoyed all the sweetness from their voluptuous abundance. If there might only be vouchsafed to him one little hour, if he might only regain the glory for a short time so that he might satiate himself with happiness, and thereby learn to disregard the pain! Then he abandoned his soul to a burning unrest; he would not acknowledge to himself whether the enjoyment he desired was worthy of a man; whether he ought not rather to thank God that his soul had not been so extravagant in the time of joy as it had now become in his unhappiness. He was not appalled by the thought that his desires were the cause of his perdition; he refused to be concerned by the fact that more wretched than all his wretchedness was the worm of desire in his soul, which would not die.

Perhaps there might be another man who at the moment of loss also remembered what he had possessed, but who had the audacity to try to prevent the loss from becoming intelligible to him. Even if it were lost, his defiant will would still be able to retain it as if it were not lost. He would not endeavor to bear the loss, but he chose to waste his strength in an impotent defiance, to lose himself in an insane preoccupation with the loss. Or in cowardice he immediately avoided humbly attempting to understand it. Then oblivion opened its abyss, not so much to the loss as to him, and he did not so much escape the loss in forgetfulness as he threw himself away. Or he lyingly sought to belittle the good that he had once enjoyed, as if it never had been beautiful, had never gladdened his heart; he thought to strengthen his soul by a wretched self-deception, as if strength lay in falsehood. Or he irrationally assured himself that life was not so hard as one imagined, that its terror was not as described, was not so hard to bear, if one, as you will remember that he did, began by not finding it terrifying to become such a person.

In fact, who would ever finish, if he wished to speak about what so frequently has happened, and will so frequently be repeated in the world? Would he not tire far sooner than would passion of that ever new ingenuity for transforming the explained and the understood into a new disappointment, wherein it deceives itself!

Let us rather, therefore, turn back to Job. On the day of sorrow when everything was lost, then he first thanked God who gave it, defrauded neither God nor himself, and while everything was being shaken and overthrown, he still remained what he had been from the beginning—"honest and upright" before God (1:1). He confessed that the blessing of the Lord had been merciful to him, he returned thanks for it; therefore it did not remain in his mind as a torturing memory. He confessed that the Lord had blessed richly and beyond all measure his undertakings; he had been thankful for this, and therefore the memory did not become to him a consuming unrest. He did not conceal from himself that everything had been taken from him; therefore the Lord, who took it, remained in his upright soul. He did not avoid the thought that it was lost; therefore his soul rested quietly until the explanation of the Lord again

came to him, and found his heart like the good earth well cultivated in patience.

The Lord took. Did Job say anything except the truth, did he
use an indirect expression to indicate what was direct? The word
is short, and it signifies the loss of everything; it naturally occurs
to us to repeat it after him, since the expression itself has become
a sacred proverb; but do we just as naturally link it to Job's
thought? For was it not the Sabeans who fell upon his peaceful
herds and killed his servants? Did the messenger who brought the
news say anything else? Was it not the lightning that destroyed the
sheep and their shepherds? Did the messenger who brought the
news mean something else, even though he called the lightning the
fire from heaven? Was it not a wind-storm from out of the desert
that overturned the house and buried his children in the ruins?
Did the messenger mention some other perpetrator, or did he name
someone who sent the wind? Yet Job said, "The Lord took"; in the
very moment of receiving the message, he realized that it was the
Lord who had taken everything. Who told Job this? Or was it not
a sign of his fear of God that he thus shifted everything over to
the Lord, and justified Him in doing it; and are we more devout,
we who sometimes hesitate a long time to speak thus?

Perhaps there was a man who had lost everything in the world.
Then he set out to consider how it had happened. But everything
was inexplicable and obscure to him. His happiness had vanished
like a dream, and its memory haunted him like a nightmare, but
how he had been cast off from the glory of the one into the wretchedness of the other, he was unable to understand. It was not the
Lord who had taken it—it was an accident. Or he assured himself
that it was the deceit and cunning of men, or their manifest violence, that had wrested it from him, as the Sabeans had destroyed
Job's herds and their keepers. Then his soul became rebellious
against men; he believed he did God justice by not reproaching
Him. He fully understood how it had happened, and the more
immediate explanation was that those men had done it, and furthermore it was because the men were evil and their hearts perverted. He understood that men are his neighbors to his injury;
would he perhaps have understood it in the same way if they had

benefited him? But that the Lord who dwells far away in heaven might be nearer to him than the man who lived next to him, whether that man did him good or evil—such an idea was remote from his thought. Or he fully understood how it had happened, and knew how to describe it with all the eloquence of horror. For why should he not understand that when the sea rages in its fury, when it flings itself against the heavens, then men and their frail accomplishments are tossed about as in a game; that when the storm rushes forth in its violence, human enterprises are mere child's play; that when the earth trembles in terror of the elements and the mountains groan, then men and their glorious achievements sink as nothing into the abyss. And this explanation was adequate for him, and, above all, sufficient to make his soul indifferent to everything. For it is true that what is built on sand does not even need a storm to overthrow it; but would it not also be true that a man cannot build and dwell elsewhere and be sure his soul is safe! Or he understood that he himself had merited what had befallen him, that he had not been prudent. For had he rightly calculated in time, it would not have happened. And this explanation explained everything by first explaining that he had corrupted himself and made it impossible for him to learn anything from life, and especially impossible for him to learn anything from God.

Still, who would ever finish if he tried to explain what has happened and what will frequently be repeated in life? Would he not become tired of talking before the sensual man would weary of deluding himself with plausible and disappointing and deceptive explanations? Let us therefore turn away from that which has nothing to teach us, except insofar as we knew it before, so that we may shun worldly wisdom and turn our attention to him from whom there is a truth to be learned—to Job and to his devout words, "The Lord took." Job referred everything to the Lord; he did not retard his soul and extinguish his spirit in reflections or explanations which only engender and nourish doubt, even if the one who dwells on them does not realize it. In the same instant that everything was taken from him he knew that it was the Lord who had taken it, and therefore in his loss he remained in understanding with the Lord; in his loss, he preserved his confidence in the Lord; he looked upon the Lord and therefore he did not see despair. Or does only that man see God's hand who sees that He gives; does not that one also see God who sees that He takes? Does only that one see God who sees His countenance turned toward him? Does not that one also see God who sees Him turn His back upon him, as Moses always saw only the Lord's back? But he who sees God has overcome the world, and therefore Job in his devout word has overcome the world; was through his devout word greater and stronger and more powerful than the whole world, which here would not so much carry him into temptation but would overcome him with its power, cause him to sink down before its boundless might. And yet how weak, indeed almost childishly so, is not the wild fury of the storm, when it thinks to cause a man to tremble for himself by wresting everything away from him, and he answers, "It is not you who do this, it is the Lord who takes!" How impotent is the arm of every man of violence, how wretched his shrewd cleverness, how all human power becomes almost an object of compassion, when it wishes to plunge the weak into the destruction of despair by wresting everything from him, and he then confidently says, "It is not you, you can do nothing—it is the Lord who takes."

Blessed be the name of the Lord! Hence Job not only overcame the world, but he did what Paul had desired his striving congregation to do: after having overcome everything, he stood. Alas, perhaps there has been someone in the world who overcame everything, but who failed in the moment of victory. The Lord's name be praised! Hence the Lord remained the same, and ought He not to be praised as always? Or had the Lord really changed? Or did not the Lord in truth remain the same, as did Job? The Lord's name be praised! Hence the Lord did not take everything, for He did not take away Job's praise, and his peace of heart, and the sincerity of faith from which it issued; but his confidence in the Lord remained with him as before, perhaps more fervently than before; for now there was nothing at all that could in any way divert his thought from Him. The Lord took it all. Then Job gathered together all his sorrows and "cast them upon the Lord," and then He also took those from him, and only praise remained in the incorruptible joy of his heart. For Job's house was a house of sorrow if ever a house was such, but where this word is spoken, "Blessed be the name of the Lord," there gladness also has its home.

Job indeed stands before us the image of sorrow, expressed in his countenance and in his form; but he who utters this word as Job did still bears witness to the joy, even if his testimony does not direct itself to the joyous but to the concerned, and yet speaks intelligibly to the many who have ears to hear. For the ear of the concerned is fashioned in a special manner, and as the ear of the lover indeed hears many voices but really only one—the voice of the beloved—so the ear of the concerned also hears many voices, but they pass by and do not enter his heart. As faith and hope without love are only sounding brass and tinkling cymbals, so all the gladness in the world in which no sorrow is mingled is only sounding brass and tinkling cymbals, which flatter the ear but are abhorrent to the soul. But this voice of consolation, this voice that trembles in pain and yet proclaims the gladness—this the ear of the concerned hears; his heart treasures it; it strengthens and guides him even to finding joy in the depths of sorrow.

My hearer, is it not true? You have understood Job's eulogy; it has at least seemed beautiful to you in the quiet moment of reflection, so that in thinking of it you had forgotten what you did not wish to be reminded of, that which indeed is sometimes heard in the world in the day of need, instead of praise and blessing. So let it then be forgotten, you will deserve, as little as I, that the memory of it should again be revived.

We have spoken about Job, and have sought to understand him in his devout expression, without the speech wishing to force itself upon anyone. But should it therefore be entirely without significance or application, and concern no one? If you yourself, my hearer, have been tried as Job was, and have stood the testing as he did, then it truly applies to you, if we have spoken rightly about Job. If hitherto you have not been tested in life, then it indeed applies to you. Do you think perhaps that these words apply only under such extraordinary circumstances as those in which Job was placed? Is it perhaps your belief that if such a thing struck you, then the terror itself would give you strength, develop within you that humble courage? Did not Job have a wife—what do we read about her? Perhaps you think that terror cannot get as much power over a man as can the daily thralldom in much smaller adversities. Then look you to it that you, as little as any man, do not become enslaved by some tribulation, and above all learn from Job to be sincere with yourself, so that you may not delude yourself by an imagined strength, through which you experience imaginary victories in an imaginary conflict.

Perhaps you say, if the Lord had taken it from me, but nothing was given to me; perhaps you believe that this is by no means as terrible as was Job's suffering, but that it is far more wearing, and consequently a more difficult struggle. We shall not quarrel with you. For even if this were true, the quarrel would still be unprofitable, and increase the difficulty. But in one thing we are in agreement: that you can learn from Job, and, if you are honest with yourself and love humanity, then you cannot wish to evade Job, in order to venture out into a hitherto unknown difficulty, and keep the rest of us in suspense, until we learn from your testimony that a victory is also possible in this difficulty. So if you then learn from Job to say "Blessed be the name of the Lord," this applies to you, even if the preceding is less applicable.

Or perhaps you believe that such a thing cannot happen to you? Who taught you this wisdom, or on what do you base your assurance? Are you wise and understanding, and is this your confidence? Job was the teacher of many. Are you young, and your youth your assurance? Job had also been young. Are you old, on the verge of the grave? Job was an old man when sorrow overtook him. Are you powerful, is this your assurance of immunity? Job was reverenced by the people. Are riches your security? Job possessed the blessing of lands. Are your friends your guarantors? Job was loved by everyone. Do you put your confidence in God? Job was the Lord's confidant. Have you reflected on these thoughts, or have you not rather avoided them, so that they might not extort from you a confession, which you now perhaps call a melancholy mood? And yet there is no hiding place in the wide world where troubles may not find you, and there has never lived a man who was able to say more than you can say that you do not know when sorrow will visit your house. So be sincere with yourself, fix your eyes upon Job; even though he terrifies you, it is not this he wishes, if you yourself do not wish it. You still could not wish, when you survey your life and think of its end, that you should have to confess, "I was fortunate, not like other men; I have never suffered anything in the world, and I have let each day have its own sorrows, or rather bring me new joys." Such a confession, even if it were true, you could still never wish to make, aye, it would involve your own humiliation; for if you had been preserved from sorrow, as no other had, you would still say, "I have indeed not been tested in it, but still my mind has frequently occupied itself seriously with the thought of Job, and with the idea that no man knows the time and the hour when the messengers will come to him, each one more terrifying than the last."

SETON POLLOCK : GOD AND A HERETIC

The contemporary English writer Seton Pollock approaches the biblical Wisdom literature "as a layman who has profited by the best scholarship available to an English-speaking student." His *Stubborn Soil* (London, 1946) is a perceptive study of Proverbs, Ecclesiastes, and Job, with a selection of newly translated texts. Pollock also wrote *The Root of the Matter: Sketches on Job* (1939). By suffering, he says, taking his clue from Job, "men are brought to a living faith, and by it their faith is destroyed." The present chapter is from the section on Job in *Stubborn Soil.*

When Job's desire was answered and the elusive Adversary spoke at last, the tables were completely turned. The indictment for which Job had appealed was no accusation such as the friends had expected, but charged him with having confused the issue by speech without knowledge. This apparent concession to the views of the three was, however, to be of no comfort to them, for they found themselves the subject of much sterner charges, while Job was not even bidden to repent, but to gird up his loins like a man to hear and answer the words of God.

At first sight there seems to be a marked similarity between the speech of the Lord and those of Elihu and the others. There is the same insistence upon the power and glory of the Almighty and the insignificance of Job, and the same inference that he has been presumptuous in taking upon himself to criticize God's ways. Was Job present when the ship of the universe was launched? Has he explored the recesses of the deep, or the mystery of death? Does he comprehend a tithe of the wonders of the physical world, the splendor of the stars, the dignity of the horse, the lonely glory of the eagle? To call in question the moral governance of this amazing universe in the face of his profound ignorance of even its physical phenomena is to cavil.

Wherein does this differ from what the friends have said? We observe at once that the friends had not been content with this argument but had added the offensive and untrue contention that Job was a wicked man; and, furthermore, they had used the argument in a spirit of obscurantism. Had they been content to remind Job of his insignificance, seeking nevertheless to strengthen him in his confidence in God, they might have been of some help to him; but they had used it to break down his spirit and to coerce him into acting dishonestly in denying the plain facts of experience to support their creed. Their vehemence had arisen out of pious panic (which is the source of obscurantism) and not out of any genuine zeal for truth.

The questions that the Lord addressed to Job left him without an answer, and the voice from the whirlwind proceeded with its devastating logic. The enigma of human suffering is not directly raised, but Job is made to think again of the cognate problem of God's dealings with the arrogant and the wicked. Can he seriously call in question what God does? Has he considered the proud beasts of land and sea, the hippopotamus, the crocodile, the war horse, and all untamable creatures? These, like the wild waves, are physical symbols of moral arrogance; and surely a God from whose hand they, as well as all proud and wicked men, spring is competent to deal with the situation, and needs no help or advice from man. Nevertheless, Job is invited to try his hand at a solution if he wishes, and God undertakes to applaud him if he succeeds.

All this throws no light upon the problem of Job's suffering, and provides no explanation for the indiscriminate way in which rewards and punishments are apportioned. The only kind of answer to be found lies in Job's own faith, in his dogged refusal to be turned from his integrity despite the disasters into which it had led him, and in his conviction that God, if only He can be found, will give the answer and vindicate him before the eyes of the whole world. It was the same in the case of the prophet Habakkuk, who could see that violence and pride destroy themselves even

within the process of history, but who could find no solace for
the suffering righteous except the daring, and seemingly foolish,
promise that the just man would live by his faith (Hab. 2:4). The
significance of these early questionings lies not in any solution
that was found but in the fact that the problem was fairly posed
and men were firmly committed to the necessity of working it out,
free of the shallow confidence of misplaced piety.

In discussing the cycle of speeches, it may have seemed that I
was suggesting that Job was always right in what he said, and
the friends always wrong; but the position is not as simple as that.
Job was right to doubt his creed, however well established it was,
when he found that it did not square with the facts, for God is
better pleased with honest heresy than with fraudulent piety; and
although the outworks of his faith were sorely shaken, his ultimate
faith in God weathered the tempest of doubt triumphantly. He
was undoubtedly wrong to conclude so hastily that God was being
unjust, darkening counsel without knowledge, and this he realized under the searching irony of the voice from the whirlwind;
but we must remember that he was not meditating in the comfort of a fireside chair. The despair from which he suffered was a
mental sickness close to madness, and he was trembling upon the
very edge of suicide. As he said himself: "What have I left to do
but to lie down in the dust and take my own life?" (cf. 7:21). Conversely, many things the friends had to say were profound, but
the spirit that informed their arguments was the narrow one that
would wrest the realities of human life to make them fit in with
the theories of religion, and all that they had said was vitiated by
their refusal to grasp the radical nature of the problem with which
they were confronted.

The progress of Job's faith can be plainly traced through the
story. It is evident that his original piety had been largely influenced by motives of fear. Having done all he could to ensure that
his own life was pleasing to God, his overscrupulous conscience
had led him to make regular sacrifices for his children to atone
for any possible follies they might commit. And when tragedy
breaks in upon him, we discover the main source of his moral
earnestness, for he exclaims: "This is what I feared—and now it
has come to pass" (3:25). His good deeds and his prayers, his
careful avoidance of evil and his sacrifices, had been the basis of

his confidence, his hope for a long and prosperous life and a peaceful, honored death. It is a typical Old Testament style of faith, which, despite the witness of the Old Testament itself against it, has persisted into modern times, and forms a very common and tenaciously held belief today.

The fear element (which is an important stage in spiritual apprehension) is a steppingstone which must be left behind if a man is to make progress. It was, of course, inherent in the ancient creed in which Job had been reared, and when that creed was shattered he found himself launched upon an entirely uncharted sea with all the terrors of a dangerous voyage ahead of him. Yet this loss of creed was necessary if he was to achieve the higher experience of "seeing God with his eyes" rather than, as hitherto, only hearing of Him "with the hearing of his ears" (42:5). Henceforth it was to be confidence in God through thick and thin, and no more merely a believing of things about God. In the words of Christian theology, it was the first step from the rule of law, with its bondage and heavy obligation, to the spirit of grace which is the spirit of liberty.

So Job, upon the threshold of a new adventure of faith, repents; but his repentance was not for any peccadilloes or imaginary sins. He has seen something of the mystery of evil and has realized his own implication in it, discovering a root of pride in his heart which had hitherto been hidden from his consciousness, but in which he now dimly recognizes the ancient and deadly plague of the soul.

If Job was humbled by his experience, the friends were humiliated. They were condemned for having falsified facts in the defense of the character of God, and we are afforded the edifying spectacle of the heretic, Job, being commanded to pray for his eminently orthodox friends. It is as well to ponder the scene when we are tempted to adopt an overrighteous attitude toward those who, appalled by the injustice and misery of the world, seem to reject the God we worship.

According to the epilogue (a happy ending which forms no part of the original poem), Job's new-found humility was sealed by his receiving gifts from his friends and neighbors, for we require peculiar grace of character when we are obliged to accept benefits from others because of our own real need, especially if we have been more used to the rôle of benefactor; but before long Job's fortunes were fully restored. Once again he had flocks and herds, and his joy was crowned by the birth of fine sons, and daughters whose beauty was the talk of all the bazaars.

Even now the curtain is not drawn aside, and Job hears no whisper of the transaction that took place in the secret council chamber of heaven. Only the reader knows that his tenacious faith, though mingled with revolt, had demonstrated the real existence of goodness as a substantive virtue, destroying the cynicism that would maintain that goodness is no more than a kind of conditioned reflex to material success.

WILLIAM BARRETT :
THE HEBRAIC MAN OF FAITH

The American philosopher William Barrett (born 1913) objects to the fact that "philosophers today exist in the Academy, as members of departments of philosophy in universities," and pleads for the ancient (Platonic) claim that philosophy is a search for deliverance "from the suffering and evils of the natural world." He views modern existential philosophy as an attempt to overcome the "increasing remoteness from life." In his *Irrational Man: A Study in Existential Philosophy* (New York, 1958), he discusses the sources of existentialism in the Western tradition and some major representatives of the movement. The passage on Job, here reprinted, is part of a chapter in that work, "Hebraism and Hellenism."

The Law is not really at the center of Hebraism. At the center lies that which is the foundation and the basis of the Law, and without which the Law, even in the most Pharisaical tradition, would be but an empty shell. [. . .] To be sure, the Law—the absolutely binding quality of its ritual and commandments—has been what has held the Jewish community together over its centuries of suffering and prevented this people from extermination. But if we go back to the Hebraic sources, to man as he is revealed to us in the Bible, we see that something more primitive and more fundamental lies at the basis of the moral law. We have to learn to reread the book of Job in order to see this—reread it in a way that takes us into our own time, reread it with a historical sense of the primitive or primary mode of existence of the people who gave expression to this work.

For earlier man, the outcome of the book of Job was not such a foregone conclusion as it is for us later readers, for whom centuries of familiarity and forgetfulness have dulled the violence of the confrontation between man and God that is central to the narrative. For earlier man, seeing for the first time beyond the routine commandments of his religion, there was a Promethean excitement in Job's coming face to face with his creator and demanding justification. The stage comparable to this, with the Greeks, is the emergence of critical and philosophical reflection upon the gods and their ways, the first use of rational consciousness as an instrument to examine a religion that had been up to that time traditional and ritualistic. The Hebrew, however, proceeds not by the way of reason but by the confrontation of the whole man, Job, in the fullness and violence of his passion with the unknowable and overwhelming God. And the final solution for Job lies not in the rational resolution of the problem, any more than it ever does in life, but in a change and conversion of the whole man. The relation between Job and God is a relation between an I and a Thou, to use Martin Buber's terms. Such a relation demands that each being confront the other in his completeness; it is not the confrontation of two rational minds each demanding an explanation that will satisfy reason.

The relation between Job and God is on the level of existence and not of reason. Rational doubt, in the sense of the term that the later philosophic tradition of the West has made familiar to us, never enters Job's mind, even in the very paroxysm of his revolt. His relation to God remains one of faith from start to finish, though, to be sure, this faith takes on the varying shapes of revolt, anger, dismay, and confusion. Job says, *"Though He slay me, yet will I trust in Him"* (13:15), but he adds what is usually not brought to our attention as emphatically as the first part of his saying: *"But I will maintain my own ways before Him."* Job retains his own identity (his "own ways") in confronting the creator, before whom he is as nothing. Job in the many shades and turnings of his faith is close to those primitive peoples who may break, revile, and spit upon the image of a god who is no longer favorable. Similarly, in Psalm 89 David rebukes Yahweh for all the tribulations that He has poured upon His people, and there can be no doubt that we are here at the stage in history where faith is so real that it permits man to call God to account. It is a stage close to the primitive, but also a considerable step beyond it: for the Hebrew had added a new element, faith, and so internalized what was simply the primitive's anger against his god. When faith is full, it dares to express its anger, for faith is the openness of the whole man toward his God, and therefore must be able to encompass all human modes of being.

Faith is trust—in the sense, at least initially, in which in everyday life we say we trust so-and-so. As trust it is the relation between one individual and another. Faith is trust before it is belief—belief in the articles, creeds, and tenets of a Church with which later religious history obscures this primary meaning of the world. As trust, in the sense of the opening up of one being toward another, faith does not involve any philosophical problem about its position relative to faith and reason. That problem comes up only later, when faith has become, so to speak, propositional, when it has expressed itself in statements, creeds, systems. Faith as a concrete mode of being of the human person precedes faith as the intellectual assent to a proposition, just as truth as a concrete mode of human being precedes the truth of any proposition. Moreover, this trust that embraces a man's anger and dismay, his bones and his bowels— the whole man, in short—does not yet permit any separation of soul from body, of reason from man's irrational other half. In Job and the Psalms man is very much a man of flesh and blood, and his being as a creature is described time and again in images that are starkly physical:

> Remember, I beseech Thee, that Thou hast made me as clay; and wilt Thou bring me into dust again?
> Hast Thou not poured me out as milk, and curdled me like cheese?
> Thou hast clothed me with skin and flesh, and hast fenced me with bones and sinews.   (10:9 ff.)

And when Psalm 22 speaks of the sense of abandonment and

dereliction, it uses not the high, rarefied language of introspection but the most powerful cry of the physical:

My God, my God, why hast Thou forsaken me? . . .
Thou art He that took me out of the womb: Thou didst make
me hope when I was upon my mother's breasts.
I was cast upon Thee from the womb: Thou art my God from
my mother's belly. . . .
I am poured out like water, and all my bones are out of joint;
my heart is like wax; it is melted in the midst of my bowels.
My strength is dried up like a potsherd; and my tongue cleaveth
to my jaws; and Thou hast brought me into the dust of death.

(Ps. 22:2, 10 f., 15 f.)

Protestantism later sought to revive this face-to-face confrontation of man with his God, but could produce only a pallid replica of the simplicity, vigor, and wholeness of this original biblical faith. Protestant man had thrown off the husk of his body. He was a creature of spirit and inwardness, but no longer the man of flesh and belly, bones and blood, that we find in the Bible. Protestant man would never have dared confront God and demand an accounting of His ways. That era in history had long since passed by the time we come to the Reformation.

As a man of flesh and blood, biblical man was very much bound to the earth. "Remember, I beseech Thee, that Thou hast made me as clay; and wilt Thou bring me into dust again?" Bound to the dust, he was bound to death: a creature of time, whose being was temporal through and through. The idea of eternity—eternity for man—does not bulk large in the Bible beside the power and frequency of the images of man's mortality. God is the Everlasting, who, though He meets man face to face, is altogether beyond human ken and comparison; while man, who is as nothing before his creator, is like all other beings of the dust a creature of a day, whose temporal substance is repeatedly compared to wind and shadow.

Man that is born of woman is of few days, and full of trouble.
He cometh forth like a flower, and is cut down: he fleeth also as
a shadow, and continueth not.   (Job 14:1 f.)

Hebraism contains no eternal realm of essences, which Greek philosophy was to fabricate, through Plato, as affording the intellectual deliverance from the evil of time. Such a realm of eternal essences is possible only for a *detached* intellect, one who, in Plato's phrase, becomes a "spectator of all time and all existence." This ideal of the philosopher as the highest human type—the theoretical intellect who, from the vantage point of eternity, can survey all time and existence—is altogether foreign to the Hebraic concept of the man of faith who is passionately committed to his own mortal being.

Detachment was for the Hebrew an impermissible state of mind, a vice rather than a virtue; or rather it was something that biblical man was not yet even able to conceive, since he had not reached the level of rational abstraction of the Greek. His existence was too earth-bound, too laden with the oppressive images of mortality, to permit him to experience the philosopher's detachment. The notion of the immortality of the soul as an intellectual substance (and that that immortality might even be demonstrated rationally) had not dawned upon the mind of biblical man. If he hoped at all to escape mortality, it was on the basis of personal trust that his creator might raise him once again from the dust.

MARVIN H. POPE : VIEWED AS A WHOLE

One of the most recent translations of, and introductions to, Job is Marvin H. Pope's volume in *The Anchor Bible* (New York, 1965). The author realizes that the book of Job, "like other great classics of world literature, can never be translated or interpreted definitively." In his formidable task he was aided by close attention to Ugaritic literature, which sheds light on linguistic problems in the Bible. Pope (born 1916) is Professor of Northwest Semitic Languages at Yale University. The statement that follows is from the Introduction to the Job volume.

A modern man reflecting on the book of Job from the vantage point of two millennia of human experience must marvel at the religious insights to be found therein.

Viewed as a whole, the book presents profundities surpassing those that may be found in any of its parts. The issues raised are crucial for all men, and the answers attempted are as good as have ever been offered. The hard facts of life cannot be ignored or denied. All worldly hopes vanish in time. The values men cherish, the little gods they worship—family, home, nation, race, sex, wealth, fame— all fade away. The one final reality appears to be the process by which things come into being, exist, and pass away. This ultimate Force, the Source and End of all things, is inexorable. Against it there is no defense. Any hope a man may put in anything other than this First and Last One is vain. There is nothing else that abides. This is God. He gives and takes away. From Him we come and to Him we return. Confidence in this One is the only value not subject to time.

But how can a man put his faith in such a One who is the slayer of all? Faith in Him is not achieved without moral struggle and spiritual agony. The foundation of such a faith has to be laid in utter despair of reliance on any or all lesser causes and in resignation which has faced and accepted the worst and the best life can offer. Before this One no man is clean. To Him all human righteousness is as filthy rags. The transition from fear and hatred to trust and even love of this One—from God the Enemy to God the Friend and Companion—is the pilgrimage of every man of faith. Job's journey from despair to faith is the way each mortal must go.

ARCHIBALD MacLEISH :
GOD HAS NEED OF MAN

When *J. B.*, the Job drama by Archibald MacLeish (born 1892), was on stage, first at Yale University in 1958, then on Broadway in 1959, the theological critics wondered whether the author had not made undue use of his poetic licence in deviating from the intent of the biblical Job. The dramatist's resolution of the enigma of human existence is "a modern romantic emphasis on love"; love is postulated "as an island of meaning in an existence threatened by no meaning." It was especially this concentration on the motif of human love as compensating for disaster, on love unrelated to religious faith, that vexed the theological critics.

However, in a sermon delivered in Farmington, Connecticut, in 1955 (reprinted below), MacLeish demonstrated his serious quest for the meaning of the biblical work. He finds the "message" of the book in man's love for God, the one thing for which God depends on man; man comes to the aid of God (the kingdom of life) in His overcoming of Satan (the kingdom of death). It is the love for God to which the author points in the prose piece. The emphasis on the motif of romantic, earthly love in the *J. B.* drama appears to be a humanist rendering of what MacLeish originally conceived to be an issue of faith.

Both the drama and the sermon show a deep attraction to the figure of Satan; the juxtaposition of God and Satan is essential to MacLeish's interpretation of Job. Let us remind ourselves again that the author, or final editor, of the book of Job dispensed with the Adversary and concentrated on the issue of the confrontation between God and Job. In retaining Satan on the stage, interpreters add color and fascination, but weaken the profoundly human concern of the biblical book.

To preach is to speak with something more than one's own voice—something that only ordination can give, that only the relation of minister to congregation can make possible. I cannot preach here this morning. I can only *say*—say the things possible to me as the kind of human being I am—not perhaps a religious man in the ordinary sense of that term but one who, because of the nature of the art he has followed and because of the character of the time in which he has lived, has had to think much about the things with which religion is concerned. *Whence* and *whither* are questions for the poet as they are questions for the priest: in a dark time, even greater questions, for the priest has answers while the man who writes the poem has only, as Yeats put it, his blind, stupefied heart.

It was a poet's question that brought me to the text I wish to speak of this morning, the most difficult and the most urgent of all poet's questions in a time like this, the question of the belief in life—which is also and inevitably the question of the belief in the meaning, the justice, of the universe—which, in its ultimate terms, is the question of the belief in God.

No man can believe in the imitation of life in art who does not first believe in life itself, and no man can believe in life itself who does not believe that life can be justified. But how can life be justified in a time in which life brings with it such inexplicable sufferings: a time in which millions upon millions of men and women and children are destroyed and mutilated for no crime but the crime of being born in a certain century or of belonging to a certain race or of inhabiting a certain city; a time in which the most shameless and cynical tyranny flourishes, in which the ancient decencies are turned inside out to make masks for cruelty and fraud, in which even the meaning of the holiest words is perverted to deceive men and enslave them? How can we believe in our lives unless we can believe in God, and how can we believe in God unless we can believe in the justice of God, and how can we believe in the justice of God in a world in which the innocent perish in vast meaningless massacres, and brutal and dishonest men foul all the lovely things?

These are questions we in our generation ask ourselves. But they are not new questions. They have been asked before us over thousands of years and by no one more passionately and more eloquently than by that ancient writer—the author of the book of Job. It is of that book I wish to speak—but of that book, not as a fragment of the Bible, but as the great, self-containing poem it actually is.

Most of us who read the book of Job read it for the magnificence of its metaphors, or for the nobility of its language in the great translation in which we know it; but the language and the metaphors are not the poem. The poem is the whole: not the language only but the action, and not alone the action but the meaning to which the action moves, and not the meaning as part of a web of meanings which the Old and New Testaments compose, but the meaning in itself.

It is commonly said, I know—and for reasons which are understandable enough—that the meaning of the book of Job is incomplete and unsatisfactory to any Christian; that the book of Job does no more than pose the tremendous question of man's lot; that we must go on to the teachings of Jesus for an answer to that question. It is understandable that men should say this, for certainly the meaning of the book of Job is a hard meaning and the terms of the dramatic action are brutal terms, terms that the modern mind may well find shocking and even blasphemous. But the fact remains that there *is* a meaning—a meaning proffered by one of the greatest poets who ever wrote—a meaning that directly touches the enormous question which haunts us all in our time as it haunted him in his.

The book begins with the passage which I read you (1:1–12). It is not a passage most of us care to dwell on, or to take in the literal sense and meaning of the words, for it makes God a party to the undeserved sufferings of a human being. Consider what is being said in those beginning verses of the first chapter. Job, it is said, was "perfect and upright and one that feared God and eschewed evil." This was God's judgment of Job also, for God describes him in these same words, you will remember, in His conversation with Satan. But notwithstanding his innocence God delivers Job into the hands of Satan, empowering the great Adversary to destroy everything but Job's person—his seven sons, his three daughters, all his people but the five servants who escape from the five massacres and disasters, all his goods and wealth, and, eventually, after the second conversation with Satan, his health also. And all this is done. And done with God's consent. And done furthermore, as God Himself asserts in the second conversation, "without cause." There can be no misunderstanding the intention of the text. The death and destruction are Satan's work, but without God's consent they could not have been accomplished, and God recognizes from the beginning that they are unjustified by any guilt of Job's.

And not only is all this explicitly said: it is also the essential precondition to the dramatic action and to the whole colloquy which follows between Job and his three "comforters." Job's agony results far more from his consciousness of this lack of cause than from the loss of his wealth or even the destruction of his children. The cry for death with which the great debate begins is not a cry for release from life but for the obliteration and cancelling out of a condition in which such brutal injustice is possible. "Let the day perish in which I was born," says Job, "and the night in which it was said, There is a man child conceived" (3:3). And it is to this same issue the comforters address their bitter comforts. Eliphaz undertakes to answer the complaint of *in*justice by foreclosing the appeal to justice. Justice, he says, is not for men to think of: "In thoughts from the visions of the night, when deep sleep falleth on men, Fear came upon me . . . a spirit passed before my face; the hair of my flesh stood up . . . an image was before mine eyes, there was silence, and I heard a voice saying, Shall mortal man be more just than God?" (4:13–17). It is not for men to debate justice with the Almighty.

But Job will not be answered in these terms. He will not forego his deep conviction that some how, some way, his suffering must be justified: "Teach me and I will hold my tongue; and cause me to understand *wherein I have erred*" (6:24). Job's challenge is the challenge of his innocence, and it is of his innocence the comforters speak. If Job insists on discussing the justice of his suffering, says Bildad, he is condemned forthwith because God *is* just, and a man who suffers, therefore, suffers necessarily for cause. "Doth God pervert judgment? Or doth the Almighty pervert justice?" (8:3). But Job, like men before him and men since, rejects the unanswerable logic of this proposition: God destroys the good as well as the evil. "The earth is given into the hand of the wicked; He covereth the faces of the judges thereof; if not, where and who is He?" (9:24). All one needs to do is to look at the world where the dishonest and the brutal flourish—and Job breaks out with that poignant cry our time has made its own: "changes and war are against me" (10:17).

But the comforters are not persuaded. Zophar picks up Bildad's argument and presses it home with the ultimate thrust. Not only are all sufferers presumably guilty: *Job* is guilty. God exacts less than Job's wickedness deserves. Job's very self-justification is proof of his guilt. But Job will not be browbeaten. He knows and fears God as well as his friends, but he respects his own integrity also:

"Though He slay me, yet will I trust in Him; but I will maintain my own ways before Him" (13:15).

And thereupon Job turns from the debate with his friends to that greater debate in which we are all inevitably engaged: the debate with God. He demands of God to show him "how many are my iniquities and sins? Make me know my transgression and my sin" (13:23). But God does not answer. "Oh that I knew where I might find Him, that I might come even to His seat! I would order my cause before Him, and fill my mouth with arguments. . . . Behold, I go forward, but He is not there; and backward, but I cannot perceive Him" (23:3, 4, 8).

And so the argument goes on, until at last God answers Job out of the whirlwind and the dust. But answers him how? By showing him the hidden cause? No, by convicting him of insignificance! Where was Job when the world was made—"when the morning stars sang together, and all the sons of God shouted for joy"? Has Job "entered into the treasure of the snow"? Can Job "bind the sweet chains of the Pleiades"? Has Job clothed the neck of the horse with thunder who "saith among the trumpets, Ha, ha; and he smelleth the battle afar off"? Does the hawk fly by Job's wisdom or the eagle?—"where the slain are, there is she" (38–39).

Power by power and glory by glory it piles up, all that unmatchable, rich fountaining and fluency of image and metaphor, heaping strength on strength and beauty on beauty only to culminate in that terrible challenge: "Gird up thy loins now like a man; I will demand of thee, and declare thou unto me. Wilt thou disannul my judgment? Wilt thou condemn me, that thou mayest be righteous? Hast thou an arm like God or canst thou thunder with a voice like Him? Deck thyself now with majesty and excellency; and array thyself with glory and beauty. . . . Then will I also confess unto thee that thine own right hand can save thee" (40:7–14). What can man reply? What does Job reply to that tremendous utterance from the blind wind? "Behold I am vile," he cries, "what shall I answer Thee? I will lay my hand upon my mouth" (40:4).

But what is this poem then? What has happened? What has been shown? Only that Job is less than God in wisdom and in power? It scarcely needed all these words, all this magnificence of words, to make that evident. And no matter how evident, how doubly evident it may be, what answer can the insignificance of Job provide to the great question that has been asked of God?

Well, of one meaning of the poem we can be certain, can we not? To the old poet who wrote this drama thousands of years ago, the injustice of the universe was self-evident. He makes this clear not once but three times. Job, he says, was a perfect and an upright man—that is to say, a man who did not merit punishment, let alone the terrible scourge of disasters with which he was afflicted. Again, God by His own admission was moved to destroy Job "without cause" (2:3). Finally, the comforters, who had argued that Job must have deserved his sufferings, must have been wicked after all, are reproved—angrily reproved—by God at the end: "My wrath is kindled against thee, and against thy two friends," God says to Eliphaz, "for ye have not spoken of me the thing that is right" (42:7).

The conclusion is inevitable: Job's sufferings—and they are clearly meant to be the most dreadful sufferings of which the imagination can conceive, the steepest plunge from fortune to misery—Job's, sufferings are unjustified. They are unjustified in any human meaning of the word justice. And yet they are God's work—work that could not have been done without the will of God.

But is this all the poem's meaning? Has the poet of that old visionary time nothing more to say to us than this—that the universe is cruel, that there is no justice, that God may plunge us into misery for no cause and then, at the end, for no cause either, give back to us twofold all that was taken away—all but the lost, all but the dead? (For this, you will remember, happens to Job at the book's end.)

No, surely this is not the only meaning. If it were, men would not have read the book of Job generation after generation, century after century, no matter how magnificent its language. But what other meaning is there? What other meaning can there be? What has the poem to say to us of our real concern: the possibility of our living in this world? If the universe is unjust, if God permits our destruction without cause, how are we to believe in life? And if we cannot believe in life, how are we to live?

This is, for all of us, the crucial question. It was the crucial question for the author of the book of Job also. "Why died I not from the womb?" cries Job; "as a hidden untimely birth *I had not been*" (3:11, 16). What answer to *that* question does the poet find? What answer does he show us in this drama of man's agony?

A deep and, I think, a meaningful answer.

Consider the drama as drama: the play as play. What is the fateful action from which all the rest follows? Is it not God's action in delivering Job, though innocent, into Satan's hands? Without this, Job would not have suffered, the comforters would not have come, the great debate would not have been pursued, God would not have spoken from the whirlwind.

But *why* did God deliver Job into Satan's hands? Why?

For a reason that is made unmistakably plain. Because God had need of the suffering of Job—had need of it for Himself *as God*.

Recall that scene in heaven with which the play begins. Satan has returned from going to and fro in the earth and from walking up and down in it. God, hearing where he has been, asks him to admire Job's uprightness and reverence. Satan replies with that oldest of sneering questions: "Doth Job fear God for nought?" Has God not protected Job and enriched him? Has God not bought Job's love and paid for it? Do you think, cries Satan, Job would still love You if You took it all away? "Put forth Thy hand now and touch all that he hath, and he will curse Thee to Thy face" (1:9 ff.).

And God gives His consent.

Why? For proof? To silence Satan? Obviously. But still, why? Clearly because God believes in Job: because God believes it will be demonstrated that Job loves and fears God because He is God and not because Job is prosperous—proved that Job will still love God and fear Him in adversity, in misfortune, in the worst of misfortunes, *in spite of everything*.

Which means? Which gives what meaning to this book?

Which means that in the conflict between God and Satan, in the struggle between good and evil, God stakes His supremacy as God upon man's fortitude and love. Which means, again, that where the nature of man is in question—and it is precisely, you will note, the nature of man that Satan has brought into question with his sneering challenge—where the nature of man is in question, *God has need of man*.

Only Job can prove that Job is capable of the love of God, not as a *quid pro quo* but for the love's sake, for God's sake, in spite of everything—in spite even of injustice, even God's injustice. Only man can prove that man loves God.

If one were to write an argument to go at the head of the book of Job in some private notebook of one's own, it might well be written in these words: Satan, who is the denial of life, who is the kingdom of death, cannot be overcome by God who is his opposite, who is the kingdom of life, except by man's persistence in the love of God in spite of every reason to withhold his love, every suffering.

And if one were then to write an explanation of that argument, the explanation might be this: Man depends on God for all things; God depends on man for one. Without man's love, God does not exist as God, only as creator, and love is the one thing no one, not even God Himself, can command. It is a free gift or it is nothing. And it is most itself, most free, when it is offered in spite of suffering, of injustice, and of death.

And if one were to attempt, finally, to reduce this explanation and this argument to a single sentence which might stand at the end of the book to close it, the sentence might read this way: The justification of the injustice of the universe is not our blind acceptance of God's inexplicable will, nor our trust in God's love—His dark and incomprehensible love—for us, but our human love, notwithstanding anything, for Him.

Acceptance—even Dante's acceptance—of God's will is not enough. Love—love of life, love of the world, love of God, love in spite of everything—is the answer, the only possible answer, to our ancient human cry against injustice.

It is for this reason that God, at the end of the poem, answers Job not in the language of justice but in the language of beauty and power and glory, signifying that it is not because He is just but because He is God that He deserves His creature's adoration.

And it is true. We do not love God because we can believe in Him; we believe in God because we can love Him. It is because we —even we—can love God that we can conceive Him, and it is because we can conceive Him that we can live. To speak of "justice" is to demand something for ourselves, to ask something of life, to require that we be treated according to our dues. But love, as Saint Paul told the Corinthians, does not "seek her own" (I Cor. 13:5). Love creates. Love creates even God, for how else have we come to Him, any of us, but through love?

Man, the scientists say, is the animal that thinks. They are wrong. Man is the animal that loves. It is in man's love that God exists and triumphs, in man's love that life is beautiful, in man's love that the world's injustice is resolved. To hold together in one thought those terrible opposites of good and evil which struggle in the world is to be capable of life, and only love will hold them so.

Our labor always, like Job's labor, is to learn through suffering to love . . . to love even that which lets us suffer.

POSTSCRIPT

The aim of the book of Job was to refute certain notions of retribution, of suffering as punishment, of providence and divine rule—notions represented by the three friends—and to teach a new understanding of faith, a new concept of knowledge, human and divine, a new appreciation of man's place in the universe, a new view of the humanity of man: a radical revision of established thinking in the author's time.

We have seen from a variety of examples how few were the thinkers, exegetes, critics throughout the centuries who were prepared to become disciples of this anonymous master and to discern his hero's dissent, his protest, and the circumstance of his final reform. Rather, the book of Job was recreated by its interpreters in their own image—with a few notable exceptions—both in times past and in the current era. Indeed, its history is a unique tale of a book conceived in a man's lonely mind and born in rebellion, yet destined to live a life of peaceful coexistence with, and adaptation to, a broad spectrum of philosophies—Jewish, Christian, humanist, secular, existentialist and nihilist, medievalist and modernist.

Perhaps it has been—so far!—too trying a task to confront the message of this book in its raw state, and most expositions have served the purpose of shielding humanity against its harsh impact.

In the long history of its interpretation, the main function of the book of Job has been to provoke reflection, to inspire the imagination of the thinker, the exegete, and the artist. Because its argument is presented not by direct statement but by allusion, and its solution, the divine "answer to Job," by implication rather than dictum

—and also because of its unsolved textual difficulties—it permitted a great variety of approach, of emphasis, of allegory, and of various degrees of subtlety.

Like the revelation to Moses on Sinai, so too did the revelation to Job engage the human mind, and the human heart in search of meaning, producing as great a profusion of discourse. The talmudic interpreters of the Sinaitic revelation imagined that each word on Sinai translated itself into "the seventy languages" of mankind; they used the parable of the statue that is viewed by a multitude of people, each person seeing it from his particular vantage point, whereas the statue sees all of them. Similarly, the reader of Job translates the book into his own mode of thinking, and lets it respond to his own needs. Deviation from what the Joban text "really meant" and its adaptation to the reader's human condition is, therefore, a historically normal and humanly legitimate pursuit, as normal and as legitimate as a corresponding approach to other biblical writings.

It has been said (by one of the authors included in this volume) that our time has become "ripe for Job." By which he meant: ripe and ready for what the original Job drama intended to convey. With a greater measure of caution it could be maintained that our time is progressing toward an increasing readiness for Job. We may indeed expect that, with the growth of scientific knowledge of the universe and of man, and greater awareness of its implications for human life, there will arise a new understanding of the book of Job. Then the literal meaning will of necessity replace allegory, transposition, and reformulation, and "text" and "interpretation" will coincide. For, as does no other work in Western literature, this book combines the cognizance of an impersonal cosmos with an affirmation of the uniqueness and the personality of man. It is the ever deeper knowledge of the first and the ever keener need for the second that may lead us to a renewed confrontation with the book of Job. Some pioneering spirits—included in this volume—are already pointing in the direction of such readiness for Job.

NOTES

Introduction: A Study of Job

1. Baba Batra 15a.
2. On this issue, see my "The Book of Job and Its Interpreters," *Studies and Texts*, ed. Alexander Altmann (Philip W. Lown Institute of Advanced Judaic Studies, Brandeis University, 1966), Vol. III; and " 'Knowest Thou?' Notes on the Book of Job," *Studies in Rationalism, Judaism and Universalism*, in Memory of Leon Roth, ed. Raphael Loewe (London, 1966).
3. William A. Irwin, "Job's Redeemer," *Journal of Biblical Literature*, LXXXI, No. 3 (1962), 217–29; and Nahum M. Sarna, "The Mythological Background of Job 18," *Journal of Biblical Literature*, LXXXII, No. 3 (1963), 315–18.
4. An English translation, by Kaufmann Kohler, appeared in *Semitic Studies in Memory of Alexander Kohut* (Berlin, 1897). An abridged version is given in my *The Rest Is Commentary* (Boston, 1961), pp. 99–112. The conclusion of the *Testament* is a version of the final section of the Septuagint translation of Job.
5. Published as Addendum II to Version I of the work, ed. S. Schechter (Vienna, 1887), pp. 150–66; the passage on Job is on p. 164.
6. Epistle of James 5:11.
7. I Clement XVII; *The Apostolic Fathers*, trans. K. Lake (Loeb Classical Library [London and New York, 1930]), I, 39.
8. In *Apocalypses Apocryphae Mosis, Esdrae, Pauli, Johannis*, ed. C. Tischendorf (Leipzig, 1866), pp. 66 f. Trans. by Justin Perkins.
9. *The Ante-Nicene Fathers*, ed. A. Roberts and James Donaldson (New York, 1913), VII, 482.
10. G. D. Mansi, *Sacrorum conciliorum nova et amplissima collectio* (Venice, 1759–98), IX, 223 ff.
11. Quoted from Duncan Black MacDonald, "Some External Evidence on the Original Form of the Legend of Job," *The American Journal of Semitic Languages and Literatures*, XIV, No. 3 (1898), 142 f.

12. Based on the reports of Wahb and Ka'b-el-aḥbar, two Yemenite Jews converted to Islam in its early period. Naftali Apt, *Die Hiobserzählung in der arabischen Literatur. Erster Teil* (Kirchhain, 1913 [Dissertation, University of Heidelberg]).

13. Duncan Black MacDonald, *op. cit.*, offers a translation of the Islamic story of Job in Tha'labi's "Stories of the Prophets" (early eleventh century), partly based on traditions that originated with Wahb and Ka'b (see preceding note).

14. Deuteronomy Rabba II, 4.

15. Baba Batra 15b.

16. *Ibid.*, 15a f.

17. Numbers Rabba XIV, 7.

18. Baba Batra 16a.

19. Sotah 31a.

20. Tanhuma Vayera 5; Baba Batra 15b f.

21. Baba Batra 16a.

22. Pesikta Rabbati 190a.

23. Baba Batra 16b.

24. Pesikta Rabbati 190a.

25. Targum on Job 1:6.

26. Pesikta Rabbati 165a.

27. Berakhot 17a.

28. His Job commentary, for centuries preserved in manuscript form, was published in *Monatsschrift für Geschichte und Wissenschaft des Judentums,* Vols. V–VII, 1856–58.

29. Ed. by Solomon Buber from a manuscript in the Bodleian Library (Berlin, 1889).

30. English rendition, *The Guide of the Perplexed,* trans. Shlomo Pines, with an Introductory Essay by Leo Strauss (Chicago, 1963).

31. Baba Batra 16a; Abot de-Rabbi Nathan I, 16.

32. English translation by M. Simon and H. Sperling, *The Zohar* (London, 1934). This translation is used in the present section.

33. Zohar II, 32b ff.

34. *Ibid.*, II, 33a.

35. *Ibid.*, II, 34a.

36. *Ibid.*

37. *Ibid.*, I, 166a f.

38. *Ibid.*

39. *Ibid.*, II, 32b.

40. "Homilies on the Gospel of Saint Matthew," in *A Select Library of Nicene and Post-Nicene Fathers of the Christian Church,* ed. Philip Schaff (New York, 1903), X, Homily XXXIII, 224. The image of Job as "wrestler" appears already in the *Testament of Job.*

41. *Ibid.*, pp. 224 f.

42. Homily XLVI. *Op. cit.*, p. 290.

43. *Op. cit.*, pp. 186–97.

44. On Adam and Job, see also "A Treatise to Prove that No One Can Harm the Man Who Does Not Injure Himself," *op cit.*, IX, 273.

45. "Homilies On the Statues." *Op. cit.*

46. Homily I. *Op. cit.*, pp. 339 ff.

47. Homily II. *Op. cit.*, p. 353.

48. Homily IV. *Op. cit.*, p. 369.

49. Homily V. *Op. cit.*, pp. 371 f.

50. Homily XVI. *Op. cit.*, p. 445.

51. "To Pammachus against John of Jerusalem," in *A Select Library of Nicene and Post-Nicene Fathers of the Christian Church* (New York, 1893), VI, 424–47. Trans. by W. H. Fremantle.

52. The Hebrew text is far from clear on this point. The Jewish Publication Society Bible and, recently, the Anchor Bible have "without my flesh."

53. *Op. cit.*, p. 439.

54. *A Library of Fathers of the Holy Catholic Church* (Oxford, 1844–50). The quotations in this section are from this translation; the references are to the book and section of the work. Biblical quotations are based on the Latin version that Gregory used. On Gregory I, see F. Homes Dudden, *Gregory the Great: His Place in History and Thought* (2 vols.; London and New York, 1905).

55. *Works of Martin Luther*. The Philadelphia Edition (Philadelphia, 1932), VI (containing the Prefaces to the Books of the Bible), 383 f.

56. *Ibid.*, p. 385.

57. *Calvini Opera, Corpus Reformatorum*, XXXIII–XXXV.

58. A modern English translation is by L. Nixon, *Sermons from Job, by John Calvin* (Grand Rapids, Michigan, 1952). Introduction by Harold Dekker. This translation is used in the present section.

59. *Calvini Opera*, XXXV.

60. On "the state and religion" in Hobbes, see Leo Strauss, *The Political Philosophy of Hobbes* (Chicago, 1952), chapter V. (The work was originally published in Oxford, 1936.)

61. Everyman Library edition (London and New York, 1914), pp. 189 ff.

62. *Ibid.*

63. See Leo Strauss, *Spinoza's Critique of Religion* (New York, 1965), pp. 258–64.

64. *Theologico-political Treatise*, VII and X, in *The Chief Works of Benedict de Spinoza*, trans. R. H. M. Elwes (London, 1900), I, 112 and 194.

65. *Ibid.*, chapters III and X.

66. *Ibid.*, chapter X.

67. English edition (New York, 1932), pp. 116 f.

68. See Joseph H. Wicksteed, *Blake's Vision of the Book of Job* (2d ed.; London and New York, 1924); S. Foster Damon, *Blake's Job* (Providence, R.I., 1966). On Blake: *William Blake*, ed. Vivian de Sola Pinto (New York, 1965).

69. *Cours familier de littérature*, XIIe Entretien (Paris, 1956), II, 441. Translated for this volume by Evelyn Simha.

70. *Answer to Job*, trans. R. F. C. Hull (London, 1954), originally published in German as *Antwort auf Hiob* (Zurich, 1952).

71. Letter to Gordon Campbell, December, 1914. In *The Collected Letters of D. H. Lawrence*, ed. H. T. Moore (New York, 1962), I, 300 ff.

72. M. Buber, *Darko shel mikra* (Jerusalem, 1964), p. 357.

Leo Baeck: JOB AND KOHELET: BOOKS OF WISDOM

1. Baba Batra 15a.
2. Gittin 68b.
3. Cant. Rabba I, 9.
4. Traditional Hebrew benediction on seeing a sage.

Martin Buber: A GOD WHO HIDES HIS FACE

1. Johannes Hempel, *Die althebraeische Literatur* (Wildpark-Potsdam, 1930), p. 179.

2. I cannot agree with H. Torczyner's view, expressed in his later (Hebrew) commentary on the book (I, 27), that "the story of the framework is later than the poem."

3. The explanation that this expression is a euphemism (according to the view of Abraham Geiger, *Urschrift und Übersetzungen der Bibel* [Breslau, 1857], pp. 267 ff., the language of later emendations, cf. Torczyner, I, 10) does not fit the facts.

4. The atmosphere of the poem is not basically historical, even if the chief characters of the story were historical persons, according to Torczyner's view (*Job*, I, 27).

5. A. S. Peake, *The Problem of Suffering in the Old Testament* (London, 1904), pp. 94 f.; cf. also P. Volz, *Weisheit* (*Die Schriften des Alten Testaments*, Vol. III [1911]), p. 62.

6. F. Baumgaertel, *Der Hiobdialog* (Stuttgart, 1933), p. 172.

7. Johannes Pedersen, *Israel* (English edition, 1926), I–II, 371.

8. Rudolf Otto, *Das Heilige* (25th ed.; Gotha, 1936), pp. 99 f.; cf. also W. Vischer, *Hiob ein Zeuge Jesu Christi* (5th ed.; Zurich, 1942); W. Eichrodt, *Theologie des Alten Testaments*, III (1939), 145 f.

9. Eichrodt, *op. cit.*, p. 146.

Robert Gordis: THE TEMPTATION OF JOB— TRADITION VERSUS EXPERIENCE IN RELIGION

1. Sotah V, 5.
2. Eliphaz had briefly referred to the idea of suffering as a discipline in one verse (5:16), but had not referred to it again or explored

its implications. Deutero-Isaiah's doctrine of the Servant of the Lord describes the Servant's suffering as inflicted by other men, not as emanating directly from God. The affinities are, however, noteworthy.

3. Abot IV, 15.

Hans Ehrenberg: ELIHU THE THEOLOGIAN

1. A reference to Karl Barth's *Theologische Existenz heute!* (1933). [Ed.]

Jean Daniélou: JOB: THE MYSTERY OF MAN AND OF GOD

1. *Moralia super Job,* Preface; *Sources chrétiennes,* p. 128.
2. *Voyage d'Ethérie,* p. 13.
3. *Le Livre de Job* (Paris, 1927), p. 2.
4. See A. Feuillet, "L'énigme de la souffrance et la réponse de Dieu," *Dieu vivant,* XVII, 82, n. 3.

Ernest Renan: THE CRY OF THE SOUL

1. I speak here of those Semites—primitively nomads, Hebrews, Moabites, Edomites, Saracens, Ishmaelites, Arabs—with whose mental characteristics (thanks to the religious and poetic works they have bequeathed to us) we are best acquainted. The Song of Songs presents indeed a commencement of lyric drama, but scarcely developed.

2. I employ here and in the translation the word "parable" not in the special sense we give to it, but as the equivalent of the Hebrew word *mashal,* which designates the sententious poetry of the books entitled "Wisdom," in opposition to the word *shir,* which designates the "Songs" and the lyric poetry.

3. There are doubts as regards the second of these expressions.

4. *Rigvéda* I, cxxiii, 4: "Aurora draws near every house; it is she who announces each day. Aurora, the active young maiden, returns perpetually; she always enjoys the first of everything, etc."

5. See especially the end of the discourse of Elihu (chapter 37), which may be regarded as a true exposition of Semitic meteorology. The manner in which all these natural phenomena are related, in this curious passage, to God as their sole agent, by means of the pronoun affixed to the third person, is singularly striking.

6. See Job 30:3–8. The existence of these races at the time of the composition of our poem is worthy of being remarked. We know that they do not figure again in the history of Israel after the epoch of David.

7. The dogma of the immortality of the soul in the philosophic sense does not appear until quite late in Christianity, and has never been reconciled in a very natural manner with the primitive Christian idea— the idea of the resurrection.

H. H. Rowley: The Intellectual versus the Spiritual Solution

1. Cf. S. L. Terrien, *Job: Poet of Existence* (New York, 1957), p. 21: "The poet of Job did not attempt to solve the problem of evil, nor did he propose a vindication of God's justice. For him, any attempt of man to justify God would have been an act of arrogance. But he knew and promoted in the immediacy of God's confrontation *a mode of life.*"

2. Cf. G. A. Barton in *Journal of Biblical Literature,* XXX (1911), 67: "He has pictured Job as finding the solution of his problem, not in a reasoned explanation or a theology, but in a religious experience. . . . His hero, Job, finds his satisfaction in a first-hand experience of God"; J. Pedersen in *Israel* (1926), I–II, 372: "Only now, when he sees God Himself does he get a real impression of His might, and in this instinctive transport he abandons all claims."

3. Cf. G. F. Oehler, *Theology of the Old Testament,* trans. G. E. Day (Zondervan Press reprint edition), p. 565: "The hope which here (*sc.* in Job 19:25–27) flashes for a moment like lightning through the darkness of temptation, is as yet no mature faith in a happy and eternal life after death, and consequently does not furnish a solution to the enigma with which the book is occupied."

4. Cf. Job 3:17, 10:21 f., 14:21 f.

5. Cf. Job 3:13.

6. Cf. Rabbi Yannai (third century): "It is not in our power to explain the well-being of the wicked or the sorrow of the righteous" (Pirke Abot IV, 15, trans. H. Danby, *The Mishnah* [Oxford, 1933], p. 454).

J. G. Herder: God and Nature in the Book of Job

1. Johann Hübner, *Neu-vermehrtes poetisches Handbuch,* etc. (Leipzig, 1712). [Ed.]

2. G. L. L. Buffon (1707–88), French naturalist, author of *Histoire naturelle* (1749–1804), a 44-volume work summarizing scientific knowledge of his day. [Ed.]

3. Joseph Priestley (1733–1804), chemist and theologian of English enlightenment. [Ed.]

Gilbert Murray: Beyond Good and Evil

1. So the Authorized Version; the original is obscure.

2. *De Sollertia Animalium,* and, more seriously, *De Esu Carnium.*

Emil G. Kraeling: A THEODICY—AND MORE

1. Pierre Bayle (1647–1706), author of *Dictionnaire historique et critique* (1695–97), emphasized "facts" as against "opinions." [Ed.]

2. A. A. Cooper, Lord Shaftesbury (1671–1713), British philosopher and moralist. [Ed.]

3. Alexander Pope (1688–1744), English poet. [Ed.]

4. R. H. Lotze (1817–81), philosopher, epigone of German idealism; attempted to harmonize idealist speculation with nineteenth-century natural science. [Ed.]

5. Max Weber (1864–1920), German sociologist; opponent of historic materialism. [Ed.]

6. Rudolf Otto (1869–1937), philosopher of religion; see "The Element of the Mysterious" in this volume. [Ed.]

7. Laurentius Valla (1404–57), Italian humanist; advocated a synthesis of classical antiquity and Christianity, theology and philology. [Ed.]

W. O. E. Oesterley and T. H. Robinson: THE THREE STAGES OF THE BOOK

1. Plato *Republic* ii. 361 f.

SOURCES AND ACKNOWLEDGMENTS

Authors and publishers referred to in the list that follows kindly gave permission to include in this volume material copyrighted in their name.

Job and Kohelet: Books of Wisdom. From Leo Baeck, *This People: The Meaning of Jewish Existence*, trans. Albert H. Friedlander (Philadelphia, 1965), pp. 95–100. Jewish Publication Society, in cooperation with Holt, Rinehart & Winston, Inc. Copyright © 1964 by the Union of American Hebrew Congregations.

A God Who Hides His Face. From Martin Buber, *The Prophetic Faith*, trans. Carlyle Witton-Davies (New York, 1949), pp. 188–97. Copyright © 1949 by The Macmillan Company.

Job the Righteous Man and Job the Sage. From Yehezkel Kaufmann, *The Religion of Israel*, trans. from the Hebrew by Martin Greenberg (Chicago, 1960), pp. 334–38. Copyright © 1960 by The University of Chicago Press; reprinted by permission.

Job and Jonah. From Leon Roth, *Judaism: A Portrait* (New York, 1961), pp. 227–30. Copyright © 1960 by Leon Roth. Reprinted by permission of The Viking Press, Inc.

The Temptation of Job—Tradition versus Experience in Religion. Robert Gordis, in *Judaism*, IV (1955), slightly abridged. Copyright © by American Jewish Congress. Reprinted by permission of the author and the publisher.

God the Creator. From Margarete Susman, "Franz Kafka," *The Jewish Frontier*, September, 1956. Trans. Theodore Frankel. Reprinted by permission of the Jewish Frontier Association.

Elihu the Theologian. From Hans Ehrenberg, *Hiob der Existentialist* (Heidelberg, 1952), pp. 45–52. Lambert Schneider. Trans. for this volume by Harry Zohn.

Job: The Mystery of Man and of God. From Jean Daniélou, *Holy Pagans of the Old Testament*, trans. from the French by Felix Faber (London, New York, and Toronto, 1957), pp. 86–103. Longmans, Green & Co. Copyright © 1956 by Editions du Seuil.

The Cry of the Soul. From Ernest Renan, *The Book of Job*, trans. from the French by A.F.G. and W.M.T. (London, 1889), pp. xxxix–lvi.

The Intellectual versus the Spiritual Solution. From H. H. Rowley, *From Moses to Qumran* (London, 1963), pp. 175–83. Copyright © 1963 by H. H. Rowley. Reprinted by permission of the Lutterworth Press.

God Himself Is the Answer. From Leonhard Ragaz, *Die Bibel: Eine Deutung* (Zurich, 1949), IV, 255–59. Copyright © 1949 by Diana Verlag; reprinted by permission. Trans. for this volume by Harry Zohn.

Of the Poem of Job. From Robert Lowth, *De Sacra Poesi Hebraeorum*, trans. from the Latin by George Gregory (London, 1847), Lecture XXXIII.

God and Nature in the Book of Job. From J. G. Herder, *The Spirit of Hebrew Poetry*, trans. from the German by J. Marsh (2 vols.; Burlington, Vt., 1832), Dialogue IV, pp. 80–98. E. Smith.

The Oneness of God with the Sufferer. From Josiah Royce, *Studies of Good and Evil* (New York, 1898), pp. 1–28. Copyright 1898 by D. Appleton and Company.

Job the Humanist. From Horace M. Kallen, *The Book of Job as a Greek Tragedy* (New York, 1918), pp. 68–78. Copyright © 1959 by Horace M. Kallen. By permission of Hill & Wang, Inc.

God, Job, and Evil. Paul Weiss, in *Commentary*, VI (1948). Copyright © 1948 by the American Jewish Committee; reprinted by permission.

Beyond Good and Evil. From Gilbert Murray, *Aeschylus: The Creator of Tragedy* (Oxford, 1940), pp. 91–95. By permission of the Clarendon Press.

Job's Victory. From Arthur S. Peake, *The Problem of Suffering in the Old Testament* (London, 1904), pp. 89–102. Robert Bryant.

A Theodicy—And More. From Emil G. Kraeling, *The Book of the Ways of God* (London, 1938), pp. 241–55, abridged. By permission of The Society for Promoting Christian Knowledge, publishers.

The Three Stages of the Book. From W. O. E. Oesterley and T. H. Robinson, *An Introduction to the Books of the Old Testament* (London, 1934). Living Age Books, published by Meridian Books; reprinted by arrangement with The Macmillan Company (New York, 1958), pp. 175–78.

In Dust and Ashes. Hayim Greenberg, in *The Inner Eye*, Vol. II, ed. Shlomo Katz (New York, 1964). Copyright © 1964 by the Jewish Frontier Association; reprinted by permission.

The Element of the Mysterious. From Rudolf Otto, *The Idea of the Holy,* trans. from the German by John W. Harvey, 2d ed. 1950. Pelican Books (1959), pp. 93–96. Reprinted by permission of Oxford University Press.

Man Is Most Comforted by Paradoxes. From G. K. Chesterton, Introduction to *The Book of Job* (London, 1916), pp. ix–xxxvii, abridged. Cecil Palmer and Hayward.

An Uncanny World. From Walter Kaufmann, *The Faith of a Heretic* (New York, 1961), pp. 162–68, 180–81. Copyright © 1961 by Walter Kaufmann. Reprinted by permission of Doubleday & Company, Inc.

Life–A Mystery. From H. Wheeler Robinson, *The Religious Ideas of the Old Testament* (London and New York, 1913), pp. 174–76. Gerald Duckworth.

Job: The Twofold Answer. From James B. Conant, *Modern Science and Modern Man* (New York, 1952), pp. 88–92. Copyright © 1952 by Columbia University Press.

Confidence. From G. W. F. Hegel, *Lectures on the Philosophy of Religion,* trans. from the German by E. B. Speirs and J. B. Sanderson (London, 1895), II, 193–94.

The Lord Gave, and the Lord Hath Taken Away. From Sören Kierkegaard, *Edifying Discourses,* Vol. II, trans. David F. and Lillian M. Swenson (Minneapolis, Minn., 1962). Copyright © 1945, 1946, 1962 by Augsburg Publishing House; reprinted by permission.

God and a Heretic. From Seton Pollock, *Stubborn Soil* (London, 1946), pp. 104–8. Sidgwick & Jackson.

The Hebraic Man of Faith. From William Barrett, *Irrational Man: A Study in Existential Philosophy* (New York, 1958), pp. 64–68. Copyright © 1958 by William Barrett. Reprinted by permission of Doubleday & Company, Inc.

Viewed as a Whole. From *The Book of Job: Anchor Bible Series,* trans. and ed. Marvin H. Pope (New York, 1965), p. lxxvii. Copyright © 1965 by Doubleday & Company, Inc. Reprinted by permission of the publisher.

God Has Need of Man. From Archibald MacLeish, "The Book of Job" (Farmington, Conn., 1955). By permission of the author.

BIBLIOGRAPHY

Material used in Selected Readings is not included.

Aked, Charles F. *The Divine Drama of Job*. Edinburgh, 1913.

Apt, Naftali. *Die Hiobserzählung in der arabischen Literatur. Erster Teil*. Kirchhain, 1913. (Dissertation, University of Heidelberg.)

Baker, John. "Commentaries on Job," *Theology: A Monthly Review*, LXVI (1963).

Ball, Charles James. *Book of Job*. A revised text and version. Oxford, 1922.

Barth, Jacob. "Die Entstehung des Buches Hiob," *Jahresbericht des Rabbinerseminars für das orthodoxe Judentum pro 5636*. Berlin, 1875.

Baumgaertel, Friedrich. *Der Hiobdialog*. Stuttgart, 1933.

Baur, G. "Das Buch Hiob und Dante's Göttliche Komödie," in *Theologische Studien und Kritiken*, 1856.

Blake, Buchanan. *The Book of Job and the Problem of Suffering*. London, 1911.

Bradley, George Granville. *Lectures on the Book of Job*. Oxford, 1887.

Brandwein, Chayim N. "Agadat Iyyov," *Tarbiz*, XXXV (1961).

Brown, Charles R. *The Strange Ways of God: A Study in the Book of Job*. Boston, 1908.

Buber, Martin. *Ijob*. Translation into German. Cologne, 1965.

Burrows, Millar. "The Voice from the Whirlwind," *Journal of Biblical Literature*, XLVII (1928).

Buttenwieser, Moses. *The Book of Job*. Translation, notes, and introduction. London, 1922.

Calvin, John. *Sermons from Job*. Trans. L. Nixon. Grand Rapids, Mich., 1952.

Cheyne, T. K. *Job and Solomon*. London, 1887.

Crook, Margaret B. *The Cruel God: Job's Search for the Meaning of Suffering.* Boston, 1959.

Damon, S. Foster. *The Doctrine of Job.* New York, 1950.

Davidson, Andrew B., and Toy, Crawford H. "Job," in *Encyclopaedia Britannica* (11th ed.), 1911.

Delitzsch, Franz. *Hiob.* English trans. Francis Bolton. 2 vols. Edinburgh, 1866; 2d ed. 1878.

Delitzsch, Friedrich. *Das Buch Hiob.* Leipzig, 1902.

Dhorme, Édouard-Paul. *A Commentary on the Book of Job.* Trans. Harold Knight. London, 1967.

Dillon, Emile Joseph. "The Poem of Job," *The Sceptics of the Old Testament.* London, 1895.

Driver, G. R. "Problems in Job," *American Journal of Semitic Languages,* XXXII (1935–36).

Driver, S. R. *The Book of Job in the Revised Version.* Oxford, 1906.

Driver, S. R., and Gray, G. B. *The Book of Job* (The International Critical Commentary). Translation and commentary. Edinburgh, 1921.

Ecker, Roman. *Die arabische Job-Übersetzung des Gaon Saadja ben Josef al-Fajjumi.* Munich, 1962.

Ewald, Heinrich. *The Book of Job.* English trans. J. F. Smith. London, 1882.

Feinberg, C. L. "The Poetic Structure of the Book of Job and the Ugaritic Literature," *Bibliotheca Sacra,* CIII (1946).

Fine, Hillel A. "The Tradition of a Patient Job," *Journal of Biblical Literature,* LXXIV (1955).

Fries, K. *Das philosophische Gespräch von Hiob bis Plato.* Tübingen, 1904.

Frost, Robert. *A Masque of Reason.* New York, 1945.

Froude, James A. "The Book of Job," *Short Studies on Great Subjects.* London, 1868.

Gard, Donald H. *The Exegetical Method of the Greek Translation of the Book of Job.* (Journal of Biblical Literature Monograph Series, VIII.) Philadelphia, 1952.

Ginsberg, H. L. "Job the Patient and Job the Impatient," *Conservative Judaism,* XXI (1967).

Glatzer, Nahum N. "'Knowest Thou?' Notes on the Book of Job," in *Studies in Rationalism, Judaism and Universalism,* in Memory of Leon Roth. London, 1966.

———. "The Book of Job and Its Interpreters," in *Studies and Texts,* Vol. III. (Philip W. Lown Institute of Advanced Judaic Studies, Brandeis University.) Cambridge, Mass., 1966.

———. "Baeck–Buber–Rosenzweig Reading the Book of Job." (*The Leo Baeck Memorial Lecture,* X.) New York, 1966.

Goodheart, Eugene. "Job and Romanticism," *Reconstructionist*, April 18, 1958.

———. "Job and the Modern World," *Judaism*, X (1961).

Gordis, Robert. "All Men's Books—A New Introduction to Job," *Menorah Journal*, Winter, 1947.

———. *The Book of God and Man: A Study of Job.* Chicago and London, 1965.

Hastings, James, ed. *The Great Texts of the Bible, Job to Psalm 23.* New York, 1913.

Irwin, William A. "An Examination of the Progress of Thought in the Dialogue of Job," *Journal of Religion*, XIII (1933).

———. "Poetic Structure in the Dialogue of Job," *Journal of Near Eastern Studies*, V (1946).

———. "Job's Redeemer," *Journal of Biblical Literature*, LXXXI (1962).

———. "Job and Prometheus," *Journal of Religion*, XXX (1950).

Jastrow, Morris. *The Book of Job, Its Origin, Growth and Interpretation.* Philadelphia, 1920.

Jung, C. G. *Answer to Job.* Trans. R. F. C. Hull. London, 1954.

Kant, Immanuel. "On the Failure of all Philosophical Essays in the Théodicée," in *Essays and Treatises on Moral, Political, Religious and Various Philosophical Subjects*, Vol. II. London, 1799.

Kaufmann, Herman Ezechiel. *Die Anwendung des Buches Hiob in der Rabbinischen Agadah. I. Theil.* Frankfurt am Main, 1893.

Kissane, Edward J. *The Book of Job.* Translation and commentary. Dublin, 1939.

Knabenbauer, J. *Commentarius in librum Job.* Paris, 1886.

Kohler, Kaufmann, trans. *The Testament of Job*, in *Semitic Studies in Memory of Alexander Kohut.* Berlin, 1897.

König, Eduard. "The Problem of Suffering and the Book of Job," *Methodist Review*, CX (1927).

Kuyper, L. J. "The Repentance of Job," *Vetus Testamentum*, IX (1959).

Lamartine, Alphonse de. "Job, ce Platon du désert," in *Témoignages sur Israël*, ed. Jacob Kaplan. Paris, 1949.

Laserson, Max. "Power and Justice: Hobbes versus Job," *Judaism*, II (1953).

Lindblom, Johannes. *La composition du livre de Job.* Lund, 1945.

MacDonald, Duncan Black. "Some External Evidence on the Original Form of the Legend of Job," *The American Journal of Semitic Languages and Literatures*, XIV (1898).

———. "The Book of Job as Lyric," in *The Hebrew Literary Genius*, chapter III. Princeton, 1933.

McKechnie, James. *Job, Moral Hero, Religious Egoist, and Mystic.* Glasgow, 1926.

MacLeish, Archibald. *J. B. A Play in Verse*. Boston, 1956.

Marcus, Ralph. "Job and God," *Review of Religion*, XIV (1949–50).

Moulton, Richard G. "The Book of Job and the Various Kinds of Literature Illustrated by It," in *The Literary Study of the Bible*. London, 1900.

Neher, André. "Job: The Biblical Man," *Judaism*, XIII (1964).

Newman, John Henry. "Peace and Joy Amid Chastisement," in *Parochial and Plain Sermons*. Sermon VIII. London, 1875.

Orlinsky, H. M. "Studies in the Septuagint of the Book of Job," *Hebrew Union College Annual*, XXVIII–XXXIII (1957–62).

Owen, John. "The Book of Job," in *The Five Great Skeptical Dramas of History*. London, 1896.

Peake, Arthur S. *Job* (New Century Bible). Edinburgh, 1905.

Pfeiffer, Robert H. *Le Problème du Livre de Job*. Geneva, 1915.

———."The Book of Job," in *Introduction to the Old Testament*. New York, 1941.

———. "Edomitic Wisdom," *Zeitschrift für Alttestamentliche Wissenschaft*, 1926.

Poznanski, Samuel. *Un commentaire sur Job de la France septentzionale*. Paris, 1906.

Pury, Roland de. *Job ou l'homme révolté*. Geneva, n.d.

Reichert, Victor E. *Job* (Soncino Books of the Bible). Translation and commentary. London, 1946.

Robinson, T. H. *Job and His Friends*. London, 1954.

Royds, T. F. *Job and the Problem of Suffering*. London, 1911.

Sarna, Nahum M. "The Mythological Background of Job 18," *Journal of Biblical Literature*, LXXXII (1963).

Shapiro, David S. "The Problem of Evil and the Book of Job," *Judaism*, V (1956).

Snaith, Norman H. *The Book of Job*. London, 1945.

Spiegel, Shalom. "Noah, Danel and Job," in *Louis Ginzberg Jubilee Volume*. New York, 1945.

Steinberg, Milton. "Job Answers God," *Journal of Religion*, XII (1932).

Stevenson, William B. *The Poem of Job. A Literary Study with a New Translation*. (Schweich Lectures.) London, 1947.

———. *Critical Notes on the Hebrew Text of the Poem of Job*. Aberdeen, 1951.

Stier, Fridolin. *Das Buch Ijjob*. Translation into German and commentary. Munich, 1954.

Stockhammer, Morris. "The Righteousness of Job," *Judaism*, VII (1958).

———. "Thomas Mann's Job-Jacob," *Judaism*, VIII (1959).

———. *Das Buch Hiob: Versuch einer Theodizee*. Vienna, 1963.

Strahan, James. *The Book of Job, Interpreted* (2d ed.). Edinburgh, 1914.

Susman, Margarete. *Das Buch Hiob und das Schicksal des jüdischen Volkes.* Zurich, 1946.

Terrien, Samuel. *The Book of Job: Introduction and Exegesis,* in *The Interpreter's Bible,* III. New York and Nashville, 1954.

———. *Job: Poet of Existence.* New York, 1957.

Thompson, Kenneth, Jr. "Out of the Whirlwind," *Interpretation: A Journal of Bible and Theology,* XIV (1960).

Torrance, James B. "Why Does God Let Men Suffer?" *Interpretation: A Journal of Bible and Theology,* XV (1961).

Tsevat, Matitiahu. "The Meaning of the Book of Job," *Hebrew Union College Annual,* XXXVII (1966).

Tur-Sinai, N. H. *The Book of Job: A New Commentary.* Jerusalem, 1957.

Ulanov, Barry. "Job and His Comforters," *The Bridge,* III (1958).

Vischer, Wilhelm. *Hiob ein Zeuge Jesu Christi* (6th ed.). Zurich, 1947.

Wicksteed, Joseph H. *Blake's Vision of the Book of Job* (2d ed.). London and New York, 1924.

Wiernikowski, Isaak. *Das Buch Hiob nach der Auffassung des Talmud und Midrash.* Breslau, 1902. (Dissertation, University of Königsberg.)

Wolfskehl, Karl. *Hiob oder Die vier Spiegel.* Hamburg, 1950.

Wood, James. *Job and the Human Situation.* London, 1966.

Yellin, David. *Hiqre Miqra: Iyyob.* Jerusalem, 1927.

Zhitlowsky, Chaim. "Job, A Poem of Jewish Free Thought," in *Gezamelte Shriften,* I. New York, 1912.

INDEX